Radical Visions

Recent Titles in
Contributions to the Study of Popular Culture

Radical Visions

AMERICAN FILM RENAISSANCE, 1967–1976

Glenn Man

Contributions to the Study of Popular Culture, Number 41

GREENWOOD PRESS

Westport, Connecticut
London

Library of Congress Cataloging-in-Publication Data

Man, Glenn.
   Radical visions : American film renaissance, 1967–1976 / Glenn
Man.
      p.   cm.—(Contributions to the study of popular culture,
ISSN 0198–9871 ; no. 41)
   Filmography
   Includes bibliographical references and index.
   ISBN 0–313–29306–6 (alk. paper)
   1. Motion pictures—United States—History.   2. Motion picture
industry—United States—History.   I. Title.   II. Series.
PN1993.5.U6M247   1994
   791.43'0973—dc20   94–3049

British Library Cataloguing in Publication Data is available.

Library of Congress Catalog Card Number: 94–3049
ISBN: 0–313–29306–6
ISSN: 0198–9871

First published in 1994

Greenwood Press, 88 Post Road West, Westport, CT 06881
An imprint of Greenwood Publishing Group, Inc.

Printed in the United States of America

The paper used in this book complies with the
Permanent Paper Standard issued by the National
Information Standards Organization (Z39.48–1984).

10 9 8 7 6 5 4 3 2 1

For Margaret, Gabriel, and
Kathleen: fellow moviegoers,
film critics, and sojourners
in the Big Picture

Contents

Acknowledgments

The University of Hawaii at Manoa has supported this project in various ways. I would like to thank the University Research Council for a seed money grant in 1985 that boosted the project in its initial stage, the University Relations Fund for grants in 1987 and 1991, and Dean Richard K. Seymour of the College of Languages, Linguistics and Literature for a Dean's Research Support Fund grant during the summer of 1990.

My gratitude also goes to the hard working, generous staff of the New York Public Library for the Performing Arts at Lincoln Center where I conducted the bulk of my research, to Charles Silver of the Museum of Modern Art Department of Film who arranged viewings for me in the Mayer Room, to Mary Corliss of the Museum of Modern Art Film Stills Archive, and to Kathy Loughney and Barbara Humphries of the Library of Congress Motion Picture, Broadcasting, and Recorded Sound Division whose kind assistance enabled me to view and analyze the films in detail.

The late Gerald Mast inspired and supported this project from its inception, offering encouragement and advice. Others who have helped along the way include Stanley J. Solomon, Seymour Chatman, Robert Self, William Rothman, Daniel Schwarz, and Jo Glorie. Thanks also to Alicia Merritt, Susan Thornton, and Dina Rubin of Greenwood, my acquisitions editor, copy editor, and production editor, respectively.

Margaret Murray Man, as always, proved to be my most interested listener, careful reader, and exacting critic.

Radical Visions

Introduction

DEFINITION AND PARAMETERS

During the years 1967–1976, an artistic renaissance energized the American commercial film. The decade's most significant films wedded modernist narrative techniques with the classical style, demystified and transformed traditional genres, and foregrounded a consciousness of the cinematic process. On a thematic level, they mirrored the attitudes of a time dominated by political radicalism and its consequences—the civil rights movement, the youth movement, the sexual revolution, the women's movement, Vietnam, Watergate, and the brutal assassinations of the Kennedys and Martin Luther King. Common themes include the breakdown of traditional values, sociopolitical oppression, the psychology of sex and violence, moral ambiguity, alienation, solipsism, paranoia, and disillusionment. The films of Arthur Penn, Mike Nichols, Sam Peckinpah, Stanley Kubrick, Robert Altman, Peter Bogdanovich, Martin Scorsese, Bob Fosse, and Francis Ford Coppola scrutinized the moral and mythic landscape of the American scene in original, bold presentations that operated as uncompromisingly as possible within the heavy commercial demands of the industry. The result were films that reassessed the American cinema's achievement, deconstructed and restructured its traditional forms, and exploded or questioned its dominant myths. As a body, they define a distinct period in American cinematic history.[1]

A major characteristic of the Hollywood film industry that acted as a prerequisite for the period's renaissance quality was the greater freedom filmmakers enjoyed to express their personal views and experiment with narrative style and technique. Several factors contributed to this new freedom. One was the breakup of the studio system, which gave rise to independent productions, lessening the predominance of a formula-factory approach; another was the establishment of the new rating code of 1968, which allowed the screen to explore former taboos in more honest and explicit ways; and a third factor was the postwar European film renaissance which influenced American filmmakers of the period to formulate eclectic styles that fused classical, neorealistic, and expressionistic elements within their narratives. The most significant consequence of the "new freedoms" during the period was that filmmakers enjoyed greater control over their works. Independent productions meant less constraint by studio methods, formulas, and the top brass. Several filmmakers wrote as well as directed their films, exerting the kind of control enjoyed by their European counterparts, Jean-Luc Godard, François Truffaut, Federico Fellini, Michelangelo Antonioni, and Ingmar Bergman. The American director emerged as an auteur, guiding the film from beginning to end, giving it direction, focus, and vision. This is not to deny the commercial pressures brought to bear on any narrative feature film in the industry or the essentially collaborative nature of the filmmaking enterprise. However, in the late 60s to mid-70s, film directors had the opportunity to involve themselves more in the total filmmaking process and to incorporate personal styles and visions into the mainstream of the American cinema.[2]

Given the opportunity, then, the new wave American filmmaker could satisfy personal artistic impulses as well as the demands of an audience hungry for a rejuvenated cinema, an audience created by the "art houses," theaters that offered foreign movies, and by the universities, which instituted the academic study of film. Both the art houses and the universities stimulated a historical awareness of cinema's development and a greater consciousness of the filmmaking process. One of the achievements of the renaissance period was the foregrounding of this awareness and consciousness. The new wave American directors brought to bear a greater degree of perceptibility of the *process* of their presentations in their narratives. They made the telling of their stories as much the subject of their fictions as the stories themselves. This does not mean that they transformed the classical Hollywood paradigm and its "invisible" style overnight, but it does mean that they challenged, subverted, and remolded the classical style to suit their individual visions and the needs of the times. This is also true for the Hollywood genres that they worked with, for their films disturbed earlier positions and formed new ones, exploring conditions and features either untapped in the past or suddenly made relevant by contemporary historical factors. It is in this sense that we can say that they demystified or undermined earlier generic patterns, but only to transform them into new stages of development, realizations of heretofore untapped potential.[3] Many of the most significant films of the decade are therefore genre films: gangster films such as *Bonnie and Clyde*, *Thieves Like Us*, *The Godfather*, and *The*

Godfather, Part II; westerns like *The Wild Bunch, Butch Cassidy and the Sundance Kid, Little Big Man*, and *McCabe and Mrs. Miller*; the science fiction of *2001: A Space Odyssey*; musicals such as *Cabaret* and *Nashville*; detective *noir* films like *Chinatown, Klute, Night Moves, The Conversation*, and *The Long Goodbye*; the woman's film of *Alice Doesn't Live Here Anymore*; and war films such as *M*A*S*H* and *Patton*.

In the fourth edition of his *Short History of the Movies* (1986), Gerald Mast divides the post–World War II years in Hollywood into three periods: "1946–1965, Years of Transition," "1964–1976, Hollywood Renaissance," and "1977 to the present, The Return of the Myths." Mast's scheme throws the renaissance years of 1967–1976 into relief in contrast to the period immediately before and the one immediately after. For the most representative films of the periods 1959–1966 and 1977 to the present rely on proven commercial formulas and function largely to sustain traditional cultural myths of American society in contrast to the radical themes and styles of 1967–1976. Spectacles, sequels, prequels, or clones of successful features compete for the attention of the American public during these periods. For example, 1959–1966 saw the rise not only of the James Bond series, but also of musicals and historical spectacles: *West Side Story* (1961), *My Fair Lady* (1964), *Mary Poppins* (1964), *The Sound of Music* (1965), *Solomon and Sheba* (1959), *Ben Hur* (1959), *Spartacus* (1960), *Exodus* (1960), *The Alamo* (1960), *The Guns of Navarone* (1961), *El Cid* (1961), *Judgment at Nuremburg* (1961), *Lawrence of Arabia* (1962), *The Longest Day* (1962), *How the West Was Won* (1962), *Cleopatra* (1963), *The Great Escape* (1963), and *A Man for All Seasons* (1966).[4]

Since 1977, films that have captured the imagination of the public have also been blockbuster spectacles or those which follow popular generic patterns, such as fantasy-adventure, horror, situation comedy, family melodrama, buddy/road films, and the teen sex romp or coming of age genre. The majority of these films mirror the present generation's bent toward heroism, optimism, and escapism, a return to the cultural myths of the pre-Vietnam, pre-Watergate era that uphold traditional values associated with the American family, capitalism, and manifest destiny. They reflect, in other words, the conservative politics that underpinned society during the Reagan-Bush era. The most representative films since 1977 have been heroic adventure fantasies such as *Star Wars* (1977), *Close Encounters of the Third Kind* (1977), *Superman* (1978), *Star Trek* (1979), *Alien* (1979), *Raiders of the Lost Ark* (1981), *The Terminator* (1984), *Ghostbusters* (1987), *Die Hard* (1988), *Batman* (1989), *Dick Tracy* (1990), *Robin Hood, Prince of Thieves* (1991); paternal melodramas such as *Kramer vs. Kramer* (1979), *Ordinary People* (1980), *E. T.* (1982); epic romances such as *Out of Africa* (1985); the teen coming of age film such as *Saturday Night Fever* (1977), *The Blue Lagoon* (1980), *Porky's* (1982), *Sixteen Candles* (1983); and the slasher/horror movie such as *Halloween* (1978) and *Friday the 13th*

(1980). Hollywood perpetuates these films' popularity by recycling them to the public in the form of sequels and imitations. Of course, I oversimplify, but it does seem on the whole that the American public is buying into the conservative myths that have sustained the Hollywood film up to this point in the 1990s. That this situation persists is evidenced by the 1992–93 releases of *Lethal Weapon 3*, *Far and Away*, *Batman Returns*, *Cliffhanger*, *Last Action Hero*, and *Jurassic Park*.

APPROACH AND METHOD

The recognition of the "New Hollywood" or "Hollywood Renaissance" is not a new one.[5] The present work expands and deepens the suggestions of earlier works and attempts to define parameters more precisely in terms of narration and narrative style, genre transformation, reflexivity, and the challenge to traditional cultural myths. It stresses the significant influence of the European art cinema on the Hollywood classical paradigm, reversing the emphasis of the Bordwell, Staiger, and Thompson and Robert Ray treatments of the period in *The Classical Hollywood Cinema, Film Style and Mode of Production to 1960* (1985), and *A Certain Tendency of the Hollywood Cinema, 1930–1980* (1985), respectively. Both treatments argue for the dominance of the classical paradigm despite the intrusions from foreign new waves.

In the following chapters, I offer a film by film discussion organized as much as possible by chronology in order to trace the historical development of renaissance strategies and themes from 1967 to 1976.[6] My readings of the films are deliberately detailed and in-depth. They are meant to be eclectic, drawing on formal, structural, ideological, and generic methodologies. I have as much as possible included close analyses of the medium and its effects. In other words, I have tried to be as cinematically specific as possible and to pay close attention to the technical apparatus which supports filmic narrative and lends it its unique spectatorial effects. I have also provided excursions into contemporary reactions to ascertain the relationship of the films to their times, especially in the first two chapters, which attempt to establish the exhilarating, oftentimes controversial atmosphere of the reception of films that marked and indeed defined the beginning of the period. Furthermore, I make reference to cultural attitudes that impact on the films and the viewing public whenever possible and relevant. If there is any chronological thematic development that can be traced from chapter to chapter and from film to film, it is that the films of the beginning of the period offer an iconoclasm that mirrors a cautious optimism that the liberal claims of the individual may eclipse those of entrenched conservative forces, while those at the end of the period offer a critique that depicts American society as a moral wasteland, reflecting a disillusionment over the waning of progressive values. However much this thematic strain hounds the foregoing discussion, my primary focus is on the complexity of the narrative process as it enters into a discourse with genre, traditional and modernist paradigms of style, and the baggage of myths that any art negotiates with its consumers.

Three films announced the beginning of the renaissance period in spectacular fashion within the space of a year, between August 1967 and April 1968: *Bonnie and Clyde*, *The Graduate*, and *2001: A Space Odyssey*. In retrospect, *Bonnie and Clyde* and *The Graduate* stand as fountainheads for the films of the period. *Bonnie and Clyde*'s deconstructivism within the familiar territory of a traditional genre repeats through the period in such films as *2001: A Space Odyssey* (1968), *The Wild Bunch* (1969), *Butch Cassidy and the Sundance Kid* (1969), *M*A*S*H* (1970), *Klute* (1971), *Little Big Man* (1971), *McCabe and Mrs. Miller* (1972), *Cabaret* (1972), *The Godfather* (1972), *Mean Streets* (1973), *Alice Doesn't Live Here Anymore* (1974), *Thieves Like Us* (1974), *Badlands* (1974), *Chinatown* (1974), *The Conversation* (1974), *The Godfather, Part II* (1974), and *Nashville* (1975).

Meanwhile, *The Graduate* spawned a group of films which explored contemporary sexual attitudes and questioned society's moral conventions and values. Along with *Easy Rider* (1969), it inspired a number of counterculture and/or youth films which retain interest and vitality: *Alice's Restaurant* (1969), *Midnight Cowboy* (1969), *Five Easy Pieces* (1970), *The Last Picture Show* (1971), *Carnal Knowledge* (1972), *American Graffiti* (1973), *Lenny* (1974), *Taxi Driver* (1976), and *Annie Hall* (1977).

In the chapters that follow, I discuss in detail sixteen of these films, while briefly mentioning others when appropriate. It may be too obvious to say that my choice of each film relies on its status as a classic of the period. Surely personal taste comes into play in these matters as well. These claims notwithstanding, each of these sixteen films summarizes in a compelling way aspects of the period's characteristics. Chapters one and two focus on *Bonnie and Clyde*, *The Graduate*, and *2001: A Space Odyssey* as the films which ushered in the renaissance decade—three films that combined technical innovation, reflexivity, genre transformation, and radical themes; chapter three selects *The Wild Bunch* and *McCabe and Mrs. Miller* as supreme examples of the period's modernist play on the western genre; chapter four singles out *Midnight Cowboy*, *Five Easy Pieces*, *Carnal Knowledge*, *American Graffiti*, and *Lenny* as legacies of *The Graduate* and its counterculture theme and aesthetics; chapter five looks at the gangster and private eye genres of the period through Coppola's American epic, *The Godfather* films *I*, *II*, and *III*, and what may be the period's most cynical version of the detective genre, Polanski's *Chinatown*; and chapter six discusses the end of the period and the culmination of its themes in *Nashville* and *Taxi Driver*.

CHAPTER ONE

1967–1968, The Wonder Year, Part I: *Bonnie and Clyde*

In rapid succession, *Bonnie and Clyde*, *The Graduate*, and *2001: A Space Odyssey* burst upon the film world in August 1967, December 1967, and April 1968, respectively. Of all the films of 1967–1968, they stand out as the year's most significant because of their originality, imagination, and artistic energy. Their effect and influence recall the impact that *Breathless*, *Hiroshima Mon Amour*, and *The 400 Blows* had on the French cinema in 1959. As their French counterparts ushered in the New Wave, the American trio announced a renaissance in the Hollywood commercial cinema and set a standard by which contemporaneous films were measured.

The three films arrived on the American scene at a propitious moment. The time was ripe for their renaissance characteristics of auteurist style, reflexivity, and genre transformation to galvanize critics and public alike and to influence directly the course of American filmmaking into the mid-1970s. Before 1967, films such as John Ford's *The Searchers* (1956), Alfred Hitchcock's *Psycho* (1960), and Stanley Kubrick's *Dr. Strangelove* (1963) possessed these renaissance characteristics, but they were isolated instances of auteurist transformations of traditional styles and genres in a Hollywood environment which didn't allow them to generate a new school or period.[1] By 1967, however, the industrial, cultural, and artistic climate had changed through the cumulative effects of the breakup of the studio system, the rise of independent productions, the new rating code, the influence of postwar European films, the establishment of the art houses, and the academic study of film in the universities. Meanwhile, the political and social consciousness of the country had been shaken by the upheavals of the midsixties: the assassination of John F. Kennedy in 1963, the civil rights movement, the women's movement, the youth movement, the sexual revolution, and the agitation over the Vietnam War. By the late sixties, America was ready to embrace a new Hollywood bold enough to forge a cinema which spoke to the emergent audience formed by these historical factors. This cinema would mirror the idealism, restlessness, and disillusionment of the times in narratives still strong in story, but conscious of fresh ways of telling.

The infusion of modernist elements into the classical paradigm elicited the now famous or infamous controversies over *Bonnie and Clyde, The Graduate,* and *2001: A Space Odyssey. Bonnie and Clyde* disturbed the establishment by its mixture of different modes. Was it a comedy, a melodrama, a tragedy? Meanwhile, some critics doubted the integrity of *The Graduate*'s structure in its change from the social satire of its first half to the lyrical romance of its second half. And *2001* was attacked for its radical ellipses, minimal dialogue, and ambiguity of meaning.[2] In retrospect, the agitation over these films was significant not only for its ultimate clarification of the new wave American narrative, but also for its revelation of the need for a different standard of reference. Public retractions of negative first reviews of *Bonnie and Clyde* and *2001* vividly illustrate a process of retooling, a modification of traditional ways of viewing commercial American films to acknowledge innovations and experimentation.

Joseph Morgenstern panned *Bonnie and Clyde* in the August 21, 1967, issue of *Newsweek* and then retracted his initial remarks in a positive review a week later. His first review objected to the film's violence and "willy-nilly" style: "Try to imagine *In Cold Blood* being played as a William Inge comedy, including an attempt at lyricism consisting of a slow-motion sequence" (65). His second review apologized for the first and praised the film's artistry: "Seeing the film a second time . . . I realised that *Bonnie and Clyde* knows perfectly well what to make of its own violence, and makes a cogent statement with it" (82). In his first review of *2001*, Joseph Gelmis judged the film's elliptical structure by conventional standards: "it is, as a whole, disappointingly confusing, disjointed and unsatisfying. . . . The film jumps erratically" ("Space Odyssey Fails Most Gloriously" 3A). In his retraction twelve days later, Gelmis admitted the need for new criteria to appreciate Kubrick's originality:

When a film of such extraordinary originality as Stanley Kubrick's *2001: A Space Odyssey* comes along it upsets members of the critical establishment because it exists outside their framework of apprehending and describing movies. They are threatened. Their most polished puns and witticisms are useless, because the conventional standards don't apply. They need an innocent eye, an unconditional reflex and a flexible vocabulary. ("Another Look at Space Odyssey" 41W)[3]

Bonnie and Clyde was the first of the three films to signal the need for "an innocent eye, an unconditional reflex and a flexible vocabulary." A watershed, it initiated a number of important trends in the films of the coming decade: the graphic depiction of violence, an openness about sexuality, the mixture of styles, the subversion and/or transformation of genres and their myths, and a marked consciousness of narration and the filmmaking process.[4] Several of these characteristics echo those of the French New Wave, and the influence of filmmakers such as François Truffaut, Jean-Luc Godard, Claude Chabrol, and Alain Resnais on the new American film cannot be overestimated. Like its French New Wave predecessors, the films of the American renaissance sport a combination of spontaneity, dash, boldness, innovation, mixed modes, existential themes, and a self-consciousness of genre and of film. *Bonnie and Clyde* sprouts from the tradition of Godard's *Breathless* (1959) and Truffaut's *Shoot the Piano Player* (1960), two films noted for their breezy homage to and playful mockery of the American gangster genre, for their topsy-turvy attitude to narrative and style (comedy turns to melodrama slides back to comedy becomes tragedy), and for their inventive use of film techniques such as jump cuts, the hand held camera, and the 360 degree pan, just to name a few. *Bonnie and Clyde* repeats this refreshing combi-nation of spontaneity and reflexivity and makes it all its own at the same time, transcending mere imitation. And just as *Breathless* and *Shoot the Piano Player* highlight the plight of their characters Michel Poiccard (Jean-Paul Belmondo) and Charlie Kohler (Charles Aznavour) as existential, so too *Bonnie and Clyde* locates this angst in the consciousness of its own central character Bonnie Parker.[5]

The sections that follow offer a discussion of *Bonnie and Clyde*'s new wave aesthetics and their complex effects, focusing on five aspects of the film's narrative: its violence, mixture of styles, formulation of a central consciousness, commentary on its mythmaking nature, and transforma-tion of genre.

VIOLENCE AND MIXED MODES: IMPLICATION AND ALIENATION

Bonnie and Clyde's achievement apes that of another American classic, *Citizen Kane*, namely in its eclectic fusion of styles and attitudes that produce splintered effects upon an audience. Like *Citizen Kane*, *Bonnie and Clyde* combines both expressionistic and realist elements within the framework of the classical Hollywood paradigm. On the one hand, these elements involve the viewer through identification (the expressionist and naturalistic presentation of Bonnie's subjectivity, for example); on the other hand, they distance the viewer in the self-consciousness of their presentation. The film's double-pronged effect upon the viewer attests to the complexity of a discourse that naturalizes and reveals the con-struction of its narrative at the same time. Its violence and mixture of styles, two of its most controversial elements, illustrate this complexity in detail.[6]

The film's violence and its mixed mode of presentation elicit a sympathetic identification with the characters at the same time that they frame distancing devices in proclaiming the film's aestheticism. Violence, for example, acts as a barometer for the audience's involvement with Bonnie and Clyde. The lovers' brutal killing at the end puts "the sting back into death" (Kael 63). Arthur Penn himself suggested that the violence of his film involves the audience in a cathartic way, purging it of its own violent tendencies (Gelmis, *Film Director* 227). On the other hand, the violence distances by the shock it elicits when the audience is brought up short after "laughing along" with the bank robbers during the crime spree (Kael 55); or the "dirty" violence is reflexive as a self-conscious attempt to deconstruct the romantic myth of violence spawned by such Hollywood genres as the western and the gangster film (Glushanok 15). The film's depiction of violence also alienates in its technical articulation of an aesthetic process, a staging in various speeds, editing, and balletic movement. Violence explodes as an aesthetic spectacle which may be received as an end in itself with its own logic of communication detached from the narrative of the film. One can see the influence of *Bonnie and Clyde*'s aestheticism of violence in the slasher/horror films of the 70s and 80s in which the narrative acts as a mere pretext for moments of gory spectacle. We can trace a clear line of development from *Bonnie and Clyde*, *The Wild Bunch* (1969), *Billy Jack* (1971), *Straw Dogs* (1971), *Dirty Harry* (1972), and *The Exorcist* (1973) to *The Texas Chainsaw Massacre* (1974), *Halloween* (1978), *Friday, the 13th* (1980), and their sequels, in which violence is at the center of each highly staged sequence and exists wholly for its own sake; shocking, yes, but also predictable and campy, detaching an audience aware of its stock conventions.

As the film's violence involves and detaches its audience, so too does its mixture of styles. When Arthur Penn was asked about the mood changes, he said that their purpose was to keep the audience on its toes, to involve them in the action, to prevent them from getting bored (Gelmis, *Film Director* 222). Certainly the yoking of humor with the horror of violence draws the audience into a sympathetic identification with the characters. Humor disposes the audience to the characters, makes them likable, while the graphic depiction of violence wrenches the audience's emotion over those they have come to care about. Jim Cook indicates how this blend of "humor and horror" could draw the audience into an involvement with the characters by illustrating its effects on a thematic level. For Cook, the narrative technique alternates between sharply distinctive sequences to "set up the tensions between illusion and reality." One example he cites is the alternation between the first and second sequences. In the first sequence, the viewer identifies with Bonnie's fantasy of an exciting life with Clyde and the exhilaration of the first raid; in the second sequence, the fantasy and the exhilaration receive a setback from Bonnie's failed sexual encounter with Clyde in the car. Another example is the alternation of moods within the fatal robbery sequence which begins with humor but ends in the horrible and shocking murder of the bank clerk, who gets it full in the face. Cook astutely implies the viewer's share in the experience of disillusionment when he says that "this horrific image reminds us that an unqualified identification with the fantasy can never exist again, certainly not for us and probably not for the characters either" (107).

However, the alternation between exhilaration/humor and violence may also have the opposite effect: instead of accenting the shared experience of disillusionment between the characters and the viewer, it may explode the viewer's identification with the gangster-lovers' fantasy of the romance of crime, so that the viewer sees Bonnie and Clyde clearly and dispassionately for what they really are. The shifts in style and mood may also alienate by the constant unsettling of the viewer's interest and by the spectacular stylishness they impart. The shifts constantly remind the viewer that this is a film she is watching as they bombard her with a chameleonlike texture: the Keystone Cop pace of the chase sequences; the graphic intensity of the violence; the zooms and pans exploring the sultry, volcanic quality of Bonnie's sensuousness; the filtered, soft-focus, muted sound, and slow motion of the homecoming scene; the rapid-fire editing in the final scene when Bonnie and Clyde exchange looks as they realize they have been ambushed; and the agonizing slow motion of their deaths. This stylistic chop suey recalls Truffaut's playful potpourri in *Jules and Jim*: the speeded-up pace for silent comedy effects; the documentary newsreel footage of World War I; the freeze framing of Catherine's face; the lyrical style in the montages of Catherine, Jules, and Jim together before the war separates them; and the slow motion of the death scene when Catherine drives off the pier.

In the overall structure of *Bonnie and Clyde*, the shifts in mood from part to part are punctuated by the banjo music of Flatt and Scruggs's "Foggy Mountain Breakdown," which signals the excitement and exhilaration of the getaway, and by the flare-ups of violence, which undercut the musical suggestion of fun and games. The banjo motif begins after Clyde's robbery of a store to impress Bonnie (Faye Dunaway) at the beginning of the film and continues through the next robbery, which is a failed attempt at a bank; the attempt fails because the bank has no money to rob. The treatment is highly comic not only because of Clyde's sheepish dismay, but also because of his extreme fluster over his need to save face with Bonnie, who has been looking forward to her first bank robbery. The next two robberies, however, are more serious affairs. In the first, Clyde is attacked by a butcher while robbing a grocery store.

He gets away and no one is fatally injured, but his bewildered remark "He tried to kill me! Why'd he try to kill me? I didn't want to kill him!" plays against the jaunty banjo music during the getaway. The next robbery is a sequence that begins comically but ends in the gang's first killing. C. W. Moss (Michael J. Pollard) commandeers the getaway car at the bank's entrance. However, he parks the car down the street away from the entrance, extremely pleased that he found an empty parking space! C. W.'s action is comic, and so is Clyde's when he goes into the bank and says, "This is a stickup" twice, and no one hears or notices him. The action turns sour, however, when C. W. has difficulty maneuvering the car out of the parking space. In the ensuing chaos, a bank clerk jumps on the runner of the car in an attempt to stop the robbers, so Clyde shoots him in the face at point-blank range. The horrible image of the shot face punctuates the shift in tone from humor to horror. In a sense, the audience is getting it full in the face after chuckling over the robbers' bungling actions.[7] As the robbers make their getaway, the soundtrack is not filled with the usual rollicking music, but with the naturalistic sounds of tires screeching and alarms going off.

The silence of the banjo at the end of this sequence foreshadows the first sustained gun battle between the gang and the police, which follows after the fatal robbery. The fierce battle involves the whole gang—Clyde, Bonnie, and C. W. joined now by Buck (Gene Hackman), Clyde's brother, and Buck's wife, Blanche (Estelle Parsons). But even in this grim sequence, the film cannot contain its humor at the expense of Blanche, who parades after the getaway car, screaming hysterically and waving a cooking utensil. Despite the comic image of Blanche, the shoot-em-up is a desperate fight for survival; and when a shaken Blanche pleads with Buck in the getaway car to quit the gang, Buck soberly informs her that the die is cast because he killed a policeman in the shoot-out.

The next robbery, however, illustrates the gang at the height of its power and fame. They rob a bank in Texas with cool professionalism. Clyde generously allows a farmer to keep his own money, and everyone makes a clean exit to the car. The getaway is a Keystone Cop–like sequence accompanied by the now familiar banjo music. Scenes of the slapstick chase are interspersed with shots of interviews of the people involved in the holdup—policemen, the farmer, bank officials, all of them proud and happy to have been part of a Barrow gang happening and posing willingly for newspaper photographers. This lively montage of chase and interviews ends with the image of a successful escape as the gang's car crosses over the Oklahoma border, the wildly jangling banjo bringing the sequence to a close on an upbeat strum.

The fun and games atmosphere continues in the next extended episode when the gang steals a car and kidnaps its owner, Eugene (Gene Wilder), and his girlfriend, Velma (Evans Evans). The sequence is a pleasant comic interlude until Eugene reveals that he is an undertaker, casting a pall over the proceedings and shifting the mood of the film. After a visit to Bonnie's folks convinces Bonnie that no other life is now possible for her and Clyde but a life of running, the shift in mood is marked by the second gun battle at a cabin at night and the ambush of the gang the next morning in a meadow, in which Buck dies a slow and painful death. As a wounded Bonnie and Clyde escape in a car driven by C. W., the banjo music plays, but in a muted way, now an ironic counterpoint to the brutality of the ambush and the grim predicament of the pair. This escape offers only a slight reprieve until the final frames when Frank Hamer (Denver Pyle) and his men riddle Bonnie and Clyde with bullets in an ambush set up with the aid of C. W.'s father.

SUBJECTIVE REALISM

The banjo music and the flare-ups of violence signal transitions in a film whose splintered structure careens from comic high spirits to desperate acts of destruction. However, modulation of mood and emotion occurs also through changes in character perception. For example, the shift from promise to disappointment, from exhilaration to frustration, can be measured by the modulations which occur within Bonnie's consciousness in her experience with Clyde and their life of crime together. The first long sequence clues us to Bonnie's central role as barometer of these changes in a series of subjective narrative techniques. These techniques function doubly as those that depict the film's violence and change of moods. They draw the audience into an identification with the character at the same time that they make the audience aware that they are doing this.

The first shot of the movie after the credits is a fade-in to an extreme close-up of Bonnie's mouth and red lips. This is an unusual shot for the beginning of a movie, for it violates the conventional opening cue of classical narration, which is usually a long shot imparting maximum information to the viewer before breaking down into medium and close-up shots within the scene. Instead of conveying information to clarify external action, the extreme closeup provides the viewer with a different kind of information, concerned more with character subjectivity than with plot, which aligns the film's narration with what David Bordwell calls "art-cinema narration."[8] The highly self-conscious shot effectively conveys Bonnie's sensuous vitality. In the sequence that follows, the camera delineates Bonnie's narcissism, boredom, loneliness, and frustration as it alternates between extreme close-ups, close-ups, and medium shots of her in her enclosed bedroom. The tight framing and the camera's refusal to give Bonnie any space in a long shot suggest the prisonlike atmosphere of her existence.

After the extreme close-up of Bonnie's red lips, the camera pans right to follow her look as she turns toward the mirror. We see her face in a close-up in the mirror just as she sees herself, narcissistically admiring her beauty; as she turns away from the mirror, the camera pulls back and then cuts to a low-angle medium close-up of her bare shoulders, her back to the spectator. She takes two steps, then falls into her bed, looking up to the ceiling, then to the metal bars of the headboard, which frame her face in a medium close-up, her look of boredom and restlessness now apparent. The metal bars figure as signs of Bonnie's perception of the restrictions of her limited environment; in her frustration, she pounds the metal bars with a clenched fist, then grabs them and pulls herself forward staring ahead, her face between the bars now in close-up and in a tighter frame; she pulls herself up over the top bar and, as she does, the camera zooms in to an extreme close-up of her eyes, which are full of longing. The extreme close-ups of Bonnie's lips and her eyes enclose this series of shots which define Bonnie's hemmed-in vitality and her intense longing for release. Up to this point, the only sounds that accompanied these images were the naturalistic ones that Bonnie made as she moved around and the chirping of birds from the outside. The sound of the birds is especially apparent during the extreme close-up of Bonnie's eyes, and it stirs Bonnie to get up and dress, the camera lingering on a medium shot of her naked back as she takes clothes from a dresser; when she goes behind a dressing screen to dress, she pouts, takes a deep breath, lets it out; she stands immobile and stares ahead emptily, as if she doesn't know what to do with herself.

But the next shot is a high-angled long one of Clyde next to a car, held for a second, then the camera cuts back to a medium shot of Bonnie still behind the dressing screen, now with hands up to her face and arms tucked to her sides, a physical parallel to her feeling of suffocation; she walks to her upper bedroom window, looks around dejectedly, then down to Clyde, the high-angle long shot of Clyde suggesting her perception of him from above. The earlier intrusions from the outside juxtaposed to the images of the enclosed Bonnie hint at the possibility of a release for her: the juxtaposition of the chirping of birds to Bonnie's look of defeat and longing and the juxtaposition of the shot of Clyde to Bonnie behind the dressing screen. Bonnie herself now sees the possibility of release as she glimpses the stealthy Clyde below; looking on with great interest, she speaks in a tone more inviting than threatening when she calls out, "Hey, boy! What you doing with my mama's car?" Bonnie offers herself to Clyde's frank look as he sees her naked body framed in the upper window; the expression of sultry pride on Bonnie's face reveals her narcissistic pleasure as she sees her sensual beauty reflected in Clyde's admiring look. Sensing her opportunity, she shouts, "Wait there!" turns quickly, races to her closet, fumbles with her dress and shoes, clomps down the stairs buttoning her dress, and pushes at the screen door—a flurry of activity that contrasts to her earlier listlessness. She coyly stops behind the opened door on the porch. The framing of her figure behind the screen underlines the previous images of entrapment: the metal bars, the dressing screen, the window frame; her hesitation mirrors her self-pride as she holds back, disguising for a moment the desperation she feels, until she steps out of the frame of the door and walks toward her destiny.

What Bonnie fantasizes her destiny with Clyde to be and what it really is result in one of the primary sources of tension in the film, until she herself finally realizes the discrepancy toward the end. But at the beginning of their relationship, Bonnie only perceives the promise of an exciting life with Clyde. The next sequence establishes this tension and the pattern of promise and disappointment, excitement and frustration. The first sign of imperfection is the slight limp in Clyde's walk, which Bonnie doesn't notice, a limp that foreshadows Clyde's impotence and a source of constant frustration for Bonnie. As they walk along the street, Clyde appeals to Bonnie's ego and fantasies as he first guesses her to be a movie star; but as he continues to guess, he touches a nerve when he knowingly identifies her as a waitress. The movie star/waitress dichotomy foreshadows the pattern of discrepancy between fantasy and reality that the film will develop. The beginning sequence initiates the pattern on the side of Bonnie's fantasy as Clyde brags to her about his criminal past.

The scene in which Bonnie goads Clyde into proving his past exploits to her is one that implies the sexual nature of Bonnie's perception of Clyde and the association she makes between his skill as a robber and his prowess as a lover. Clyde is Bonnie's answer to her desire for a life pitched at a higher level of intensity, one that will fulfill her keen sensuality and vitality. Physical objects emblematic of the sexual nature of Bonnie's perception are the bottles of soda pop on which the two coolly suck, the stick of match in Clyde's mouth which he nervously twitches up and down, and, most obviously, the gun which Clyde shows off to Bonnie. As Clyde rests the gun against the inside of his thigh, Bonnie fingers it and challenges him, "You wouldn't have the gumption to use it, would you?" After Clyde proves his gumption by robbing a store and stealing a car, Bonnie is so exhilarated that she can't keep her hands off Clyde as he drives the car; the car careens wildly to the fast-paced tones of the banjo music on the sound track, an apt correspondence to Bonnie's sense of thrill and adventure. As the car comes to a jolting halt, Bonnie tears at Clyde's clothing, but he shoves her away violently, shattering her illusion of his sexual prowess and frustrating her smoldering sensuality. Bonnie's first instinct at this disappointment is to ask Clyde to take her home; instead, he begins the pattern of fantasy/frustration all over as he persuades her to stay with him, reminding her of the dull life

Gun prowess and power: Clyde's sublimation of sexuality/Bonnie's romantic longings. *Courtesy of Museum of Modern Art Film Stills Archive; Copyright Warner Brothers, 1967.*

that awaits her back in West Dallas. Clyde's appeal to Bonnie represents the film's verbal articulation of the camera's visual communication of Bonnie's narcissism and desire for release in the first sequence.

Despite the power of Clyde's appeal and the initial excitement of the first three robberies, Bonnie continues to fluctuate between the intoxication of her new liberation and the disappointments which ensue. The life that Bonnie chooses as an escape from her environment proves to be yet another deprivation. At first, the deprivation is associated with Clyde's impotence; later, it will be associated with the dead end, no way out, impotent nature of crime itself. Two scenes effectively summarize Bonnie's sexual dissatisfaction. The first parallels the scene of Bonnie alone in her room at the beginning of the film. In this scene, she's with Clyde and C. W. in a motel room, but she may just as well be alone. The scene begins with a subjective shot of Bonnie and ends with a subjective one of Clyde, a double-pronged method of suggesting Bonnie's situation: an extreme close-up of Bonnie's longing look as she lies awake in bed, listening to Clyde snore, and a zooming close-up of Clyde's face as he opens his eye, but continues to snore. The moment is as privileged as the one of Bonnie at the beginning of the film. It exposes not only Bonnie's vulnerability but Clyde's as well, and it draws the viewer in sympathy to the characters by this revelation of their frail humanity, Bonnie's checked romantic sensibility and the illusion of Clyde's bravado.[9] As in the first scene of the film, the camera not only affects us into an identification with the characters through its subjective narration, but also makes us aware of its self-conscious effort to do so.

The other scene which dramatizes Bonnie's sexual dissatisfaction recapitulates the pattern of fantasy/frustration. In the "We're in the Money" sequence, Bonnie's identification with the golddiggers' promise of wealth and good times in an era of economic depression contrasts sharply with Clyde's angry and nervous concern over his first killing. Even when Clyde offers her a ticket out before the situation worsens, Bonnie still refuses to see the reality, choosing to perceive only the thrill and promise of crime. To Clyde's "You ain't going to have a minute's peace," she replies, "You promise?" Her reply virilizes Clyde for a moment, and he begins to make love to Bonnie in a highly erotic scene. But this only leads to disappointment since Clyde fails to follow through and then rejects Bonnie's attempts to arouse him again.

Eventually, Bonnie begins to see that their life of crime together is leading nowhere and that no other life is possible for them. Two sequences indicate this major change in Bonnie's perception, the kidnapping of Eugene and Velma and Bonnie's visit to her mother. Bonnie is the central consciousness in each sequence, the camera focusing on her face and eyes as they register her dawning awareness and insight. In the sequence with Eugene and Velma, Bonnie makes the two feel at ease at the beginning by saying, "Don't be afraid; you're not the law; you're just folks, just like us." Bonnie would like to believe that she and Clyde are "just folks," who can lead ordinary lives. But her reaction to Eugene's profession as an undertaker indicates a flash of awareness that they are not like everyone else, that, as hunted criminals, they are doomed. The camera focuses on Bonnie's face as she turns to the back seat to ask Eugene what he does; when he gives his answer, her inquiring look changes to a stare of recognition. She turns around, the camera cutting to her and Clyde in the front seat as she says, "Get them out of here!"

The premonition of death chills Bonnie into urging Clyde to let her visit her mama, who is "getting so old." Perhaps Bonnie's visit to her mother is an attempt to recapture the sense of "jes folks" quality which could restore her and Clyde to the world of ordinary living. But the visit only impresses upon her the vanity of this wish. In the sequence, the camera cuts to close-ups of Bonnie's face and her reactions to what Clyde and her mother say in their farewell conversation. For example, when Clyde says to her mother, "We ain't headin' to nowhere; we're just running from," the cut to Bonnie's face indicates her concerned look of near-disbelief in what he says, and her realization that she can't refute it. When he next says, "Don't believe what you read in all them newspapers; that's the law talkin' there; they want us to look big, so they can look big when they catch us," her alerted look on "when they catch us" indicates her awareness that their capture is the inevitable ending to their life of crime. Her mother puts the final emphasis on the true nature of their situation when she says, "You try to live three miles from me, and you won't live long, honey; you best keep on runnin', Clyde Barrow." In the cut from mother to daughter, Bonnie's stunned look registers not only awareness but resignation.

In this sequence, cinematic style works hand in hand with the change in Bonnie's perception. The soft-filtered cinematography, muted sounds, and slow motion suggest an unreal nostalgic atmosphere, corresponding to Bonnie's realization that this life is now closed to her. The very next sequence is the violent shoot-out at the cabin and in the meadow. Coming as it does after the enlightening visit to her mother, the shoot-out accents the change in Bonnie's perception and the pervasive feeling of doom in the final part of the film.

SELF-CONSCIOUS MYTHMAKING

The self-conscious art of *Bonnie and Clyde* is everywhere apparent in its mixture of styles and subjective narration, but the most insistent form of the film's reflexivity is its commentary on its own mythmaking nature. From its beginning, the filmmakers proclaim, "This is a movie we are making about Bonnie and Clyde." The movie never pretends to be an

The explosion of Bonnie's romance of crime. *Courtesy of Museum of Modern Art Film Stills Archive; Copyright Warner Brothers, 1967.*

accurate historical account of the gangster pair. It doesn't recreate the actual Bonnie and Clyde; it mythologizes them. Commenting on the mythmaking nature of his film, Arthur Penn said, "I don't think the original Bonnie and Clyde are very important except insofar as they motivated the writing of a script and our making of the movie" (Penn 20), and

I suppose that what intrigued me was the enterprise of Bonnie and Clyde, the bravura with which they decided to assault the system. And I have to say again and again, I don't mean to suggest that they had heroic character, because I don't believe that they did. But if *they* didn't, I wish that Bonnie and Clyde had had it, and I certainly mean that they should have it in this film. (Hanson 11)

The brilliantly conceived titles and credits of *Bonnie and Clyde* are reflexive in gesture. The credits begin with real-life photographs of the period, which change to "photographs" from the movie itself. The clicking sound of a camera not only punctuates the changes in credits and photographs, but also signals the movement of the film as it winds its way through the projector and flickers onto the screen. The names of the principal actors and actresses who play the Barrow gang—Warren Beatty, Faye Dunaway, Michael J. Pollard, Gene Hackman, and Estelle Parsons—and the title *Bonnie and Clyde* appear in white first, then turn to red before fading away. The association of red with the members of the gang (flair, passion, violence, death?) is a consciously conceived directorial comment. And the photograph of Warren Beatty as Clyde is immediately followed by the credit *Produced by Warren Beatty*, emphasizing the moviemaking process, which in this case involves acting and production.

In addition to its titles and credits, the movie comments on its mythmaking quality in its references to the role which the media play in the creation of legends in the forms of photography, journalism, poetry, and film itself. Each medium of expression for mythmaking is given its due. Members of the gang take pictures of themselves posing with their guns and cars to send to the newspapers, contributing to their growing status as gangsters. They immortalize Frank Hamer by taking his picture with them and sending it to the press. Bank personnel, customers, and police officers involved in the robberies pose eagerly for photographers. Newspaper accounts exaggerate or fictionalize the gang's exploits. One account credits them with near simultaneous robberies in Chicago and New Mexico; another reports Bonnie and Clyde holding up a bank when they are actually recuperating from their wounds. In anger, Clyde vows to get even with the press by robbing the bank they're credited with robbing after they get well. If Clyde had ever carried out his intention, his action would have been an example of the ultimate reflexivity of the media—when people and their culture reflect the media's presentation by way of imitation; in other words, when life imitates art. (One is reminded, of course, of the influence of *Bonnie and Clyde* itself on the culture of its time in the fashion industry's imitation of its clothes style and in the counterculture's adoption of the lovers as its rebel-heroes.)

The mythologizing nature of the press in creating legends in *Bonnie and Clyde* recalls John Ford's *The Man Who Shot Liberty Valance* (1962) and Penn's earlier film, *The Left-Handed Gun* (1958). At the end of Ford's film, a newspaper editor, confronted with the truth and the legend of the identity of the gunman who shot Liberty Valance, decides to print the legend and hide the truth. In Penn's film, a journalist covers the exploits of William Bonney (Billy the Kid, played by Paul Newman) and sends his reports to the East, where they are read by an eager public. At one point, the journalist reads a report of Billy's death in a newspaper to Billy himself, who takes this as a compliment on his already legendary stature. Billy further shows his appreciation of the publicity surrounding him by plastering the walls of his hideout with clippings and posters advertising his picture and the reward for his capture.

Literature is another mythologizing medium in *Bonnie and Clyde*. Bonnie's poem about the pair's exploits refers to the press's tendency to feed the legend: "If a policeman is killed in Dallas, / And they have no clue or guide; / If they can't find a fiend, / They just wipe their slate clean / And hang it on Bonnie and Clyde." When Clyde reads the poem in the newspaper, he realizes that he has made it, that his place in history is secure, that he is a legend come to life in print. He says to Bonnie, "One time I told you I was gonna make you somebody. That's what you done for me. You made me somebody they're gonna remember." The idea of his legendary status energizes Clyde, and, potent as he couldn't be in real life, he is finally able to make love to Bonnie, the agent of his immortality.

Finally, *Bonnie and Clyde* employs film itself to comment on its mythmaking quality. Like the press, movies are a source for both personal and national mythmaking. C. W. and Blanche are fans of *Screenland Magazine* (C. W.'s favorite movie star is Myrna Loy). The movie-within-the-movie, *Gold Diggers of 1933* (1933), reinforces Bonnie's personal fantasy of thrills and mobility while it bolsters the nation's optimism in a time of economic depression. The Busby Berkeley–choreographed opening number, "We're in the Money," sung by Ginger Rogers and danced to by a chorus line dressed in costumes made of coins, glosses over the nation's lack of prosperity and feeds Bonnie's romance of crime. As Bonnie sits in the darkened theater absorbed in the screen fantasy, she is oblivious to Clyde in the rows immediately behind her; he is absorbed not in the fantasy on screen but in the anger and fear caused by his first killing.

But if the "We're in the Money" sequence answers Bonnie's romantic sensibility, *Gold Diggers of 1933* as a whole reflects her fractured sense of thrills followed by disappointment. For *Gold Diggers of 1933* blends fantasy and reality in its plot of three chorus girls who pursue and marry rich men. The opening number is a rehearsal for a show that has yet to open. As the chorus sings "We're in the Money," the sheriff and his men move in to close the show because of its unpaid bills. Trixie (Aline MacMahon) says to Faye (Ginger Rogers), "They close before they open," to which Faye replies, "the depression, dearie. . . ." However, the setback is temporary, and the show opens to great success. After several turns of plot, the three gold diggers, Carol (Joan Blondell), Polly (Ruby Keeler), and Trixie, get their rich men. But the closing number, "Remember My Forgotten Man," enacts the drama of the depression. Carol sings of her "forgotten man," who went off to war and came home only to face a jobless existence. Choreographed sections include weary and wounded soldiers marching in heavy rain followed by a scene of men filing through a breadline. Paradoxically then, the movie begins in denying the depression, but ends in deploring its effects. In this way, the 1933 musical comments upon the movie of which it is a part in two ways: as it reflects *Bonnie and Clyde*'s own mythmaking quality, it also evokes the later film's pattern of disillusionment.

TRANSFORMATION OF GENRE

Bonnie and Clyde shifts, expands, and deepens the dynamics of its genre in several ways. Its mixture of styles hybridizes the genre's basic melodramatic mode; the subjective pattern of desire and frustration within Bonnie's consciousness internalizes the genre's classic structure of rise and fall; Bonnie's self-awareness and resignation to her plight play against the genre's convention of the blind, relentlessly defiant gangster; and, finally and most significantly, the narrative shifts the genre's predilection for a prosocial accounting of the gangster's waywardness to an empowerment of the gangster as an individual at odds with a system of containment and repression.

The film's mixture of styles and the pattern of Bonnie's internal drama have been discussed. Let me just add here a note on Arthur Penn's conscious linking of the film's structure with Bonnie's perspective. In the interview with Richard Gelmis, Penn said that he gave the film "a kind of underpinning it didn't have originally" by structuring it around Bonnie's perceptions and reorganizing the kidnapping and homecoming episodes. Originally, the script had positioned the two scenes earlier. Without the reorganization and the focus on Bonnie's vision, Penn felt that the picture was merely "a bunch of incidents" that didn't come together. At the time of the revision, he told Robert Towne, "I think the scene with the undertaker should be a foreshadowing of their death. The comic scene should end abruptly with a chill. Bonnie has to be impelled to go home and see what is there, to see whether there is anything left" (Penn 223–224). As Bonnie's consciousness registers the sense of impending doom in these scenes, it also marks the beginning of the end for the gang and the turning point in the film's structure.

In its depiction of Bonnie's insights near the movie's end, the film transforms yet another aspect of the genre. As Bonnie moves to an awareness of crime's dead end, she accepts and resigns herself to the inevitable. After all, she ended her poem with "Some day they'll go down together; / They'll bury them side by side; / To few it'll be grief— / To the law a relief— / But it's death for Bonnie and Clyde." Bonnie's awareness and resignation undercut the blind hubris and stubborn resistance of the traditional gangster. In Mervyn Leroy's archetypal gangster film *Little Caesar* (1930), Rico (Edward G. Robinson) defies prosocial forces to the end.[10] In his death throes, Rico proudly resists, "I told you little bodyguards like you, you wouldn't put no cuffs on me." His final words "Oh, Mother of Mercy, is this the end of Rico?" is a concession to the moral message of the classic gangster film of the 30s and 40s that crime doesn't pay, rather than following organically out of the kind of subjective scrutiny that we see in *Bonnie and Clyde*. In Howard Hawks's *Scarface* (1932), Paul Muni's Tony Camonte kills without remorse ("Do it first, do it yourself, and keep on doing it"), relentlessly defiant in the siege before his death: "Ha, ha, ha; hey, look at the monkeys there; they think they gonna get Tony Camonte. Yeah, ha, ha, ha!"[11]

The genre's formula of a protagonist blind to the illusion of ego and success persists in films of more recent vintage: Dillinger (Warren Oates) in *Dillinger* (1973), Michael Corleone (Al Pacino) in Coppola's *The Godfather II* (1974), Tony Montana (Al Pacino) in Brian De Palma's remake of *Scarface* (1983), and Al Capone (Robert De Niro) in De Palma's *The Untouchables* (1987). In *Bonnie and Clyde*, Clyde himself follows the traditional pattern. When Bonnie asks him near the end of the film what he would do if he could start clean all over again, Clyde replies that he would do it all again but only different. Bonnie, struck by Clyde's incomprehension, reacts with a silence that is as sad as it is wise.

The most significant transformation of the genre in *Bonnie and Clyde* is the shift from the claims of a civilized but repressive community to those of the violent but energetic and imaginative individual. John Cawelti cites three reasons why film genres undergo transformation: generic exhaustion; an historical awareness of popular cultures, of genres, and of film; and the decline of the underlying mythology on which the traditional genres have been based since the late nineteenth century ("*Chinatown*" 510–511). The last two seem to explain especially *Bonnie and Clyde*'s transformation of the gangster genre in the late 60s. The historical awareness of popular cultures, genres, and film explains the film's alteration of the genre by art cinema subjectivity and new wave techniques, while the decline of traditional, cultural myths explains the film's subversion of a prosocial myth that tends to dominate in the discourse of the gangster movie.

In the classic gangster film of the early 1930s, the myth of the self-made individual pursuing the American dream of financial success and the myth of community solidarity vie with one another in conflict.[12] In the first instance, the gangster is an attractive larger than life figure; the intensity of his will and passion overshadows those of others around him as he pursues the American dream of material success and power (Schatz, *Hollywood Genres* 86). On the other hand, the gangster gains his power through illegal activities which upset the stability of society. The cultural myth of community solidarity urges the gangster's only temporary success, his social downfall, and his ignominious death. As Robert Warshow observed in his classic essay "The Gangster as Tragic Hero," "We gain the double satisfaction of participating vicariously in the gangster's sadism and then seeing it turned against the gangster himself" (131–132). The tension between the myth of the individual and the myth of the community erodes (although not completely) before the onslaught of prosocial elements either inserted artificially or incorporated according to the demands of plot and character. In the latter case, the gangster's hubris, his overweening pride and lust for power at all costs, becomes the primary cause of his downfall and not the rapacious capitalism that motivated his personal desires in the first place. The gangster's tragedy is personal, not social. Society itself is depicted as an uncomplicated enforcer of public order and morality, dispensing systemic punishment. The conventional elimination of the gangster acts as a warning to all those who would disturb the status quo. Perhaps the most forceful indictment of the gangster in the prototypical films lies in the dramatization of his humiliating and brutal downfall. In *Little Caesar*, titles preceding Rico's death stress his failure, "Months passed—Rico's career had been like a sky-rocket—starting from the gutter and returning there." Rico's last words punctuate his ignominious defeat, "Oh Mother of Mercy, is this the end of Rico?" After police riddle the body of Tony Camonte in *Scarface*, Hawks emphasizes the irony of Camonte's downfall after his tremendous success by panning from his dead body in the street to the Cook's Tours sign above flashing "The World Is Yours."

The prosocial punishment of the gangster follows from his personal responsibility for the unleashing of anarchy within the system. In other words, the punishment or tragedy is internally motivated. Other prosocial elements, in contrast, make their way into the films from the outside, tacked on through prologues, epilogues, and extradiegetic dialogue. They seem inserted in order to satisfy public pressures to police the sensationalism in Hollywood films before the enforcement of the Production Code after 1933. The prologue, which precedes or follows the credits of the pre-1934 gangster films, crusades the message that the character depicted is a menacing social force that must be eradicated. In both *Little Caesar* and *The Public Enemy*, a prologue before the titles (apparently tacked on after the films were released) emphasizes the iconic nature of Rico and Tom Powers (James Cagney):

Perhaps the toughest of the gangster films, *Public Enemy* and *Little Caesar* had a great effect on public opinion. They brought home violently the evils associated with prohibition and suggested the necessity of a nation-wide house cleaning. Tom Powers in *Public Enemy* and Rico in *Little Caesar* are not two men, nor are they merely characters—they are a problem that sooner or later we, the public, must solve.

The Public Enemy contains an original foreword after the credits, which is an apology for what may be taken as a glorification of the gangster: "It is the ambition of the authors of *The Public Enemy* to honestly depict an environment that exists today in a certain strata of American life, rather than glorify the hoodlum or the criminal." In *Scarface*, the foreword after the credits challenges the government and the audience to civic duty and action in order to counteract the "increasing menace to our safety and our liberty." The epilogue of *The Public Enemy* underlines the lesson of Tom Powers's brutal death: "The *END* of Tom Powers is the end of every hoodlum. The Public Enemy is not a man, nor is it a character—it is a problem that sooner or later, *WE*, the public must solve."

Scarface contains the best example of inserted dialogue that indicts the gangster and undercuts his appeal. In response to his underling's remark that Tony Camonte is "a story, public's interested in him, he's a colorful character," the police chief replies:

Colorful? What color is a crawling louse? Say listen, that's the attitude of too many morons in this country; they think these big hoodlums are some sort of demigods; what do they do about a guy like Camonte? They sentimentalize, romance, make jokes about 'em. They had some excuse for glorifying our old Western badmen; they met in the middle of the street at high noon, waited for each other to draw. But these things sneak up and shoot a guy in the back and run away. When I think what goes on in the minds of these lice, I want to vomit.

Similarly, in a scene that has almost nothing to do with the narrative, but has everything to do with the film's prosocial message, a group of citizens meet with a publisher to protest his newspaper's coverage of Camonte's criminal activity. This gives the publisher (and the social-conscious filmmaker) the opportunity to launch into a lecture on the dangers of censorship and on the people's and government's duty to enact and enforce legislation to solve the gangster problem.

The prosocial myth became more pronounced in the years following the enforcement of the Production Code in 1933. In the mid-30s and early 40s, the studios varied the classic formula to comply more stringently with public morality. Schatz points out three variations of the gangster film which occurred after 1933: the gangster as cop variation, the Cain and Abel variation, and the middleman variation (*Hollywood Genres* 99–102). The gangster as cop variation switched the focus to the lawman figure, who assumed the tough, intelligent individualism of the gangster prototype. Examples include *G-Men* (1935) with James Cagney, *Bullets or Ballots* (1936) with Edward G. Robinson and Humphrey Bogart, *Public Enemy's Wife* (1936) with Pat O'Brien, and *Racket Busters* (1938) with George Brent and Humphrey Bogart. The Cain and Abel variation pitted the gangster figure against an equally strong prosocial figure, whose values eventually held sway over the gangster's bad ways. This variation included *Manhattan Melodrama* (1934) with Clark Gable and William Powell, *Dead End* (1937) with Humphrey Bogart and Joel McCrea, *Angels with Dirty Faces* (1938) with James Cagney and Pat O'Brien, *Cry of the City* (1948) with Victor Mature and Richard Conte, and *Key Largo* (1948) with Edward G. Robinson and Humphrey Bogart. The middleman variation highlighted a person caught between prosocial and criminal forces, usually a criminal who decides to go straight but finds it difficult to shake off his past ties. Examples of this variation include *The Roaring Twenties* (1939) with James Cagney and Humphrey Bogart, *Johnny Apollo* (1940) with Tyrone Power, *Kiss of Death* (1947) with Victor Mature and Richard Widmark, and *Dark City* (1950) with Charlton Heston.

In the late 40s to early 60s, the gangster film did not significantly alter the prosocial undercurrent of the genre. In some films of the period, the gangster/criminal figure was an extension or mirror of a general corruption in society, a legacy of the *film noir* experience so dominant in many films in various genres during the period. But this in no way deflected from the dangers of the gangster; it was only that now the disease of gangsterism infected everyone. *Kiss of Death* and *White Heat* (1949) portrayed the gangster as psychologically aberrant; *Brute Force* (1947), *The Big Heat* (1953), *Pickup on South Street* (1953), and *Underworld, USA* (1961) played up the criminal's amoral sense and brutal violence; *Al Capone* (1959) and *The Rise and Fall of Legs Diamond* (1960) followed the classic pattern of the gangster's rise and fall, done in semidocumentary style and, in the case of *Al Capone*, narrated by the police figure responsible for Capone's downfall; *Baby Face Nelson* (1957), *Machine Gun Kelly* (1958), *The Bonnie Parker Story* (1958), and *Pretty Boy Floyd* (1960) offered gangster biographies which merely exploited the genre's melodramatic elements and violence.

By the mid-60s, the time was ripe for the overthrow of the prosocial myth because of a growing public's need for a new myth of the individual. *Bonnie and Clyde* supplied just such a myth, for it touched the nerve of an audience traumatized and radicalized by the political and social upheavals of the decade. As the movie subverts the legitimacy of an establishment responsible for social injustice and oppression, it raises the figures of Bonnie and Clyde to mythic stature as rebel heroes.[13] The film establishes its sympathy and identification with the gangster protagonists in several ways: in its personal and humanizing portrayal of Bonnie and Clyde; in its presentation of the lovers as heroes against the system; in its depiction of a cold and reactionary establishment in the persons of Frank Hamer and Malcolm Moss, respectively; and in the imaginative recreation of the pair's death that counters the prosocial implications of the classic gangster's annihilation.

When gangster films utilize names of the gangsters themselves for their titles, the titles are usually nicknames or last names. The effect of this is to depersonalize the gangster and tout him/her as a monster/creature and/or social disease that society needs to eliminate. Just think of *Little Caesar*, *The Public Enemy*, and *Scarface*, the granddaddies of the genre. This practice of using nicknames or last names persists throughout the genre's history: *Dillinger* (1945 and 1973), *Baby Face Nelson*, *Machine Gun Kelly*, *Pretty Boy Floyd*, *The Rise and Fall of Legs Diamond* (1960), *Bloody Mama* (1970), *The Godfather I and II* (1972 and 1974), and *Capone* (1975). In contrast, the simple first name title of *Bonnie and Clyde* personalizes the protagonists, an effect reinforced by the first shot of the film, the highly subjective extreme close-up of Bonnie's lips. The apparatus draws us into the personal world of the characters, filtering events through Bonnie's consciousness and making us care for these people who share our common aspirations and limitations as human beings. For all her pizzazz, Bonnie has as her most endearing quality her vulnerability, which blinds her to the real nature of the dashing but impotent Clyde and to the exciting but dead-end life of crime. Clyde himself reveals a vulnerability that makes him part of our common humanity. His swagger and charm cannot conceal his impotency once Bonnie tries to make love to him. At one point, the camera reveals his pathetic pretense of sleep at night, a defensive posture to Bonnie's restlessness beside him. In Bonnie's own phrase, she and Clyde are "jes folks" like us, flawed dreamers, a representation that blurs the figure of the gangster as a social problem and sharpens his always lurking appeal to our sense of mayhem and possibilities.

Though *Bonnie and Clyde* offers its protagonists as ordinary and close to us in their vulnerability, it also champions them as heroes against the system. The makers of the film were conscious of this formulation. Arthur Penn said that it was his intention to pit Bonnie and Clyde against

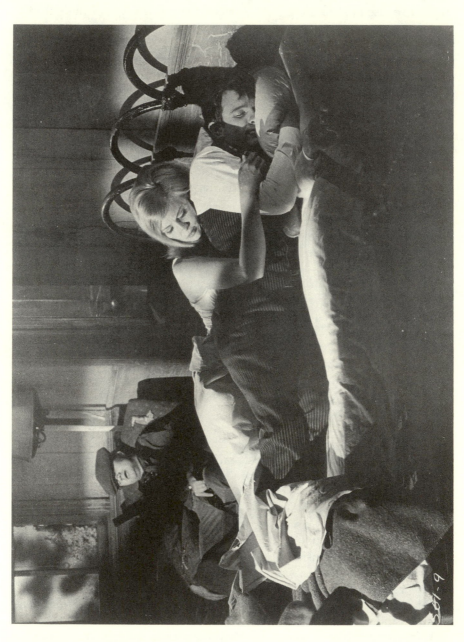

Complex mise-en-scène: the rebel heroes' vulnerability as ordinary folk—Bonnie's frustration/Clyde's pretense at sleep. *Courtesy of Museum of Modern Art Film Stills Archive: Copyright Warner Brothers. 1967.*

a system (represented by the banks and the police) that privileged a few while victimizing the many:

These very rural people were suffering the terrors of a depression, which resulted in families being up-rooted, farms being foreclosed, homes being taken away, by the banks, the establishment of their world, which in part was represented by the police. In the context of our film, Bonnie and Clyde found themselves obliged to fulfill some kind of role which put them in the position of being folk heroes— violators of the status quo. Retaliators for the people. And, in that context, one finds oneself rooting for them. . . . (Penn 20)

The "system" in *Bonnie and Clyde* favors financial corporations which can withstand the financial instability of the depression at the expense of the ordinary folk whose properties fall into the hands of the banks. Early in the movie, a farmer tells Bonnie and Clyde that the abandoned house the pair had slept in the night before was his place before the bank took it. In defiance of the bank, Clyde shoots the sign that says, "Property of Midlothian Citizens Bank. Trespassers Will Be Prosecuted," then lends the farmer and his hired hand the gun to shoot the windows out of the house. As the farmer turns to leave, Clyde consciously adopts the role offered to him in this felicitous moment: "This here's Miss Bonnie Parker; I'm Clyde Barrow. We rob banks."

In robbing banks, Bonnie and Clyde thumb their noses at a system that takes advantage of the depression, foreclosing on the individual workingman and leaving him with little dignity in the process. By their dash and dare, the pair recovers a sense of distinction, purpose, and romance for a generation of down-and-outers. When C. W. drives them into the Oakie camp after the penultimate gun battle, the displaced gather around the pair and, in hushed tones, express wonder at this unexpected advent. Two of them shyly, delicately touch the shot-up, disheveled bandits as if they were deities. By a process of association, *Bonnie and Clyde* appealed to a whole generation of moviegoers infected by its own anti-establishment zeitgeist in the 1960s.

The two characters responsible for the deaths of Bonnie and Clyde, Frank Hamer and Malcolm Moss, typify the establishment. The depiction of Frank Hamer is in keeping with the institutional intractability of the banks. The Texas Ranger's cool demeanor and unswerving sense of purpose overwhelm and eclipse the effervescence of Bonnie and Clyde. He tricks the pitiful blind Blanche into giving him C. W. Moss's last name in order to determine the pair's hiding place, leaving her to talk on unwittingly as if he were still with her after receiving the information. Blanche had been the one who discouraged the gang from killing Hamer when he was its captive. Meanwhile, Malcolm Moss represents the flip side of the establishment coin. He is the hot reactionary to Hamer's cold efficiency, and his intense disapproval of C. W.'s tattoo (read also "long hair" for the 60s counterculture) sums up the 60s generation gap: "How come you make yourself all up with that tattoo? What the hell made you do a damn fool thing like that?"

The machinations of the unfeeling Hamer and the temperamental Moss work in concert to destroy the threat to their status quo. In doing so, they snuff out the vital flame that makes living bearable in a civilly restricted environment. As Robin Wood says, Bonnie and Clyde are

representatives of a spontaneous-intuitive aliveness that society even at its best can contain with difficulty or not at all: an aliveness that expresses itself in the overthrowing of restrictions, in asocial, amoral freedom and irresponsibility. We all respond to it; or if we don't, we might as well be dead. (*Arthur Penn* 75)

When Bonnie and Clyde die up there on the screen, something dies in us as well—that spark that enabled us to identify with them in the first place and of which they were an expression—a breadth of imagination, an expansiveness of spirit that we deny ourselves in our conventional existence. That is why the depiction of their death is so crucial, for it must reimburse us for our emotional investment in the lives of these characters. It must signify more than the exploitation and object lessons of so many other gangster films of the past. It must transport Bonnie and Clyde into the myth that the movie had been making them out to be from the beginning, forcing from us a personal identification with them at first, then feeding us the values they represent so that the hunger we felt could only be satisfied by their mythic stature at the end, by an image we could store in our imaginations in the dark to bolster our spirits in the daylight. Here again is Arthur Penn, this time on the death scene:

In the final sequence in *Bonnie and Clyde*, I wanted a balletic quality. I thought that after we had seen a succession of realistic, rugged killings what I wanted to dramatize in those last ten seconds was the movement from life to myth.

Just shooting them down, as we had shot down other people in the film, would have simply terminated it. It would not have suggested that there was something that was going on into an extended sense of time, movement, myth, resonance in the culture. I felt I had to do this balletically. (Gelmis, *Film Director* 222)

The slow movement of the death ritual that seems interminable in its brutality is nonetheless hypnotic in its dancelike quality, for it keeps before our eyes the image of the two lovers as they move "from life into myth." Paradoxically, the ambush set by Hamer and Moss blasts the life out of Bonnie and Clyde and propels them into our imaginations forever.

Bonnie and Clyde opened the way for a new American cinema that would challenge and energize the classical narratives, genres, and myths of Hollywood. Its new wave characteristics and its shocking, honest treatment of sexual and violent themes paved the way for other film-makers to punctuate the American scene with bold, unsettling achievements of their own. However, *Bonnie and Clyde* was not alone in generating a new period in the American film. *The Graduate* and *2001: A Space Odyssey* stand side by side with it in announcing the renaissance decade.

CHAPTER TWO

1967–1968, The Wonder Year, Part II: *The Graduate* and *2001: A Space Odyssey*

THE GRADUATE

The Graduate was released with hardly any fanfare at the end of 1967 during the Christmas season. Little anticipation had built for this movie adapted from a minor novel featuring an unknown leading man whose physical appearance challenged the conventional image of a romantic hero. Of interest was the movie's neophyte director, Mike Nichols, who had made an auspicious debut a year earlier with a successful adaptation of Edward Albee's hit play, *Who's Afraid of Virginia Woolf?* Bolstered by strong performances by Elizabeth Taylor, Richard Burton, Sandy Dennis, and George Segal, the film proved that Nichols could work well in the cinematic medium and that he was not afraid to strike down taboos in the process. *Who's Afraid of Virginia Woolf?* included rather than watered down the explicit language of the play, and thus helped pave the way for the new rating code of 1968.[1]

Nichols's second film was even more innovative in style and subject matter. *The Graduate* dealt explicitly with American middle-class sexual mores and spawned a series of youth-oriented films about sex, protest, and the generation gap. Like *Bonnie and Clyde*, it deeply affected an audience in reaction against traditional attitudes and conventions. Critics such as Stanley Kauffmann and Hollis Alpert welcomed *The Graduate* as a significant breakthrough in American film. Kauffmann tabbed the movie as "a milestone in American film history" ("Cum Laude" 38), praising its "cinematic skill" and "sheer connection with us" ("Postscript" 37). He viewed the film as part of a "moral revolution," an "index of moral change," because Ben is a moralist who resists, in the healthiest sense, the social role of taboo ("Cum Laude" 22). Meanwhile, Hollis Alpert touted *The Graduate* as "the freshest, funniest, and most touching film of the year" and claimed that "the American film may never be quite the same again" ("Mike Nichols Strikes Again" 24). In a second review of the film six months after it opened, Alpert noted its phenomenon as a youth movie drawing multiple attendance by young people; letters to Hoffman and Nichols, he said, stress an identification with Benjamin's particular parental and societal hang-ups ("*The Graduate* Makes Out" 14). A moving example of American youth's investment in the movie came in a letter to the editor of the *New York Times*. In response to Renata Adler's statement that no one identifies with movie characters anymore in her article "How Contemporary Are Movies?" Miriam Weiss, a junior at Stony Brook at the time, wrote:

One movie she did not mention—*The Graduate*—affected me more deeply than any other movie I've ever seen. If any of the films of the past year was truly a young people's film, it was *The Graduate*. *Bonnie and Clyde*, too, but especially *The Graduate*. You don't have to be young to dig it, but it helps. I myself both laughed and cried when I saw the picture.

I identified with Ben, or, as I might have said when I became articulate again, I thought of him as a spiritual brother. He was confused about his future and about his place in the world, as I am. He was chasing an ideal in spite of all the obstacles that society put in his path in the attempt to co-opt or eliminate him. (The great scene in this respect comes at the end when Elaine shouts, "It's not too late for me!") ("She Identifies with *The Graduate*" D19)

Narrative Style

Alpert was one of the first to note *The Graduate*'s most significant quality, its challenge to conventional narrative style. He said that Nichols had made a "remarkable breakthrough . . . in the traditional Hollywood mode" (24). In *Old Hollywood/New Hollywood*, Thomas Schatz echoes Alpert when he compares *The Graduate*'s narration to that of modern literature "with its convoluted narrative style, its thematic ambiguity, and its concentration on character rather than plot" (19). One explanation for *The Graduate*'s modernist style is that it stems from Nichols's experimentation in cinematic narrative as a journeyman director fresh from the theater. This view is not without some significance given the development of Nichols's style from a self-conscious to a more transparent classical one, from *The Graduate*, *Catch 22* (1970), and *Carnal Knowledge* (1971) to *Silkwood* (1983), *Heartburn* (1986), *Working Girl* (1988), and *Regarding Henry* (1991).[2] However, the explanation that Nichols's accomplishment in *The Graduate* rests on his experimentation in search for a classical style, though interesting, is a simplistic misrepresentation of his achievement as a significant modernist auteur. In only his second film, Nichols effectively combines New Wave techniques with the postneorealism of Fellini and Antonioni. *The Graduate*'s satiric look at the sexual mores of the emotionally and spiritually bankrupt middle class recalls Fellini's *La Dolce Vita* (1960) and *8½* (1963). However, Antonioni seems to be the most direct source for Nichols's depiction of bourgeois malaise. *The Graduate*'s images of characters caught in the web of their environment have the look and feel of Antonioni's visual motifs of alienation as his own characters play out their listless or desperate actions in unaccommodating locales. In *L'Avventura* (1960), for example, the cool classic architecture of the hotel in Taormina heightens Claudia's (Monica Vitti) sense of separation as she searches for Sandro (Gabriele Ferzetti) in its long elegant corridors and empty rooms. In *L'Eclisse* (1962), the final montage of areas of Rome where the two protagonists-lovers (Alain Delon and Monica Vitti) have met during the course of the film, but in which they do not now appear, represents the end of their brief affair, their estrangement, and the hopelessness of love in modern society. In *The Red Desert* (1964), the choking atmosphere of Ravenna's industrial landscape suggests the moral morass of its characters; one retains the image of Giuliana (Monica Vitti), who, after a frustrating and humiliating tryst with her lover, Corrado (Richard Harris), walks down to the docks dwarfed by huge mechanical structures and the rusty hull of a ship in water polluted by slime, to say nothing of the penultimate image of Giuliana and her son, Valerio, struggling over the wasted factory grounds of the industrial park, their movements punctuated by the yellow poisonous smoke billowing from the stacks in the background. In *Blow Up* (1966), the cool white and blue of Thomas's (David Hemmings) photography studio and the drab exterior browns of the buildings in London emphasize not only Thomas's nomadic existence but also the general lack of communication between him and the other characters who people his world.

In *The Graduate*, the Southern California environment of swimming pools, scuba diving suits, barbecues, and bourbon reflects the plastic souls of its middle-class inhabitants. Two famous Antonioni-like shots capture perfectly the sense of entrapment felt by its most apparent victims, Ben and Mrs. Robinson. In the first shot, Ben stands at the bottom of his family's swimming pool in a scuba diving suit after being forced to show it off to his birthday guests. To escape the materialistic ogling, Ben remains on the floor of the pool, refusing to surface. As the underwater camera pulls away from a medium to a long shot, Ben recedes into a little figure in the watery tomb, isolated and insignificant. In the second shot, Mrs. Robinson stands huddled in a corner of a hallway after her revelation to Elaine, her daughter, that she is the woman with whom Ben had an affair. The shot begins as an extreme close-up of Mrs. Robinson's pale, rain-soaked face; the camera then pulls back suddenly to a deep focus over-the-shoulder medium long shot, Ben's head and shoulder in the foreground left, Mrs. Robinson's vulnerable figure in the background right enclosed by two white walls. Ben leaves the frame, and the shot is held for some time on Mrs. Robinson. The image contains a threefold significance, for Mrs. Robinson is trapped, first of all, in the upper-middle-class convention that urges a relationship of financial convenience for one's offspring (Ben lacks purpose and direction, and Elaine opts later to marry a medical student); further, Mrs. Robinson is caught in the hypocritical attitude that her lover, by the very fact that he participated in her infidelity, is not good enough for her daughter; and finally in the immediate context, Ben's resolve to see Elaine despite her mother's wishes forces upon Mrs. Robinson the humiliating necessity to reveal herself as the other woman to her daughter in order to preserve Elaine from someone as unworthy as Ben.

The Graduate's Antonioni-like use of environment and setting represents one of several visual and aural manipulations to form a satiric commentary on American middle-class culture. Indeed, the film's tone and style are so self-consciously wrought that the formulation of its commentary on American society is as well a commentary on itself as cinema.

A comparison of the narration of Nichols's film with the narration of the Charles Webb novel highlights the former's reflexive quality. Webb's narration is covert and scenic; it reports action and dialogue whose discourse time corresponds more or less with story time. It eschews overt commentary, relying on the implications inherent in the action and dialogue to communicate intention. The effect of this transparent style is that the story seems to tell itself, the narration or discourse remaining hidden or "invisible." The novel's temporal summaries, its compression of time, are the most overt form of its discourse.[3]

Because it relies mainly on scenes to tell its story, Webb's narration is not only transparent but objective as well, a reporting of what the characters say and do, with little or no internalization of action. The beginning of the novel is a good example of the summary and scene method of its narration:

Benjamin Braddock graduated from a small Eastern college on a day in June. Then he flew home. The following evening a party was given for him by his parents. By eight o'clock most of the guests had arrived but Benjamin had not yet come down from his room. His father called up from the foot of the stairs but there was no answer. Finally he hurried up the stairs and to the end of the hall.

"Ben?" he said, opening his son's door.
"I'll be down later," Benjamin said.
"Ben, the guests are all here," his father said. "They're all waiting."
"I said I'll be down later."
Mr. Braddock closed the door behind him. "What is it," he said.
Benjamin shook his head and walked to the window.

"What is it, Ben."
"Nothing."
"Then why don't you come on down and see your guests."
Benjamin didn't answer.
"Ben?"
"Dad," he said, turning around, "I have some things on my mind right now."
"What things?"
"Just some things."
"Well can't you tell me what they are?"
"No." (5)

The scene continues as Ben finally gives in and goes down to mix with the guests; he eventually escapes back to his room, only to be followed by Mrs. Robinson, who asks him to drive her home.

In contrast to the objective transparent narration of the novel, the film employs a self-conscious narration to express the subjectivity of its main character, provide satiric commentary, and reflect upon itself as film. *The Graduate* begins with its protagonist in a situation common to modernist narrative: the boundary or crisis situation. As David Bordwell says in *Narration in the Fiction Film*, "The (art) film's causal impetus often derives from the protagonist's recognition that she or he faces a crisis of existential significance" (208). Benjamin Braddock's "recognition" after his graduation from a distinguished eastern college is the realization of his indifference to everything that his education has prepared him for. He feels trapped in a mercantile middle-class environment that expects him to start reaping the profits of his college achievements and in his own purposelessness and ennui.

The cinematic conventions of an expressive realism convey Ben's feelings to us in the credits and graduation party sequences that open the film. As in *Bonnie and Clyde*, *The Graduate* begins with an extreme close-up of its protagonist's face, eschewing the more conventional establishment shot. Ben's eyes stare straight ahead as if he is looking off into infinite space without seeing anything. His head rests against a white background which the camera's pulling back to a medium long shot reveals as a seat back in an airplane about to land in L.A.; the shot also reveals other people in their own seats, like Ben indifferently staring off into space, each locked in his/her separate seat yet part of the same crowd. This scene cuts to a medium profile shot of Ben as he rides the conveyor belt to the luggage area. The shot is held for a long time, the camera tracking slowly with the conveyor belt as the titles and credits flash on screen left against the white wall alongside the belt, Ben's profiled figure on screen right. This long-held shot and Ben's expressionless face underline the sense of monotony expressed in the preceding shot in the airplane. Furthermore, the cool colors of white (the wall) and blue (Ben's suit) evoke a sense of alienation.[4]

After the credits, another extreme close-up of Ben's face dominates the frame as he sits in his room, facing the camera with an aquarium in the background. The camera remains stationary in this position as Ben's parents move into the frame in front of Ben in even more extreme close-ups, with Ben's face in the background. First, his father enters the frame and sits to talk to Ben, his profile in the foreground screen left. Then Ben's mother enters, her body occupying the whole frame and blocking out the faces of both men. These ever increasing close-ups indicate Ben's feelings of entrapment, of his parents' crowding him; in this case, asking him why he isn't coming down to the party and insisting that he do. The camera itself allows Ben little space, a motif which continues into the next scene. With his face in close-up, the hand-held camera follows Ben as he walks through the party, at times hugging him in extreme close-up as he talks to a guest. The cramped space emphasizes Ben's feelings of suffocation as the guests demand his attention, fawning over him and giving him advice. In one instance, the combination of camera movement and sound operates to convey the hemmed-in quality of Ben's condition. As Ben escapes from the pool area through the living room and upstairs to his room, the camera catches him in close-up while, on the sound track, a woman reads his accomplishments from his college yearbook. As the camera follows him up the stairs, the voice of the woman reading from the living room does not diminish on the sound-track in a realistic manner, but remains at the same volume and clarity until Ben slams the door of his room, shutting out all noise in absolute silence. The woman's approving and fawning voice is an index to all that Ben finds distasteful, since his college successes have not prepared him for his present feeling of indifference and indecision. The consistent volume on the sound track stands for Ben's internalization of the insistencies of the congratulations and expectations which overwhelm him.

The next series of shots develops the theme of suffocation through the motif of water, here associated not with rebirth or life, but with drowning and a death-in-life. When Ben returns to his room, he finds relief from the stress of the party below, but not from his general state of ennui. He walks over to the fish tank and sits next to it. The shot that follows is yet another close-up of Ben's face, now staring into the fish tank, not looking at anything in particular. The camera is level with the aquarium on the opposite side from Ben. This entire shot is underwater, so to speak, since the fish tank encompasses the frame. Through the water, then, we see Ben's face in close-up on the right side of the screen and the door to his room on the left side. The door opens and Mrs. Robinson walks in on the pretense of looking for the bathroom. Ben turns his head toward the door. For a second, Ben and Mrs. Robinson are framed by the fish tank, before the camera cuts to a medium shot of Ben rising and telling her that the bathroom is down the hall. The shot through the fish tank links Ben and Mrs. Robinson with the water motif and anticipates their later affair, which Ben uses to escape from his indecision and to rebel against his parents for their attempts to make him conform to their conventional world. The association of the water motif and Ben's motives to escape and rebel is further illustrated by the scuba diving scene and by the use of sound bridges from the scene before and to the scene after.

Just before the scuba diving incident, Ben takes his leave of the Robinsons after he has driven Mrs. Robinson home and she has propositioned him. The sound bridge to the scuba diving scene is Ben's father's voice speaking to his guests, introducing Ben in his new scuba diving suit, "Ladies and gentlemen, your attention please, for this afternoon's feature attraction. . . ." As indicated, Ben is so humiliated by the experience that he stays underwater at the bottom of the pool. As the underwater camera pulls away from Ben's "drowning" figure, the next sound bridge offers Mrs. Robinson's voice saying, "Hello," and Ben's responding, "Ah, I don't know quite how to put this; I was thinking about that time after the party." Then the camera cuts to Ben in a phone booth talking to Mrs. Robinson and arranging a meeting at the Taft hotel. The sound bridges effectively unify this sequence of three scenes to illustrate Ben's motivation for his affair, rebellion against his parents and escape from loneliness and boredom.

Ben's escape, however, is only temporary. It ends when he learns more about Mrs. Robinson. She is a victim in her world as he is in his own, and she is a victimizer as well, controlling the affair and forbidding Ben to see Elaine. The figure of Mrs. Robinson through the fish tank in water, then, suggests another meaning parallel to an appreciation of Ben's point of view. Like Ben, Mrs. Robinson is drowning, but in a loveless marriage, tied to its convenience and material comforts. The affair with Ben offers her an escape as well. In a poignant moment in the course of one of the few conversations they have before lovemaking, Mrs. Robinson reveals that she had wanted to be an artist; instead, she traded her soul in the back seat of a Ford for marriage to Elaine's father. The parallelism breaks down, however, for the victim, now a bored alcoholic housewife who sleeps around, has turned victimizer and hypocrite in reaction to Ben's relationship with Elaine.

In addition to the water motif, other related images and sounds reinforce the theme of suffocation in the Ben/Mrs. Robinson relationship: the shot of Ben from behind and under Mrs. Robinson's leg as she sits on the bar stool in her family room and begins to seduce him; Ben's gasping for breath in Mrs. Robinson's family room after he confronts her with his suspicion that she is seducing him and in the phone booth after he calls her to take her up on her offer; the shot of Ben underwater again after diving into the pool in response to his mother's suggestion that she will invite all the Robinsons over to dinner if he doesn't ask Elaine out for a date; and a rain-soaked Ben and Mrs. Robinson in the traumatic revelation scene with Elaine.

As the preceding discussion shows, *The Graduate*'s cinematic techniques in the opening sequences effectively develop an expressive realism to chart Ben's dilemma and to formulate its wry observation of the Southern California life-style. Other striking cinematic techniques that illustrate a psychological or internal realism include the film's use of soft focus/deep focus, editing, and, in one instance, the extreme telephoto lens. Nichols employs the soft focus/deep focus technique twice with interesting results. In the first instance, he uses it to convey the triangular relationship of Ben, Mrs. Robinson, and Mr. Robinson. When Mrs. Robinson propositions Ben in Elaine's room, Mr. Robinson's car arrives in the driveway, and Ben flees the room, down the stairs, and into the hallway leading to the family room. The camera is in the family room facing the hallway and shoots Ben out of focus as he runs toward the room. He comes into focus as he enters the room and flings himself down at the bar in the foreground as Mr. Robinson enters the hallway from the front door in deep focus. The two discuss Ben's present situation, and Mr. Robinson urges Ben to sow a few wild oats before he settles down. Mrs. Robinson comes down the stairs and appears in the background out of focus between the two men, who are seated on a couch in the foreground. The association of soft focus with Ben and Mrs. Robinson implies their shared knowledge in contrast to Mr. Robinson's ironic ignorance.

In the second instance, Nichols uses the soft focus/deep focus technique for dramatic and psychological effects. In the sequence in which Elaine discovers that her mother was Ben's lover, Ben leads her to the truth, "Elaine, you know that woman, the woman I told you about last night?" as Mrs. Robinson appears in the doorway in soft focus behind Elaine with Elaine's face in the foreground; Elaine turns to see her mother, who is now in deep focus; when Elaine turns back to face Ben, her face is in the foreground still but in soft focus, which gradually becomes focused as she reaches full awareness of Ben's relationship with her mother.

Two montage sequences in the film still seem fresh today as expressions of a perceptual realism. The first is the cat-quick cutting in the seduction scene when a naked Mrs. Robinson surprises Ben in Elaine's room, the cutting alternating between Ben's look of embarrassed disbelief and parts of Mrs. Robinson's body. The other sequence is the five-minute montage compressing the period of the affair, alternating between Ben and Mrs. Robinson in the hotel room and Ben at home listless and daydreaming about the affair while lying on his bed, or, more significantly, drifting on an air mattress in the pool. The montage is clever in its matching shots from one location to the other. For example, as Ben walks from the swimming pool into the house going from right

Deep focus/soft focus mise-en-scène: Elaine's discovery of Ben's affair with her mother, Mrs. Robinson. Courtesy of Museum of Modern Art Film Stills Archive; Copyright Avco Embassy, 1967.

to left, the scene cuts to Ben in the hotel bathroom walking from the bathroom into the bedroom from right to left; or as Ben lies in bed in the hotel room, the scene cuts to him lying in the same position in his bedroom; and, in the most striking match, as Ben leaps onto the air mattress in the swimming pool, the scene dovetails to him on top of Mrs. Robinson in bed. The montage not only summarizes the affair, but also, and more importantly, conveys through its daydreaming mood Ben's further isolation and monadism which the relationship with Mrs. Robinson exacerbates rather than solves. Icons of containment dominate in the sequence: the rectangular pool and mattress on which Ben drifts, his cluttered room at home and the cool spartan room of the hotel, and the two beds, the one at home reflecting the vise of Ben's boredom, the other the vise of passionless love.

Later, when Ben rises out of his passivity into an active pursuit to win Elaine, Nichols uses an effective technique to express Ben's anxiety as he nears his goal. He photographs Ben head-on through an extremely long telescopic lens as he runs to the church where Elaine is getting married. The lens flattens depth perception so that as Ben runs toward the camera he seems like a man on a treadmill, not getting anywhere. The shot emphasizes his frustration as he races against time to interrupt the marriage ceremony and claim Elaine for his own.

Narrative Structure

Though *The Graduate*'s mixture of styles doesn't approach *Bonnie and Clyde*'s rollercoaster changes between comedy, violence, and melodrama, its own does include a dramatic switch from hard-edged satire to romantic drama. Like *Bonnie and Clyde*, Nichols's film came under attack for its inconsistent style and seeming lack of unity. Some critics praised the first half of the film for its sharp and ironic observation of middle-class society but deplored the romantic maneuverings of the second half. For them, the film falls short of the promise of its first half and is problematic because of its fractured structure. Richard Schickel's commentary on *The Graduate* in *Life*, "Fine Debut for a Square Anti-Hero," is an example of such a mixed review:

A film which starts out to satirize the alienated spirit of modern youth, does so with uncommon brilliance for its first half, but ends up selling out to the very spirit its creators intended to make fun of.... From anti-hero he turns into a romantic hero ... the emotional distance from which we previously viewed him—a distance absolutely essential for satire—suddenly disappears. (16)

Schickel, however, misses the point. Ben is consistent as an anti-hero throughout the movie. In the first half, he is the alienated and passive anti-hero, while in the second half, he is committed and active. He remains an individual out of sync with the system from beginning to end. His consciousness unifies the Mrs. Robinson and Elaine parts of the film, and the two styles are appropriate to his separate experiences with each woman. Nichols himself said in an interview that he deliberately changed the mood and style of the second part to reflect the change in Ben's feelings from one relationship to the other. When asked about the criticism of the movie's "structural slippage," Nichols replied:

It was deliberate on our parts. The picture changes in every way. The whole section with Mrs. Robinson is hard and glossy and Beverly Hills and cold and sexy in that way that things can be sexy when you get laid without a great deal of feeling. And with Elaine and his fantasy of Elaine, everything changes into a kind of fantasy prettiness. (Gelmis, *Film Director* 288)[5]

In the first half of the film, Ben flounders in the abyss of his ennui, his parents' control, and his spiritless affair with Mrs. Robinson. The satiric tone is entirely consistent with his own outlook on a material culture he perceives as hollow and crass. In the second half, he finally discovers a goal for which he can feel a passion that is not false—Elaine, the woman who inspires whatever is decent in him and who answers to his truest self and deepest desires. The tone and mood of a romantic quest are entirely appropriate for Ben's feverish pursuit of Elaine in the face of obstacles posed by a society based on conventional taboos: Elaine's resistance to a reconciliation with Ben because of his affair with her mother; Mr. and Mrs. Robinson's disapproval of Ben, whom they deem unfit for their daughter; and Elaine's marriage to the WASPish medical student, Carl Smith, her penultimate and her mother's preferred choice for a comfortable, conventional, soulless coupling. The playing out of Ben's drama of pursuit, first in Berkeley where Elaine is a student and then in Santa Barbara at her wedding, is the playing out of a drama of his salvation, of his rescue from the hypocrisy of the world of his parents and Mrs. Robinson; it is a battle fought against the phantoms within as well as those without as Ben struggles to preserve a sense of selfhood, to uphold his integrity within a corrupt and corrupting world.

Ben's pursuit of Elaine in the film's second half is not irrelevant but integral to the satiric theme begun in the first half. He is still pitted against an establishment intent on forcing him to submit to its control. Only now his resistance is active and openly defiant, whereas it was passive and unarticulated before. This active rebellion maintains his integrity and, in the process, Elaine's as well. Ben's instinctual primal cry to her in the church, "Elaine, Elaine!," stirs her to respond from the depths of her own being, "Ben!" Elaine's heart-wrenching response shatters her conventional adherence to her just-proclaimed marriage vows and exposes the lie of her merely ceremonial action at the altar. When Elaine undercuts her mother's ironically triumphant "It's too late!" with her retort, "Not for *me*," she acknowledges the same self-awareness as Ben and, like Ben, has the courage to act on it, in contrast to her mother's self-deluding capitulation.

The unity gained by *The Graduate* from the thematic suturing of its two parts and from the consistency of Ben's characterization belies its seemingly fractured structure. From the perspective of more than two decades, the contemporaneous complaint of its lack of unity strikes one as more significant for what it reveals about its detractors' classical sensibilities than about any structural flaw the movie may possess. Instead of the classic Hollywood structure of a firmly resolved, goal-oriented plot, *The Graduate*'s structure betrays its neorealistic bias. It is episodic, character-centered, and open-ended.

The Graduate's episodic quality is most apparent in the first half, which parallels Ben's sense of purposelessness as he drifts from day to day and from one event to another: the graduation party, the birthday party, the affair with Mrs. Robinson, his date with Elaine, each punctuated by his lying around in his bed or on the air mattress in the pool. Later, however, the movie's structure does take a turn into the classic Hollywood plot of boy-meets-girl, gets girl after many obstacles and misadventures. If there is any fracture in the film's structure, it is here, in the turn from an episodic development to a classical one, but the change in structure still serves and develops the central concerns of the first half—Ben's existential crisis and the satiric look at his social environment. In other words, it still serves to create an objective realism: the internal development of character and the impingement of social realities on the individual. Ben's decision to marry Elaine motivates the classical plot of the movie's second half, but more importantly, it signals Ben's change into a figure of action and underlines, in its open defiance, his enlightened attitude toward the society of his parents and the Robinsons. In the end, the resolution to the classical plot also means the resolution to the interrelated themes of character development and the restrictive social order. When Ben "gets the girl," he posits an authentic identity against the bankrupt values of the surrounding middle-class material culture.

The extent of *The Graduate*'s accomplishment as a satire, its iconoclasm, may be measured when compared with Hollywood's screwball comedies of the 1930s and 1940s. Though *The Graduate* is not strictly a screwball comedy, it shares several characteristics with the genre. Ben and Elaine enact the "battle of the sexes," two strong-willed individuals verbally jousting after Ben arrives in Berkeley uninvited but hopeful. Beyond their personal disagreement are class differences, which traditionally separate the hero and heroine of the screwball comedy. Elaine and her parents judge Ben morally and financially unsuitable after the affair. Like other screwball comedy heroines, Elaine becomes engaged to a snobbish and shallow exemplar of the upper class for merely conventional reasons before being rescued by the hero from the snares of such a union. Finally, both Ben and Elaine overcome their superficial differences through the recognition of shared values. In *The Graduate*, these values include the same ones that motivate Peter Warne (Clark Gable) and Ellie Andrews (Claudette Colbert) to overcome their class differences in Capra's *It Happened One Night* (1934). Thomas Schatz describes these values as "individual self-assertion, direct and honest human interaction, and a healthy disregard for depersonalizing social restrictions" (*Hollywood Genres* 152). Ben's rescue of Elaine recalls most directly Peter/Gable's offer of an appropriate alternative for Ellie/Colbert to her stuffy upper-crust fiance, King Westley (Jameson Thomas), but it also has an affinity to Dexter Haven's (Cary Grant) rescue of Tracy Lord (Katherine Hepburn) from the clutches of the insipid social climber George Kittredge (John Howard) in Cukor's *The Philadelphia Story* (1940).

Like the screwball comedies of the 30s and 40s, *The Graduate* combines personal drama and social criticism. But unlike them, it doesn't blunt the social criticism as they do by ultimately focusing on the personal conflict and its resolution; as *The Graduate* resolves its personal drama, it also makes its most telling strike against society's taboos. Ben arrives at the church *after* the wedding vows, unlike Gable, who arrives *before* the wedding in *It Happened One Night* to influence Colbert's father, who in turn talks Colbert into running off to Gable as he walks her down the aisle. In the earlier screwball comedies, though the characters achieve transformation into a new innocence and more generous self, they do so finally both within conventional institutions and within the fantasy of romance that characterizes the genre. The former satisfies the prosocial demands of the times (Colbert escapes before she exchanges wedding vows, making it possible for her to *marry* Gable, only after which the walls of Jericho can come tumbling down), while the latter reveals the utopian nature of the couple's transformation. As Stanley Cavell puts it, the vision of "reciprocity or equality of consciousness between a man and a woman," of their "mutual freedom"

gives the films of our genre a Utopian cast. They harbor a vision which they know cannot fully be domesticated, inhabited, in the world we know. They are romances. Showing us our fantasies, they express the inner agenda of a nation that conceives Utopian longings and commitments for itself. (18–19)

In *The Graduate*, social institutions are not preserved but shattered. Ben and Elaine perform their act of defiance without the support of any denizens of society like that of Colbert's enlightened capitalist father, and they make a mockery of conventional rituals such as wedding vows that have become empty of meaning.[6]

Meanwhile, the ending of *The Graduate* complicates the escape of Ben and Elaine from the church and confers an anti-utopian cast on their achievement. The ending to *The Graduate* is not as resolute as the endings of earlier screwball comedies. The last sequence on the bus undercuts the exhilaration and excitement of the escape from the church, scaling down its climactic energy and pace. After locking in the wedding party behind the glass doors of the church, Ben and Elaine mount a bus and hustle to the rear; as the bus starts up, they stare ahead, not saying a word to each other, the camera lingering on them for some time before cutting to the outside rear of the bus. The last scene does not celebrate their tremendous act as the "walls of Jericho" scene celebrates Gable's and Colbert's act of running off together in *It Happened One Night*, or as Grant's and Hepburn's second marriage ceremony crowns the mutual recognition of their inescapable compatibility in *The Philadelphia Story*, sealing the fantasy of the romance which is their narrative. Instead, the bus scene situates the couple in the here and now. Ben's and Elaine's stare certainly indicates exhaustion, a denouement of physical tension and exertion, but it may also imply a question occurring to both, "What do we do now?" As the bus drives off, it doesn't drive off into the sunset, but into an uncertain future. The movie audience is also left with the question, What will Ben and Elaine do now? The cynical among them may agree with Jacob Brackman, who sees Ben's rescue of Elaine as just another one of Ben's distractions, a solution incommensurate with the complexity of his problem. For Brackman, the rescue resolves nothing, while it creates problems with which an unchanged Ben is powerless to deal:

Will Ben and Elaine now become like their parents? Or will Ben return now to the anguish that he had before? Or has he settled a complex issue by focusing on a solution not commensurate? Was his problem at first only a shallow one—post grad blues? With Elaine, has Ben cowardly simplified the complex issues? (39–40)

If Brackman's questions imply an attitude too extreme even for Ben's detractors in the audience, yet they find a spokesman in no less than Nichols himself, whose own interpretation is that Ben and Elaine will capitulate finally to the world of their parents:

At the end he is just as lost as he was in the beginning. People say the second half of the film is romantic. But it's not. It's setting a trap. I think 10 minutes after the bus leaves, the girl will say to him, "My God, I have no clothes!" At

Sober realization: The Graduate's anti-utopian ending. Courtesy of Museum of Modern Art Film Stills Archive; Copyright Avco Embassy, 1967.

least they're out of the terrible world they lived in, but they're not to be envied. I think Benjamin will end up like his parents. (Aldridge 15D)

It is not enough for Nichols's satiric bent that Ben and Elaine thumb their noses at the establishment; they must be gestured at as well. Nichols's and Brackman's response to *The Graduate*'s ending favors a reading of the film that is more in line with the satiric outlook of the first part, an outlook that is unmerciful in its sharp observation of its characters and the society they inhabit. In the end, this predilection for satire ignores the significance of Ben's rescue of Elaine and makes both the butt of the joke along with everyone else in the film, rather than its preferred standard of measure.

Brackman's extreme view exposes the lack of enthusiasm he feels for a film which he obligingly discusses at length in a clinical fashion for the purpose of accounting for its huge success. Meanwhile, Nichols's natural inclination for satire blinds him to the overwhelmingly positive effect of the film's second half. Let us take the dictim of D. H. Lawrence to heart in this instance, "Never trust the artist. Trust the tale" (2). In an interview Nichols gave after the success of *The Graduate* and during the filming of *Catch 22*, he noted that whenever he expresses his opinion that Ben and Elaine will be just like their parents in five years, people in the audience are "stunned and enraged" (Gelmis, *Film Director* 288). The opinion stuns and enrages them because their shared experience with Ben and Elaine resists a detached, self-satisfied response that takes the whole affair at the end lightly; it resists the clinical preoccupation with the satiric elements of the movie and revels in the existential implications of Ben's character and his actions; it resists the coded images of death in the film, the emotionless, glossy landscape and its plastic characters, and opts for the vivacity offered by Ben and Elaine in their momentous act. Recall Miriam Weiss's passionate statement in 1968, quoted earlier in another context:

I identified with Ben, or, as I might have said when I became articulate again, I thought of him as a spiritual brother. He was confused about his future and about his place in the world, as I am. He was chasing an ideal in spite of all the obstacles that society put in his path in the attempt to co-opt or eliminate him. (The great scene in this respect comes at the end when Elaine shouts, "It's not too late for me!") (D19)

Audiences cheer Ben and Elaine and express dismay and shock at Nichols's wry remarks because they experience what for them is as true in the film as its satire, the suggestion of possibilities beyond the ordinary and conventional, the promise of a pleasure beyond the daily rituals of life. Ben and Elaine grasp those possibilities and take the audience along with them.

The engagement with Ben's movement from a death-in-life existence to a life-in-death affirmation recalls François Truffaut's statement on the inherent pleasure principle in movies and the reason we go to films at all:

There exists, in the very idea of cinematic spectacle, a promise of pleasure, an idea of exaltation that runs counter to the downward spiral of life that goes through infirmity and old age to death. I am using shorthand and of course, oversimplifying: the spectacle moves upward, life downward. (*The Films of My Life* 16)

Truffaut is referring here to all the promises of pleasure that the cinema offers: first, the promise of fantasy, of magic, of a larger, more intensely lived existence; second, the promise of aesthetic pleasure in the formulation of the images and sound; and last, the thematic promise which movies offer when they affirm the human spirit. *The Graduate* counters the "downward spiral of life" in the promise of its "cinematic spectacle." It is a movie first of all, images produced by flickering light projected onto a screen in a darkened theater, a wonderfully achieved aesthetic event that feeds the fantasy that we ourselves project; and it affirms the individual's need and ability to preserve a sense of integrity and innocence in the midst of compromise and disillusionment.

The Graduate fulfills its "promise of pleasure" in the penultimate scene when Ben rescues Elaine at her wedding. For all the controversy it has elicited, the final scene in the bus does not detract from the dominant impression gained by the audience from the preceding action. The wordless condition of Ben and Elaine at the end tones down the excitement of the chase, but it doesn't negate, undercut, or even mute their achievement. Both are stunned by their action and need time to absorb its significance. Their act is not a slight one. Ben and Elaine will never, can never, be the same again. When Elaine shouts, "Not for *me!*" to her mother's "It's too late," the gulf which separates them will not be easily bridged in the future. Whatever Ben and Elaine do now will radiate from the choice they have made. Though they may move among the society of their parents and perhaps even adopt some of its accoutrements, they will experience it on their own terms, terms more authentic than conventional.

The bus scene is appropriate in its open-endedness. If the movie had concluded with Ben and Elaine in heady flight, it would lessen their achievement, and confer upon it the aura of fantasy, wish fulfillment, utopia. The doubts and questions raised at the end locate the couple's future actions in the real world, where they should be, where they hold meaning for the audience. Ben and Elaine must now consider what they have done and the difficulties that lie ahead. Their achievement can be measured only by its continued expression in the world of their fathers and mothers. The test is not over; it has only just begun. To maintain their integrity, Ben and Elaine must sustain commitment to their original choice in their daily acts within the whirlpool of society. They have, however, taken the first step. The future is uncertain; the road lies perilous before them. The coded implication of the final image, though, is satisfying. The bus drives off into the distance and away from the bewildered crowd.

2001: A SPACE ODYSSEY

Stanley Kubrick's science fiction epic 2001: A Space Odyssey, which premiered in Washington, D.C., on April 2, 1968, completed the trinity of films that shook up the industry, the critics, and the American public in the late 1960s. In some ways, it went further than its two predecessors in producing controversy, mirroring the times, undermining conventional narration, transforming its genre, and celebrating itself as film. Complaints about the film betrayed a longing for a classical narrative structure: it was incoherent, boring over long stretches in which nothing happens; its meandering plot led nowhere; and it existed for its special effects, which detracted from the development of story and characterization.[7] To counteract the befuddlement caused by his film, Kubrick urged an experiential response, a taking in of sensual, emotional, and subconscious elements coupled with a resistance to categorization:

2001 is a nonverbal experience; out of two hours and 19 minutes of film, there are only a little less than 40 minutes of dialog. I tried to create a visual experience, one that bypasses verbalized pigeonholing and directly penetrates the subconscious with an emotional and philosophic content. . . . I don't want to spell out a verbal road map for 2001 that every viewer will feel obligated to pursue or else fear he's missed the point. (Agel 328)

The need to find a rational key for 2001, however, is so strong that many have sought out Arthur Clarke's novel as an "explanation" of this film.[8] But a comparison of the novel and film only serves to underscore the contrast between the two works and to confirm the film's open-endedness and sense of mystery. The novel chronicles the discovery of each of the three monoliths, the first by the man-apes on earth, the second by the Americans in Clavius on the moon, and the third by the astronaut Bowman on Japetus, one of Saturn's moons (in the movie, the third monolith is found in orbit around Jupiter). Each section of the novel is told from the perspective of a main character, Moonwatcher in section one, "Primeval Night"; Dr. Heywood Floyd in section two, "TMA-1"; and astronaut Dave Bowman in sections three, four, five, and six, "Between Planets," "Abyss," "The Moons of Saturn," and "Through the Star Gate." The novel jumps four million years from the man-apes to twenty-first-century man, but, unlike the filmic narration, the novel's omniscient narration accounts for everything. It demystifies the four-million-year gap in a chapter entitled "The Ascent of Man," which traces in a summary way man's development from Moonwatcher's discovery of rudimentary tools and weapons to twenty-first-century man's highly sophisticated technology of space travel and nuclear systems. We later learn in chapter 37 that the monolith on earth was a teaching and controlling device, a tool of extraterrestrial beings to instill intelligence in the man-apes at the beginning of the evolutionary process; that the monolith on the moon was a cosmic alarm, signaling another monolith on Japetus that man has reached the end of one stage in his development and is ready for the next stage; and that the monolith on Japetus, the Star Gate, is the device left by the aliens three million years ago to instigate the next stage in man's development to a superhuman being. Chapter 16 explains HAL and the concept of machine intelligence; chapter 31 clues us into the reason for HAL's faulty behavior; chapter 32 offers scientific theories about extraterrestrials, the possibility of man's development into machine intelligence before heading into the realm of spirit; chapter 44 explains the mystery of the room Bowman finds himself in after entering the Star Gate; and the last chapters indicate clearly Bowman's transformation into a baby, Star-Child, the force who returns to earth, detonates the bombs circling the globe, and prepares the way for a superhuman race.

The novel is written in a linear manner, with clear connective links, a coherent plot, and conflicts logically resolved. It clarifies the evolutionary theme by positing an extraterrestrial force external to man as responsible for mankind's development from animal intelligence to human intelligence and on to superhuman intelligence. The movie is a study in contrast. Its gaps are unfilled, its images obscure. Radically different from the novel, it offers another experience, the kind one encounters in a poem, especially a modern poem, whose structure is open and elliptical, and whose meaning evolves by way of association, its imagery and metaphors forming parallels, contrasts, and analogies.

An example of such a poem is T. S. Eliot's *The Wasteland* (1921). Instead of a linear and logical structure, the poem employs an associative structure where meaning derives from a complex series of analogies. The poem is difficult to read in the conventional way because of its lack of connective links, its highly allusive quality, and its built-in ambiguity. *2001* approximates the characteristics of a poem like *The Wasteland*, since, as I suggest, the proper way to view the film is to "read" it as a cinematic poem. In this way, one avoids the two extreme and inadequate approaches to it. The first explains away the film's ambiguity by referring to the rationalism of Clarke's work, while the second experiences it as a light and sound extravaganza, a sensual, emotional immersion in the "flow" of its special effects. On the one hand, a "reading" of the film as a cinematic poem prevents reducing it to the level of plot and preserves its open and suggestive quality. On the other hand, it rescues the film from the misunderstanding that it is an amorphous collection of images to induce a "trippy" experience.

As a cinematic poem, *2001* is coherent primarily on the level of analogy; however, one can perceive the classical underpinning to its modernist form. The movie is linear in its movement; its structure evolves out of the classical principle of continuity editing, a principle which preserves a chronological progression of images, but which also recognizes the inevitable ellipses between images and sequences in the editing process. Continuity editing depends on the viewer to fill in these gaps. As the gaps widen or occur more suddenly, the viewer supplies more of the transitions between shots. Films employ extreme ellipses all the time, but the degree of work the viewer does varies. For example, *Lawrence of Arabia* (1962) and *The Deer Hunter* (1978) contain radical ellipses, but both films provide prior coded information to aid the audience in linking shots and sequences. In *Lawrence of Arabia*, Lawrence's British commander in Cairo has assigned him the task of advising the Arabs in their fight against the Turks in World War I. To carry out his assignment, Lawrence must travel from Cairo to Medina and cross sixty miles of desert to find Prince Faisal, the leader of one of the largest tribes. The film makes the transition from army headquarters in Cairo to the desert in a cut from the flame of a match to the red dawn of the desert. On the wide screen in close-up, Lawrence's face is in profile on the right, while the flaming match he holds up is on the left. As he blows out the flame, the scene cuts to the flaming desert. The transition is breathtakingly sudden, but easily understandable on the level of plot, action, and character motivation. In *The Deer Hunter*, the main protagonists, Mike, Nick, and Steven, spend their last weekend before being shipped to Vietnam celebrating Steven's marriage. On the morning after the wedding, Mike, Nick, and their friends, Stan, Axel, and John, embark on a hunting trip, the last ritual before the trio leaves for the war. Their long day ends when they return to John's bar and, in a quiet interlude, John plays a Chopin to the now sober and pensive men. The soothing, lilting notes of the piano mix with the whirring of the fan above the pool table, which blends into the faint whirring of helicopters, a sound bridge to the next scene; the peaceful moment in the bar in Clairton, Pennsylvania, then cuts to the violence of helicopters bombarding a Viet Cong village, where Nick and Steven reunite with Mike after months of combat. The radical shift in location and time is startling in its suddenness, but the viewer negotiates the ellipsis rather smoothly once the surprise passes. The first hour of the film had provided ample anticipation of the three protagonists' time in Vietnam.

The ellipses of *2001*, however, put greater demands on the viewer to fill its gaps because *2001* lacks the conventional verbal clues in dialogue and narration that provide information about situation and character motivation. The consequent effect is a deemphasis on linear action and a classical cause and effect process. Instead, the focus shifts to a figurative association of details over the course of the entire film text. The important links in *2001* are thematic rather than chronological. Nothing in the way of plot time and character motivation prepares the viewer for the famous cut from Moonwatcher's bone to the spaceship in the twenty-first century. The cut traverses an enormous juncture which the viewer recognizes; but why from the Dawn of Man to the twenty-first century? Unlike the radical ellipses of *Lawrence of Arabia* and *The Deer Hunter*, the cut doesn't work in the conventional sense of character motivation and accompanying actions. The cut does operate, however, on a figurative and thematic level, in the association of Moonwatcher's bone with the orbiting spacecraft. Moonwatcher's bone is both a tool and a weapon, and the sign of man's first step toward a higher intelligent being. The cut suggests the ultimate development of man's technological skills from the rudimentary bone to the elegant spaceship, a tool to explore space and a defense mechanism in the cold war between the two superpowers, America and Russia. The cut also suggests an irony—for all the time that has passed and for all the sophistication man has acquired, nothing has changed. In their double function, the bone and the spacecraft reflect man's capacity for both creation and destruction. Furthermore, the cut is not only an operative in the thematic patterns within the cinema text, but also a commentary on the text itself, a self-reflexive gesture celebrating the techniques available to cinema to effect both a radical transition and a figurative association.

Modernist Ambiguity

The enormous body of commentary on *2001* illustrates the rich variety of readings stimulated by the figurative associations strung out over the entire film text. That these interpretations clash and may be irresolvable is not an important issue. What is important is what it reveals about the film's essential characteristic, its ambiguity, an elasticity which permits a number of possible meanings in keeping with its sense of exploration and openness in the face of the unknown. To embrace the film's ambiguity instead of attempting to explain it away is to acknowledge its raison d'être. In the interview with Gelmis, Kubrick himself pointed out this feature, one which he called "inevitable" and "unavoidable":

I didn't have to try for ambiguity; it was inevitable. And I think in a film like *2001*, where each viewer brings his own emotions and perceptions to bear on the subject matter, a certain degree of ambiguity is valuable, because it allows the audience to "fill in" the visual experience themselves. In any case, once you're dealing on a nonverbal level, ambiguity is unavoidable. (Gelmis, *Film Director* 303)

Different and equally valid approaches to the status of the monolith and to the evolutionary theme itself lay open the ambiguity at the heart of *2001*. In the first case, one source of ambiguity is the tension between a viewing of the monolith as literal and a viewing of it as metaphoric. From the perspective of Clarke's novel and the "simple level of plot," the monolith represents an artifact of super extraterrestrial creatures intent on controlling man's progression from brute animal to intellectual being. The first monolith instills a sense of higher consciousness in Moonwatcher's tribe and teaches it the use of tools and language. The second monolith signals the aliens that man is ready to achieve the next step in the evolutionary process; while the third monolith leads Bowman to the final stages in the process, and the last transforms him into Star Child, a superhuman being of pure intelligence. By this viewing of the film, the power behind the monolith controls man's development, while he remains passive for the most part, acting out a higher consciousness only with the aid of the monolith. However, with the Clarkean perspective out of mind, the monolith may take on the quality of a figurative object; once that happens, its meaning becomes more open and mysterious. Does it represent an external or an internal force in relation to man? Does it represent the natural evolutionary forces within earthly life or an extraterrestrial power? Given its perfect geometric form, could it not represent and celebrate man's perfection of technology so evident in the grace and precision of his machinery and in his capacity to reach the outer limits of the solar system? Given its severe, dark, blunt form, could it not represent and warn of the dangers of technology to dull the imagination and the emotions in favor of a razor sharp sense of logic and reason so evident in the robotlike astronauts? Or is the monolith a mere marker for man's progress and the mysterious possibilities open to him as Robert Kolker suggests in *A Cinema of Loneliness* (1988): the monoliths are "imaginary markers of humanity's evolution, dark and featureless because one of the valid connotations of the future is the unknown, a blindness to possibilities" (123).

Critics faced with the possibility of both a literal and a figurative reading of the monolith handle the contradictions in various ways. Thomas

Allen Nelson, for example, resolves the contradiction by distinguishing between the monolith's "overt" and "covert" meanings. Its overt meaning derives from the conventional narrative based on Clarke's novel and Kubrick's level-of-plot explanation—the monolith is an otherworldly device, a teaching tool, a cosmic alarm, and a gateway to a life of pure energy. Meanwhile, its covert meaning derives from its analogous association with other objects, such as bone, fountain pen, spaceship, computer, and crystal glass. In other words, its covert value derives from the cinematic elements which project it as a visual and aural phenomenon in the film world and from our response to its shape, its color, and the sound of Ligeti's music (104–105). The monolith's covert meaning stems from what Nelson calls the film's enormous "visual ambiguity," in contrast to its minimal "explanatory clarity." I would call it its "cinematic ambiguity" to suggest the function of the whole cinematic apparatus in the visual and aural projection of the monolithic figure.

The implication of Nelson's idea of the monolith's covert meaning is that it is an object associated with man's scientific accomplishments over time, signifying his progress and development as a being of higher consciousness. To say this is just a step away from conceiving of the monolith as a metaphor for the internal spark within man that drives him to higher achievements.

David Boyd, meanwhile, deals with the contradictory interpretations of the monolith as external and internal force by acknowledging both factors as necessary for mankind's leap forward—in other words, an evolution that necessarily includes both environmental conditioning and internal adaptation. And so he argues that the actions involved in the leap forward are both the external influence of the monolith and man's own internal will to power (212). This reading preserves the distinction between monolith and man, but it also recognizes the power within Moonwatcher and Bowman that acts in concert with the monolith as if the monolith were a trigger for internal action rather than a godlike force controlling human behavior.

Finally, Don Daniels cleverly argues that an interpretation of the monolith as an extraterrestrial force acting as a deus ex machina would subvert the film's evolutionary theme—would in fact be anti-evolutionary, since evolution necessarily includes the process of internal development. He then suggests that the monolith be taken as a metaphor for nature, for the natural order of progression which includes man's development to a higher being: "But there are suggestions that the slow progress to intelligence is a natural one and that the aliens are part of nature itself. 2001 celebrates the rare signatures of a natural order within the chaotic mystery of the universe" (9).

These attempts to resolve the tension of meanings inherent in the monolith image serve only, in the end, to reemphasize the open-ended quality of the figure, just one example of the ambiguity at the heart of the film. The theme of evolution itself possesses this same open-endedness, given two major and conflicting interpretations concerning the nature of mankind's progression to a higher level of existence. The first interpretation views the action of evolution in the film as a development toward pure mind, intellect, energy, or spirit—a transcendence of materiality. In Daniels's phrase, the theme is "the growth of intelligence in the universe" (2). In this scheme, the apes evolve out of the trap of mere animal instinct into greater consciousness, conceptual thought, and reflection, while modern man extricates himself from the materiality of technology in gaining an even higher level of consciousness and thought. Jack Fisher in "The End of Sex in *2001*" emphasizes the ethereality of Star Child, identifying it as a sexless creature: "intelligence raised to its infinite power, the Messiah without the humanity of being born of woman . . . without anyone resorting to physical sex. He is now Star Child, a product of philogenesis: mind birth" (65).

Kubrick himself identified the next stage in evolution as approximating advanced forms of intelligent life or "disembodied immortal consciousness," attributes finally that we associate with God:

Such cosmic intelligences, growing in knowledge over the aeons, would be as far removed from man as we are from the ants. They could be in instantaneous telepathic communication throughout the universe; they might have achieved total mastery over matter so that they can telekinetically transport themselves instantly across billions of light years of space; in their ultimate form they might shed the corporeal shell entirely and exist as a disembodied immortal consciousness throughout the universe.

Once you begin discussing such possibilities, you realize that the religious implications are inevitable, because all the essential attributes of such extraterrestrial intelligences are the attributes we give to God. (Gelmis, *Film Director* 305)

The higher state of being, which Kubrick describes and which Star Child supposedly looks forward to, is not so much superhuman as anti-human. This is one of the problems with such an interpretation of the film's end. However, on the basis of the Clarkean synopsis, the subject of extraterrestrial influence and man's aping of its qualities from primitive bone weaponry to spaceship technology to starlike existence remains uppermost in the logic of the narrative. Furthermore, sounds and images back up the idea of a godlike and intellectual development of mankind in the film: Ligeti's eerie and mysterious notes, Strauss's grand heroic statement, and the emotionless, sexless demeanor of the scientists and astronauts operating within an antiseptic environment.

On the other hand, other elements in the film suggest a different goal of humankind in the twenty-first century, a goal that would save man his humanity rather than have him slough it off cocoonlike. This view agrees with the first on one account—that the movement is away from technology—but the purpose is quite the opposite: to achieve not pure intelligence but a fuller consciousness of what it means to be human and to rescue the emotions, imagination, passion, and subjectivity from erosion by analysis, logic, and objectivity. In this view, the stonelike and stoic features of the astronauts represent a dangerous signal rather than a progressive looking forward. Man has unwittingly made himself into an image of his machines. We see him robotlike depicted in Floyd's highly cultivated professional and scientific manner and in Poole's and Bowman's expressionless faces, in their service to routine, and in their clipped, unembellished, functional speech. These three characters indicate that man has chosen to close off open and heartfelt communication in his acceptance of the professional conventions which dictate his relationship to others. Politics and cold war expediency lock Floyd into circumspect answers to the questions of the Russian scientist concerning the activity on the American base of Clavius, while the Jupiter mission conditions Poole and Bowman to function as its human levers. Given this view, Kolker can say that the leap forward from ape to twenty-first-century man is no leap at all because "man is shown joyless and dead—man has become his machines" (124), while Daniels sees the depiction of man in the film as "goalless rationalists with a supreme distrust of the emotions and a child-like faith in rational reality and the intellect. . . . There are no hopes or goals for these supermen, only a mechanical extension of the race into the local universe" (3–5).

The irony that HAL, the film's supercomputer, expresses more human characteristics than the astronauts themselves has been well documented. HAL is, in turn, gently warm in his solicitations, proud, deceptive, murderous, cunning, and fearful of dying. The expression of human traits in a machine underlines the absence of them in the men, but we must not forget that HAL is still a machine and that he represents the "disembodied voice of three centuries of scientific rationalism . . . intelligence uncontrolled by the strictures of morality" (Daniels 6). As a machine, he is programmed to achieve the success of the Jupiter mission. The astronauts are like HAL, and vice versa: they are human machines to his machine humanity, and they are as much automatons to the demands of the mission as he is.

One development away from this machinelike state would be to recover the affective and moral sensibilities, to reawaken a sense of wonder, to embody a new freedom in which man's powers are fully integrated rather than dissipated in the service of one faculty. It would mean working out a new consciousness within each individual to break the bonds of objectivity and convention in order to realize a new self. Four sequences provide glimpses of Star Child's significance as future

Antiseptic space station/politics and cold war expediency. *Courtesy of Museum of Modern Art Film Stills Archive; Copyright MGM, 1968.*

"man alive" in touch with his feelings as well as with his intellect, imbued with curiosity and imagination, and awakened to a subjectivity
which is individual and not co-opted. The first sequence is Bowman's
conflict with HAL after his rescue of Poole's body from space. Since
every conventional means of entering *Discovery* has been closed off by
HAL's interference, Bowman has to use imagination and daring to enter
through highly unconventional means. In other words, when man's most
highly developed machines fail him, he must fall back on his own personal resources. (Bow)man succeeds and, in doing so, sparks the inception of a more inclusive sense of being. When he kills HAL, "he rejects
science, technology, and rationalism as only partial aids in the search for
life" (Daniels 7).

In the second sequence, Bowman takes a ride through Star Gate, which
may be taken as a psychedelic trip, an intensification of awareness and
sensory experience. Bowman's heightened visual perception during the
ride through the corridor represents the awakening of his sensual powers
shown in the shot-reverse-shots of his alert, stunned eyes and the colorful, varied shapes and dimensions he sees. The third sequence begins
after Bowman's trip through Star Gate when he finds himself in a Louis
XVI room. The sequence details a literal sloughing off of the old before
rebirth. Bowman sheds first the space pod, then his space suit, and finally
the aged and decrepit body we last see dying in bed. The crystal glass
he finders and drinks from parallels the human artifacts fashioned
throughout the ages—bone weapon, spaceship, pen, computer, technological accomplishments rejected and done away with in one swift moment when the crystal shatters in its fall from the table. Furthermore, the
Louis XVI room is, of course, a reminder of the Age of Reason; its cool,
elegant decor is a sign of the coded structures of civility in an urban,
modern society. Star Child's issuance from the confinement of the room
to universal space represents (Bow)man's liberation from the steel precision and logic of technological man, the legacy of eighteenth-century
rationalism.

The image of the fetal Star Child wrapped in its womb, floating in
space, is the fourth and final sequence which provides a hint of a future
integrated consciousness by the recovery of the affective sensibilities, for
the wide-eyed fetus may be viewed for what it is—a warm, wet, sensual
being—in contrast to Fisher's view that it is sexless, cerebral, and a sign
of pure intelligence.

Whether one subscribes to the interpretation of the new order of being
as bodiless intelligence or as the recovery of the sensual, the emotional,
and the imaginative in human life is not as important as the recognition
of the rich texture of the film, which makes possible the perception of
different shades of meaning. Though the fetus image at the end may
serve the purposes of either perspective, perhaps we should emphasize

(Bow)man's psychedelic trip: an awakening and intensification of sensory experience. *Courtesy of Museum of Modern Art Film Stills Archive; Copyright MGM, 1968.*

instead its mystery and unexplored future meaning. Thomas Allen Nelson, for example, focuses finally on Star Child's elusiveness:

This enhanced being carries no tools, speaks no tongue, and contemplates space without the mediation of the primitive's instincts or the rationalist's machine logic. The mirror world has been broken and beyond its reflexivity stands the unknown and unexplored. . . . The Star-Child in his bubble rotates like a planet, and his huge eyes look not only toward Earth below, his home and destination, but directly into the camera, like a humanized monolith mutely imploring the audience to ponder its mystery. (132)

Transformation of Genre

The ambiguities offered by *2001*'s open and unconventional structure, by its deep sense of exploration and mystery, by the tension between literal and figurative interpretations, and by Kubrick's deliberate deemphasis of rational explanations in favor of a faith in the possibilities opened up by the film's purely cinematic elements deepen and take on an even greater significance in the context of *2001*'s place in the genre of science fiction films.

Just as *Bonnie and Clyde* did earlier and as westerns would do later in the period, *2001* represents a commentary on its genre. It is both a culmination and a transformation of the science fiction film in its working out of the two major attitudes toward science in the genre, an attitude of celebration and an attitude of criticism. On the one hand, *2001* glorifies the wonders of technology; on the other, it inquires pessimistically into the effects of technology on people's lives. The incorporation of both a proscience and an anti-science attitude on the film's generic level fuels the ambiguity we find operating in its figurative associations and theme. Both attitudes have played their parts in the genre's development since the early 1950s. According to Vivian Sobchack in *Screening Space, The American Science Fiction Film*, Second Edition (1987), and in "Science Fiction," *Handbook of American Film Genres* (1988), proscience science fiction films celebrate man's scientific achievements and create the illusion of an authentic technological world. They are optimistic in the belief that man and science can extend human life beyond earth to the stars (*Screening Space* 21–22). Sobchack says that the primary visual project of science fiction films is to "produce wondrous and unfamiliar imagery"; to emphasize the "wonderfully functional and functionally wonderful aspects of advanced science and technology." Big budget sci-fi films, especially, foreground technology and spectacular machinery and also "the latest technological developments in the cinema's own means of expression" ("Science Fiction" 230). We can trace this aspect of sci-fi films from Melies's 1902 *A Trip to the Moon* and 1904 *An Impossible Voyage* to its full-blown development in the 1950s with *Destination Moon* (1950), *When Worlds Collide* (1951), *War of the Worlds* (1953), *The Conquest of Space* (1955), *This Island Earth* (1955), and *Forbidden Planet* (1956), and on to such movies in the 1960s as *The Time Machine* (1960), *From the Earth to the Moon* (1964), and *Fantastic Voyage* (1966). Besides fashioning an authentic technological universe through cinema's own technology of special effects, these films project a faith in science through the depiction of scientific actions and machinery called upon to overcome threats to humankind. Positive scientific machinery includes the space ark in *When Worlds Collide*, constructed to take a group of people to colonize a planet before another planet collides with earth; the death ray reflector constructed to defeat the alien Martians in *The War of the Worlds*; the wondrous and time conquering gadgetry of *The Time Machine*; and the microtechnology of *Fantastic Voyage*. However, these movies may also contain grim warnings of the misuse or dangers of science. *The Time Machine* warns of the destructive aspect of science as George (Rod Taylor) sees the devastating effects of World War II in 1940 and experiences the detonation of an orbiting atom bomb in 1966 as he travels into the future from 1899. In *Forbidden Planet*, the giant machines of the Krels can create materials from the sheer thought of its user, but this power backfires since it can create materials from the unconscious as well as the conscious mind. Given this capability, the machines fashion monsters from the ids of their masters, which turn on their makers and destroy them. The Krels' machines vividly personify both the creative and the destructive forces within man and his technology.

Whatever slurs against science these films possess are overridden, however, by their generally optimistic tone and stunning visual sets and effects, celebrating not only their subject but also their "means of expression," the technology of cinema itself. *2001* represents the culmination of this celebration. More than any previous film, it creates convincingly a complete world of future space. One may describe the film's plot as overly simple and its theme as pretentious, but one can only marvel at the film's unqualified success in creating the world of *2001* in meticulous visual detail. The scenes in space and on spaceships are as much performed for their authenticity as for their contribution to plot or theme. Some would say even more so. Through its careful detail and deliberate pace, the sequence on the Pan Am shuttle and at the Howard Johnson space station at the beginning of the film's second part illustrates the transference of earthly habits to space and invests the audience with the wonder of the possibility of space travel in its lifetime. The sequences aboard *Discovery* reveal what life directed almost completely by computer technology would be like; the sequences outside *Discovery* illustrate the use of such sophisticated equipment as the space suit and space pod. Kubrick's fashioning of a complete world of the future, grandly announced by Richard Strauss's *Thus Spake Zarathustra* and gracefully inhabited by waltzing spaceships to the tune of *The Blue Danube*, testifies to the glory of man's achievements at this stage of his evolutionary development.

However, the anti-scientific elements in *2001* are serious enough to qualify its magnificent celebration. Kolker says that *2001* is two films in one, a "technological fantasy" and a "pessimistic inquiry into the forms of the immediate future" (117). The pessimistic inquiry exposes the technological for the threat it poses to the spontaneity of the human spirit: "Perfect order and perfect function decrease the need for human inquisitiveness and control. A perfectly clean world is clean of human interference" (121).

As noted in the discussion of the evolution theme, the characters' automated responses and stunted speech measure the dangerous effects of science. They lay bare the paucity of feeling in a supertechnological environment. Man has become an automaton, his own machine, a monster destroying himself. In this way, the anti-science of *2001* is like the anti-science we find at the core of the creature/monster and the "takeover" films of the genre. Both subgenres fashion a narrative in which mankind is threatened by an external force. In the creature/monster film, the threat is one of physical attack and destruction; in the takeover films, the threat is more insidious since it means the assumption or takeover of one's body, identity, volition, or humanity by aliens. In the creature/ monster film, the antagonist may be either earthly or extraterrestrial, while in the takeover film, the antagonist is almost always extraterrestrial. The creature/monster films include two general kinds of external forces operating against humankind—the "creature" defined as an animal or intelligent threat apart from man and the "monster" defined as a human being horribly transformed through scientific accidents or experiments (Sobchack, *Screening Space* 44, 52). Creature films include *The Thing* (1951), *The Beast from 20,000 Fathoms* (1953), *Creature from the Black Lagoon* (1954), *It Came from Beneath the Sea* (1955), and *Them!* (1954); monster films include *The Amazing Colossal Man* (1957), *The Fly* (1958), *The 4-D Man* (1959), and *The Most Dangerous Man Alive* (1961). A film like *Tarantula* (1955) has both a creature and a monster. The creature/monster in these films personifies the threat that science poses in the devastation it can inflict through misuse and irresponsible behavior by those who have access or control. In *The Beast from 20,000 Fathoms*, a nuclear device tested in the Arctic Circle releases a prehistoric rhedosaurus, a carnivorous dinosaur; in *Them!*, atomic testing mutates desert ants into giants; in *It Came from Beneath the Sea*, H-bomb tests radioactivate a huge octopus that threatens humans because its natural prey, fish, detect its radiation as it approaches. *The Amazing Colossal Man* develops from exposure to a nuclear blast; in *Tarantula*, scientists, experimenting with an "atomically stabilized" nutrient to develop a way to feed the world's growing population, inject themselves with it and develop giantism; in *The Most Dangerous Man Alive*, a gangster wanders into an atomic test area for "cobalt mutation," and the explosion that follows causes him to absorb steel, making him superhuman.

In addition to personifying the threat which a destructive application of science poses to man, the creature/monster films also personify the threat of the "other," which in the 1950s translated into the anxieties caused by Communism and the cold war (Sobchack, "Science Fiction," 233–234). The takeover films, meanwhile, extend the threat of the "other" to include forces closer to home that mold the individual to social conformity. Examples include *It Came from Outer Space* (1953), *Invaders from Mars* (1953), *Invasion of the Body Snatchers* (1956), *I Married a Monster from Outer Space* (1958), *Invisible Invaders* (1959), and *The Day Mars Invaded the Earth* (1962). In 1950s America, these films mirrored the anxieties caused by forces that erode originality and independence: established bureaucracy, McCarthyism, white-middle-class American values, and technological advancement. The aliens take over by inhabiting the body or simulating the physical characteristics of human beings. Though they look human, they are not. These "simulacra" lack emotion, volition, and spontaneity and give themselves away by merely walking through the daily activities of their human counterparts without the usual tics or idiosyncrasies that distinguish a personality. Carlos Carens in *An Illustrated History of the Horror Film* calls this the "ultimate horror" of "dehumanisation" that exposes contemporary society's most realized fear, a "collective anxiety about the loss of individual identity, subliminal mind-bending, or downright scientific/political brainwashing" (134).

2001 both extends and transforms the anti-science attitude of the creature/monster and take over films when viewed as a satire on technology's capability to cause physical destruction and to corrode man's affective, moral, and imaginative sensibilities in molding him to approximate his machine environment. Just as the creature/monster films posit the threat of nuclear disaster, so too *2001* dramatizes the cold war tension between the American Floyd and the Russian scientist in the Howard Johnson space station. Just as the creature/monster films pose the threat of the "other," so too, *2001* poses this threat; however, it transforms the external threat of these films to an internal one, for the "other" in *2001* is man himself. The values of logic, reason, and order have grown monstrously out of proportion and turned man into his own worst enemy. Sobchack points out that in the monster films, the man-monster is evil not because of what he is, but because of what he *does* in wreaking violence (*Screening Space* 52). In *2001*, man is "evil" not for what he does, but for what he *is* or has become, evident by his expressionless face, his stunted speech, and his mechanical functioning.[9]

In relation to that of the takeover films, *2001*'s depiction of the loss of an integrated humanity approximates the loss of identity we find in a film like *Invasion of the Body Snatchers*, where alien pods assimilate people's bodies, but not their humanity and individuality. *2001* attributes this loss not to alien creatures, but to man himself. In stunting certain powers needed to prevent the taking over of the self by his rational faculties, man has allowed technological advancement and its values to seep into his everyday and personal existence; he has become his own simulacrum.

2001 AND *HAIR*: COUNTERCULTURE VISIONS

Just as the creature/monster sci-fi films of the 1950s mirror the paranoia of the time, so too *2001*, as an anti-utopian vision, reflects the late 1960s dissatisfaction with traditional authoritarian discourses—patriotism (Vietnam), paternalism (women's movement), racism (civil rights movement), puritanism (sexual revolution). As an expression of the sentiments sweeping the country at the end of the 1960s, *2001* looks forward to the liberalism of the science fiction films of the 1970s before *Star Wars* (1977) and *Close Encounters of the Third Kind* (1977), films highly critical of social and political institutionalism—*The Planet of the Apes* series (1968–1973), *Zardoz* (1973), *Rollerball* (1975), *The Stepford Wives* (1975), and *Logan's Run* (1976)—and those concerned with terrestrial issues such as overpopulation, food shortage, old age, and conservation—*The Omega Man* (1971), *Frogs* (1972), *Silent Running* (1973), and *Soylent Green* (1973).[10] In the context of its time, the ambiguities of *2001* give way to the clear vision that it is indeed an expression of the threat of a centralization in society or in government that saps man's full potential. The fetus image at the end signals the coming of a new dawn that approximates the beginning of life before the encroachment of environment, making possible the growth of one's full humanity in the future ahead.

The radicalism of *2001* parallels that of its contemporary on the Broadway stage, the hit musical *Hair*. *Hair* opened off-Broadway at Joseph Papp's New York Shakespeare Festival Public Theater in November 1967 between the openings of *Bonnie and Clyde* (August 1967) and *The Graduate* (December 1967); it later premiered on Broadway at the Biltmore Theater on April 29, 1968, just three weeks after the premiere of *2001*. The public and critics alike linked the science-fiction film and the "American tribal-love rock musical" as significant artistic as well as cultural "events." Both stood the conventions of classical narration and musical theater, respectively, on their heads. And both became anthems for the counterculture.

William Kloman, in his contemporary *New York Times* article, "*2001* and *Hair*—Are They the Groove of the Future?" noted the pair's parallel achievements. *Hair*'s plot of a boy who joins a hippie community, forms a menage-à-trois, goes into the army, and dies in Vietnam is a throwaway around which "a collage of dramatic effects" can be formed. The audience is asked not to respond to plot in the conventional sense, but to lose itself in the sensuality, emotionalism, the "flow of activity"; to groove "without anticipation or imposition of logical structures" (D15). In both content and form, the musical asks us to free ourselves of preconceptions, to lay aside the categories that bind us, and to open our sensibilities to the current of images, sound, light, and movement in order to get in tune with ourselves, our planet, and our universe. In the book and lyrics by Gerome Ragni and James Rado, the opening instructions for the setting indicate the concept of the universe that runs through the play in its songs:

Note should be taken of the spiritual theme running through the play; outer space, astrology, the earth, the heavens, interplanetary travel, mysticism, as seen in the songs "Aquarius," "Walking in Space," "Early Morning Singing Song," and "Exanaplanetooch." (ix)

The psychedelic experience of *Hair*, which extends in space from New York City to the rest of the nation, the world, and the universe, receives its impetus from the celebration of strobe lights, incense, balloons, nude bodies, choreographed movements, and, especially, music.

Kloman sees *2001* as a similar "happening." His claim that the film is "deeply subversive" applies not only to its form and structure, but also to its psychedelic elements and its offer to the audience to adopt an open attitude and immerse itself in the flow of images, "shapes and motion," sounds, and special effects—in other words, in the possibilities of the medium itself (D15). As such, the audience reflects upon itself in the figure of the astronaut Bowman, as he travels through the Star Gate with his startled open expression during the display of colors and figures, and as he sheds the constrictions of the everyday at the end in order to renew an innocence by which he can enter into a fuller experience on the earth and among the stars. The song "Aquarius" from *Hair* refers to the affect which openness and embracement make possible when it celebrates the dawning of universal peace and love. The heavenly sign for this event is the alignment of Jupiter and Mars, which recalls the alignment of the heavenly bodies in *2001* at those moments when man taps his potential to expand and develop a higher consciousness. In 1968, both *Hair* and *2001*, strange yet compatible bedfellows, looked forward to this new age of Aquarius at a time when everything seemed possible:

When the moon is in the seventh House
And Jupiter Aligns with Mars

Then Peace will guide the Planets
And love will steer the stars
This is the dawning of the age of Aquarius
The Age of Aquarius/Aquarius/Aquarius
Harmony and Understanding/Sympathy and Trust Abounding
No More falsehoods or derisions/Golden living dreams of visions
Mystic Crystal Revelation/And the Mind's true liberation
Aquarius/Aquarius.

CHAPTER THREE

Westerns in Modern Dress: *The Wild Bunch* and *McCabe and Mrs. Miller*

In the years following the advent of *Bonnie and Clyde*, *The Graduate*, and *2001: A Space Odyssey*, American moviemakers vigorously extended and explored the trio's legacy of apocalyptic themes, stylistic experimentation, and reflexivity of narrative form and genre. As those films had used the traditional genres of the gangster film, the screwball comedy, and the sci-fi film both to structure their narratives and to transform, even subvert, the genres' conventions, so too movies such as *M*A*S*H*, *Cabaret*, and *Chinatown* would advantageously employ only to overturn the conventions of the war film, the musical, and the detective/*noir* film, respectively.[1] However, no genre during the period was more exploited, explored, and exploded than the western, the genre which more than any other represents an index to the historical development of the American film and to the basic myths and contradictions underlying American society.[2] In the 60s and 70s, the main type of western which evolved from the classic strain was the "professional western," of which the Italian spaghetti western was an imported example. American westerns of this type included *The Magnificent Seven* (1960), *The Professionals* (1966), *El Dorado* (1967), *The Wild Bunch* (1969), *Butch Cassidy and the Sundance Kid* (1969), *The Great Northfield Minnesota Raid* (1972), *The Missouri Breaks* (1976), and *The Long Riders* (1980). The most prominent Italian spaghetti westerns of the 60s were those of Sergio Leone: *A Fistful of Dollars* (1964), *For a Few Dollars More* (1965), *The Good, the Bad, and the Ugly* (1967), and *Once Upon a Time in the West* (1969). Thomas Schatz says that the professional western hero combines the "values of entrepreneurial capitalism and rugged individualism"; he is either an enterprising outlaw looking out for his own good or a lawman who "develops an antagonistic rapport with the bureaucrats who hire him." In both roles, the professional westerner subordinates social instincts to self-interest, in contrast to the classic westerner who combines the values of the individual with those of the community ("The Western" 32).

The world of the professional western accommodates its anti-heroes by incorporating the amoral society of its precursor, the spaghetti western. These westerns had depicted a dark, corrupt, and treacherous world in which heroes were indistinguishable from villains and marked, not by moral purpose and righteous courage, but by superior strategems, unscrupulousness, and skill in violence. John Cawelti sees the worldview of the spaghetti western as even seeping into the John Wayne "Godfather westerns" of the 60s and 70s. Though the "godfather" hero of *True Grit* (1969), *Chisum* (1970), *Rio Lobo* (1970), *Big Jake* (1971), and *The Cowboys* (1972) is imbued with a clear sense of moral purpose in his quest for personal justice, this purpose is really a cloak for unabashed aggression and violence, quite unlike that of the classic western hero, whose violence is necessary but reluctant. In the "Godfather western," ruthless aggression and concern with power are positive values because society's weakness and corruption necessitate a hero who combats the ruthlessness, violence, and cruelty with superior force of his own ("Reflections" 113–117).

In addition to these westerns, the period also produced two other types, the Indian raid or "Vietnam" westerns and those which dismissed the traditional formula altogether in favor of the realistic depiction of cowboy or frontier life. Examples of the latter include *Jeremiah Johnson* (1968), *Will Penny* (1968), and *Monte Walsh* (1970). Meanwhile, *Soldier Blue*, *Little Big Man* (1970), and *Ulzana's Raid* (1972) illustrate the Indian raid westerns, which overturned the prosocial myth of manifest destiny and the American cavalry's taming of the West through the exposure of the jingoism and racial-cultural chauvinism of the military move westward. The depiction of the U.S. cavalry as imperialistic paralleled Americans' perception of their government's militaristic stance in Vietnam and tied these westerns to the anti-war protests of the late 60s and early 70s (Schatz, "The Western" 33).

However, of all the westerns during the period, one type dominated because of its renaissance qualities of apocalyptic themes, stylistic experimentation, and reflexivity of narrative form and genre: the auteurist or personal western, examples of which overlap with the categories mentioned. The personal western places the individual vision and style of its filmmaker foremost; its plot follows but transforms the classic conflict between heroism and villainy; and its protagonist extends and deepens the ambiguity of the classic hero through a violence which is honorable not for its social merit as in the past, but for its expression of a personal moral code.[3] Auteurist westerns during the period would include George

Roy Hill's *Butch Cassidy and the Sundance Kid* (1969); Arthur Penn's *Little Big Man* (1970) and *The Missouri Breaks* (1976); Sam Peckinpah's *The Wild Bunch* (1969), *The Ballad of Cable Hogue* (1970), and *Pat Garrett and Billy the Kid* (1973); and Robert Altman's *McCabe and Mrs. Miller* (1971) and *Buffalo Bill and the Indians: or Sitting Bull's History Lesson* (1976). Of these, two stand out as supreme examples of the personal western, *The Wild Bunch* (1969) and *McCabe and Mrs. Miller* (1971).

THE WESTERN HERO

Before discussing *The Wild Bunch* and *McCabe and Mrs. Miller*, it is necessary to trace the evolution of the western hero from his classic beginnings in the late 1930s to his transformation into the Wild Bunch and John McCabe in the 1970s. *Stagecoach* (1939), *My Darling Clementine* (1946), and *Shane* (1953) will serve as examples of classic westerns; *Red River* (1948), *The Naked Spur* (1953), *The Searchers* (1956), and *The Man Who Shot Liberty Valance* (1962) as complicated variations of the classic hero; and *A Fistful of Dollars* (1964) as the movie that takes the western hero as far afield from the traditional as he can go before the advent of *The Wild Bunch*.

The classic western hero feels both the need for individual integrity and the need to build and preserve the social order. In *Stagecoach*, the values of the wilderness and the community meet in the person of Ringo Kid (John Wayne). Wanted by the law for a crime he did not commit, Ringo is the "good bad man." On the one hand, he supports the community by saving the stagecoach from Indian attack and ridding Lordsburg of the dreaded Plummer gang. On the other hand, he destroys the Plummer gang not from the demands of social obligations, but from those of personal revenge for the murder of his father and brother. The ambiguity of Ringo's position is further emphasized when the town marshal releases him after he has taken the law into his own hands and killed the Plummer family, thereby officially sanctioning his primitive action. At the end, the conflicting elements enjoy rich play. Though embraced by society because of actions on its behalf, Ringo and the heart of gold prostitute Dallas (Claire Trevor) preserve their individuality by leaving Lordsburg. As they ride away, Doc Boone (Thomas Mitchell) confirms their status as outsiders by saying, "Well, they're saved from the blessings of civilization." However, the implication is that they will marry and begin a new branch of civilization elsewhere, marriage being the ultimate social action which threatens the western hero's autonomy.

In Ford's *My Darling Clementine*, Wyatt Earp (Henry Fonda) recalls Ringo's ambiguity in his own classic hero's status. On the one hand, he becomes a lawman and saves Tombstone from the evil Clantons; on the other hand, he does so for the personal motive of revenge for his brother's death. However, unlike *Stagecoach*, which tends to preserve the tension between the conflicting forces of the community and the individual even as it leans toward the latter, *My Darling Clementine* ultimately favors the prosocial myth over the myth of the individual. For example, Earp may have a personal rather than a social motive for bringing the Clantons to justice, but his brother James, who was killed, represents familial values: like Ma, he did the cooking, and he bought a brooch for his girl back home. To avenge James's murder, then, is to uphold the sanctity of the American family as well as to establish law and order in Tombstone. Furthermore, Earp falls in love with Clementine Carter (Cathy Downs), the embodiment of civilized virtues and, in the process, improves his dress and manners. His procession with Clementine to the half-built church and his dance with her after represent a symbolic wedding of the westerner with the easterner, the civilizing of the wilderness by the city. However, the crowning gesture of Earp's prosocial status is his speech over the grave of his brother in Monument Valley in which he states that his purpose for bringing the Clantons to justice is so "every kid has a chance to grow up safe." Though the valley's desert environment reflects Earp's solitary ruggedness in contrast to the rhetoric of his speech, the strength of Fonda's earnest face and honest eyes and the passion of his tone and inflections impart a resonance to the social value of Earp's motives which overcomes the suggestions of his surroundings.

In contrast to the predominantly prosocial figure of Wyatt Earp is Doc Holliday (Victor Mature), a former doctor turned gambler and drinker whose dark side overshadows the civilizing elements within. The contradictions within Holliday's character are apparent: he quotes Shakespeare and cultivates champagne, but this is undercut by his heavy whiskey intake and violent temper. Two women vie for him, the virtuous Clementine and the half-breed Chihuahua (Linda Darnell). In rejecting Clementine and choosing Chihuahua, Holliday affirms the darkness within and represents a threat to the social stability wrought by Earp. However, his death at the end eliminates that threat. Doc, the good bad man, like Chihuahua, the bad good woman, must die to preserve the classic purity of the prosocial myth advanced by Earp, Clementine, and the churchgoers in the half-finished church.[4]

While *My Darling Clementine* opts for the claims of the community and *Stagecoach* veers somewhat toward those of the individual, George Stevens's *Shane* preserves a perfect balance between the two. The film dramatizes these claims through the internal conflict within Shane in his attempt to quit his former life as a gunfighter and help the Starretts eke out a civilized existence in the wilderness. Despite the strength of his motivation, Shane's past keeps interfering with his attempt to salvage his instinct for home and family. For example, Ryker and his gang recognize Shane's affinity to them and ask him to join up after he successfully vanquishes one of their men in a fistfight. Their hired gun, Wilson (Jack Palance), recognizes Shane immediately as one of his kind. Furthermore, Shane's resistance to a full commitment to family relations tempers his obvious attraction to Marion and Joey. When he hears Joey say, "Mom, I love Shane," he silently leaves the house to go to the barn; after he looks longingly on Joe and Marion celebrating their tenth anniversary and dances with Marion, his gunfighter's past dissipates his pleasure when one of the farmers reports Wilson's presence in town. Finally, after being tempted to let Starrett face Wilson (as a possible way to gain Marion and Joey?), Shane decides to do what he does best—to take up guns against Wilson in order to save Starrett from certain death. In killing both Wilson and Ryker and in leaving town, Shane affirms and preserves the balance between the values of the community and his integrity as an individual. At one and the same time, he saves the community by ensuring Starrett's leadership and eliminating Ryker's threat, and he places himself beyond society's pale by taking up guns again and going to "a place he hasn't been before."

Though Ringo, Earp, and Shane may emphasize different aspects of the contradictory elements within the western hero, they all embody the classic characteristic of moral integrity. They repress or use in the service of the law whatever dark elements exist in their persons. The worst the classic hero can do in the eyes of society is to alienate himself from the community, but he does this to preserve his sense of integrity. In the next group of westerns, *Red River*, *The Naked Spur*, *The Searchers*, and *The Man Who Shot Liberty Valance*, the dark forces within the western hero surface, in some cases dominate, and lead to the anti-heroes of the 60s and 70s. In *Red River*, the John Wayne character, Dunson, represents the individual obsessed with his own ways, the westerner's code taken to extreme. Dunson's obsession undercuts his ability to function as a proper leader of men. He lacks the empathy to respond to human weaknesses and needs, a quality necessary to bind a community of men and women together. Matthew Garth (Montgomery Clift), on the other hand, complements Dunson's hardness and intractibility with his sensitivity and flexibility, and it is he who preserves the community and mediates between the solitary hero and society. As an initiate hero who fluctuates between the forces of civilization and the wilderness but remains, finally, on the side of hearth and home, Garth takes over the traditional hero's function in society and underscores that hero's alienation and inability to function any longer as a viable force between the two poles.[5]

In *The Searchers*, Martin Pawley (Jeffrey Hunter) acts as another initiate hero who mediates between the alienated westerner, Ethan Edwards (John Wayne), and the community, represented by his intended, Laurie Jorgensen (Vera Miles). Ethan's racism, savagery, and obsessive behavior undercut his moral integrity as a classic hero. His hatred of Indians clouds his relation to Debbie (Natalie Wood), his niece, abducted and raised by the Indians, as his motives change from a desire to rescue to an obsession to kill her during a five-year search. His return to society at the beginning threatens familial values since he knows that Martha, his brother Aaron's wife, still loves him with a love she is powerless to suppress as she greets him with warmth and longing. In this context, the Indian Scar's rape and slaughter of Martha and the family reflect Ethan's own would-be destruction of his brother's household, and his consequent vengeful search for Scar represents a sublimation of his subconscious guilt.

The end disturbs to say the least. The tension caused by the forces threatening to the community remain. Martin and Laurie will marry and affirm the values of family and community, but Ethan remains alienated from those values and their ever potential menace. Ethan rescues Debbie after all, but by returning her to the community, he places within its midst the possibility of infection. For Debbie's insecure glance at the Jorgensens and her shrinking posture on entering their home signify the ambiguity of her identity as Indian or white. As Martha's unrequited love for Ethan made her a threat to the integrity of the family, so Debbie's unresolved identity marks her integration as problematic.

Through Dunson and Ethan Edwards, *Red River* and *The Searchers* reveal the western hero's sap of moral energy which diminishes his importance as society's champion and increases his role as its subverter. *The Man Who Shot Liberty Valance* strikes the inevitable knell by deconstructing the myth of the western hero and then signals its demise by nostalgically yearning for it at the end. Tom Doniphon (John Wayne) may embody codes of both East and West, but his ultimate sympathies lie with the wilderness code of survival by violence and rugged individualism. In this way, he identifies more with the outlaw Liberty Valance (Lee Marvin) than with the eastern lawyer Ransom Stoddard (James Stewart). When Doniphon shoots Valance, he enables Shinbone to develop into a modern town in an evolving territory and then a state of the union. Stoddard epitomizes this modern trend as he progresses from lawyer to Shinbone's territorial representative to Congress to governor and finally to U.S. senator. Doniphon makes all this possible by killing Valance, but in the process he destroys the forces of the frontier responsible for holding back the encroachment of society. In other words, in empowering civilization, he obliterates qualities vital to his own existence; he kills himself.

Hallie (Vera Miles) is the character who acts as mediator between the values represented by Doniphon on the one hand and Stoddard on the other. In choosing Stoddard over Doniphon, she necessarily chooses the inevitable ascendency of civilization in the march of progress. However, her heart lies in the past with Doniphon, a commitment symbolized by the cactus rose she places on Doniphon's coffin at the end of the film. Hallie's ambiguous position may ultimately be the film's position. However, both sides of the ambiguity—civilization and nostalgia for its opposite—agree on the westerner's inevitable annihilation and his elegiac status.

While *Red River*, *The Searchers*, and *The Man Who Shot Liberty Valance* trace the westerner's alienation from society, *The Naked Spur* and *A Fistful of Dollars* place him within society, but a society that reflects the worst tendencies of the wilderness forces within the westerner, for the westerner's negative tendencies have become society's tendencies as greed, savagery, and violence permeate its structures and relationships. In *The Naked Spur*, Howie Kemp (James Stewart) is a bounty hunter obsessed with getting reward money in order to purchase back a ranch he had lost when he was double-crossed by his former lover after he left to fight in the Civil War. As he searches for Ben (Robert Ryan), a wanted killer, he draws together a band of characters that represents a microcosm of society held together by common motives of greed for the bounty and opportunities for double-dealing. The only decent person seems to be Nina (Janet Leigh), but she is at first slavishly devoted to Ben, the murderer, then to Howie after he asserts his power over Ben and the others. When love "saves" Howie from his obsession and he and Nina leave Ben's body behind and strike out for a new life in California, the suddenness of his decision strikes a false note. What stays with one, finally, are the image and idea of Kemp's single-minded obsession with money to avenge former deeds against him, and the pervasive weakness and moral chaos in society as a whole, as evidenced by the actions of individuals within the group and by the betrayals in Kemp's past life.

Before *The Wild Bunch*, Clint Eastwood's Man with No Name played upon the cool professionalism of the estranged westerner as no one else had up to that time. Hired out to the highest paying entity (usually outlaws), the stranger had no scruples in a world rife with deception and killings in the trio of 1967 Sergio Leone films *A Fistful of Dollars*, *For a Few Dollars More*, and *The Good, the Bad, and the Ugly*. The conventional response to Eastwood's character is that he represents the westerner as unambiguous anti-hero, lacking any decent qualities because of the ascendancy of cynicism in his nature. Yet this is too simple. For in *A Fistful of Dollars* (shamelessly adapted and copied in almost every detail from Akira Kurosawa's 1961 *Yojimbo*), the stranger helps the villain's mistress and her family escape from further enslavement, motivated by the memory of a past loved one whom he couldn't save from the same predicament. Even in Leone's morally fractured and spiritless environment, the stranger's good deed recalls the sense of decency, albeit limited, in a Dunson, an Ethan Edwards, a Tom Doniphon, and a Howie Kemp, which, though a gradually disappearing element, endows these frontier figures with varying degrees of ambiguity. In *The Wild Bunch*, this sense of decency will prove only a vestigial memory in Pike, leader of a desperate gang of thieves threatened by changing times and the narrowing of the West.

THE WILD BUNCH (1969)

In 1913, a year before the great war, a bunch of outlaws and its aging leader, Pike Bishop (William Holden), ride into the town of Starbuck on the Texas border to rob the railroad office. What was to be a last big haul turns into a nightmare as railroad men and bounty hunters ambush the bunch as it makes its way out of town. Among the ambushers is Deke Thornton (Robert Ryan), a former member of the gang now helping the railroad in exchange for parole from prison. Five of the gang, including Pike, Dutch (Ernest Borgnine), Lyle (Warren Oates), Tector (Ben Johnson), and Angel (Jaime Sanchez), manage to escape over the border into Mexico only to discover that the sacks they took from the railroad office contain metal washers. Undaunted, they determine to make one more "last" score and strike a deal with a Mexican general, Mapache (Emilio Fernandez), to rob an army supply train and sell him the rifles for a bag of gold a case. The train robbery is a success. However, Mapache discovers that the bunch had given one case of rifles away to the revolutionaries he is fighting. As a trade-off, he takes Angel captive and tortures him, since Angel has ties to the rebels. The bunch decides to rescue Angel as an act of duty and honor to one of their own. In the ensuing gun battle, Pike and his men kill Mapache, his German adviser, and many soldiers but are themselves wiped out. Deke Thornton and the bounty hunters arrive, and Deke, no longer beholden to the railroad, decides to ride with Freddy (Edmond O'Brien), the oldest bunch member, who has joined up with the Mexican rebels.

Upon this story, Sam Peckinpah has fashioned a western rich in the context of the genre. *The Wild Bunch* is not an anti-western as some have claimed. It upsets traditional western myths of the hero and of society, but these myths had been on the decline in the regression of the western hero from the late 40s to the mid-60s, from *Red River*'s Tom Dunson to *A Fistful of Dollars*'s Man with No Name. The cynical professional outlaws of *The Wild Bunch* are the culmination of this development. Instead of making an anti-western, Peckinpah transformed the western into an original modernist variation, replete with existential theme and self-reflexive gestures.

Existential Integrity

The "heroes" of *The Wild Bunch* are brutal outlaws with no socially redeeming features, who operate in an environment which itself lacks civilized virtues. The role of women in the movie points to the absence of a viable social structure dispensing communal values. Pike can remember a time when he loved a woman, but this western undercuts the redeeming love of woman we find in such past films as *My Darling Clementine* and even in those which present the decline of the hero such as *The Naked Spur*, *The Man Who Shot Liberty Valance*, and *A Fistful of Dollars*, for Pike's young love was a sordid affair with a married woman whose husband caught the two together and killed his wife and wounded Pike. The only women the men relate to in this sordid world are prostitutes, those who, like Angel's Teresa, sell themselves out to generals for a "better" life, or those who work the brothels, as does the young girl Pike buys before the climactic gun battle. Pike courteously walks a woman across a street at the beginning, but only to disguise the intended robbery; indeed, the film mocks the traditional role of society's matrons when the Starbuck ambush mutilates members of the Christian Women's Temperance Movement as they march down the street, the bunch using them as shields to escape. The "law" itself proves ruthless and barren of socially redeeming features as the railroad men and bounty hunters fire indiscriminately on the ordinary citizens of the town in their bloodlust for the reward money. The corruption is so widespread that children take on the characteristics of the adults: they torture a scorpion as the bunch rides into Starbuck; they ape the gunplay and violence during the fighting; and in the gunbattle at the end, a child kills Pike by shooting him in the back. No tension exists between the wilderness and civilization in the movie because the greed and savagery of the wilderness are now so encompassing that civilized values are inoperable.

At the same time that its values have been lanced from the landscape of the western in *The Wild Bunch*, civilization as a *physical force* has overtaken the narrowing frontier. Significantly, the time of the film is the year 1913, just before World War I severed any ties the world had with the past and plunged it headlong into the modern age. The bunch runs into signs of this modernity in the technology that replaces the essential and traditional equipment of the westerner: the automobile for the horse and the machine gun for the six-gun. The hearsay of airplanes foreshadows the eclipse of the frontier as a field of operation. In his classic study of the western in 1954, Robert Warshow had already identified "limitation" as the western's essential theme in contrast to "freedom and expansiveness": "We are more likely now to see the Westerner struggling against the obstacles of the physical world . . . than carelessly surmounting them" (144). *The Wild Bunch* presents the final gasp of the westerner as the encroachment of the "physical world" in the form of civilization blurs the borders of the frontier. The outlaws' flight into Mexico may afford them one last chance, but it also propels them to their inevitable annihilation.

Though Peckinpah's film signals the death knell of the westerner prefigured in Ford's 1962 *The Man Who Shot Liberty Valance*, it resists, as its predecessor did, a total sellout of the westerner to his fate. In Ford's film, Tom Doniphon is eulogized through nostalgic memories of Hallie and Stoddard Ransom and through the work of the film, which produces the flashback revealing his primary role in the shooting of Liberty Valance. Meanwhile, *The Wild Bunch* allows its brutal protagonists the honor and integrity usually reserved for the traditional western hero. Though the world of the movie denies a code of civilized values by which past westerners could attain distinction, it still offers this band of outlaws a personal code of honor by which its members gain a measure of dignity and glory. At the very least, the members of the bunch have the opportunity to be loyal to each other and to persist in that loyalty in the face of threats to undermine it. In the end, they take the opportunity to die with dignity in their decision to rescue Angel, who himself had acted honorably by accepting the consequences of giving guns meant for Mapache to his countrymen.

At the beginning of the film, however, Pike and his men are in disarray, sadly botching the robbery and making a mess of the affair. It is not insignificant that the causes for this failure were the betrayals committed by Pike, its leader, and by Deke, its former member. Pike enumerates the code he expects each member of the bunch to follow when Tector threatens to kill Old Freddy Sykes: "You're not getting rid of anybody. We're going to stick together, just like it used to be. When you side with a man you stay with him, and if you can't do that you're like an animal. You're finished. *We're* finished!" After the botched robbery, Pike, in a flashback, recalls his failure to live up to his own code when he ran out on Deke Thornton, his best friend. In other flashbacks, we find out that authorities tortured Thornton in prison, forcing him to join Harrigan, the railroad officer, in planning the setup in Starbuck to kill or capture his former partner. Pike's betrayal of Thornton, the violation of his code, leads directly to the ambush and unsuccessful robbery.

A major pattern in the narrative consists of Pike's attempt to salvage his compromised honor and integrity. Paul Seydor in *Peckinpah: The Western Films* (1980) suggests that the film's flashbacks represent Pike's awareness of his failures since they deal with personal losses that resulted from past mistakes, calculation, or equivocation. In the first, he ditches his best friend to avoid capture; in the second, he remembers leaving Crazy Lee, Old Sykes's grandson, in the railroad office with the command to hold the clerks and customers hostage while the rest of the bunch escapes, virtually condemning him to death; and in the third flashback, he loses the woman he loves through his thoughtlessness when he shows up two days late for their assignation and then through his carelessness when he doesn't take precautions to prevent her husband from coming upon them unawares (87–94).[6] In order to make up for his past mistakes, Pike desires a successful last score as a testament to the loyalty and fortitude the bunch would need to bring it off. And the munitions train operation reflects the group's perfect cooperation and execution. No doubt the caper's success salves Pike's wounded pride, but it does not really compensate for the personal betrayals of his past or repair his crippled honor. It is only when Mapache takes Angel prisoner that Pike receives an authentic opportunity to redeem himself. Seydor says that, for Pike, Angel is Deke Thornton, Crazy Lee, and Old Sykes wounded and left to die (and I would add Aurora, his lost love). Instead of compounding his guilt by abandoning Angel, Pike decides to reclaim his comrade, and in doing so become a human being (98). The camera visualizes the bunch's solidarity in its choice to die with honor rather than leave in dishonor as Pike, Dutch, Lyle, and Tector march to Mapache's stronghold in sync to the roll of drumbeats and the singing of a Mexican song.

In contrast to its confusion in the first gunbattle, the bunch controls the action in the last. When Pike challenges Mapache to surrender Angel, the Mexican general appears to comply but slits Angel's throat instead. The four gringos shred Mapache to pieces with lead. Stunned, Mapache's soldiers freeze as the four men form a phalanx in the middle of the arena, guns held up, preventing the army from drawing on them. Pike and his men are giddy with the realization that they are in control; they *could* slowly withdraw and escape, but they entertain this option fleetingly if at all. With nowhere left to go, they know their time has come; besides, they must play the game to its end. In deciding to avenge Angel's death, they themselves die, but in dying, they gain stature through an act made by choice and without compromise.

The Ethics and Aesthetics of Violence

Pike's and the bunch's moral stature at the beginning and at the end is defined not only through such story elements as events, action, and characterization, but also through cinematic discourse, especially in the way the film portrays the violent action in the two gunbattles. The extensive commentary on the film's violence plays on the public topic of its morality or immorality; in other words, whether it is gratuitous, overly graphic, and harmful or whether it is educational, repulsive in a positive way, and aesthetically pleasing.[7] None of the commentary deals with the *generic* function of the violence, how it defines the westerner or those who live by violence. In his classic essay on the western, Robert Warshow discusses this generic function. For Warshow, the "point" of violence in western movies is not the violence itself, "but a certain image of man, a style, which expresses itself most clearly in violence"; as an audience, "our eyes are not focused on the sufferings of the defeated but on the deportment of the hero" (153). Warshow would minimize the "anxieties over the problem of violence" in the western and would suggest instead "that even in killing or being killed we are not freed from the necessity of establishing satisfactory modes of behavior" (154).

In the traditional western, "satisfactory modes of behavior" include certain rituals one adhered to in a violent situation: one never drew unless provoked and then only when drawn upon; one never shot anyone in the back; one never backed down from a challenge especially when insulted; one never flinched or showed fear. In other words, the hero deported himself well and with honor. In *The Wild Bunch*, Pike and his men do observe certain standards in their violent action; they kill, but they are not sadistic or cruel. In distinguishing their violence from Mapache's, Dutch says, "We don't hang nobody." However, Dutch's sensitivity about degrees of violence is only an echo of the elaborate ritualization of classical gunfights. Peckinpah is not really interested in formulating a new ritual of violence among ruthless outlaws, because, frankly, among these men, the only rule is to shoot first or be killed. Instead, Peckinpah transforms the ritualization of content into a ritualization of cinematic style. The moral status of these men in battle is defined not so much through their action as through the stylization of action in the process of the film's discourse. In the first gunbattle, the cinematic apparatus's depiction of the violence reflects the vulnerability of the bunch and the compromised nature of their robbery; in the final gunbattle, it reflects their honor and integrity.

The cinematic presentation of the first gunbattle functions thematically as it reinforces the fragmentation of the situation and the lack of control not only of the bunch but of everyone involved. Pike and his men are the most compromised, riding as they are into an ambush, but Harrigan's own plans go awry when the temperance union marches down the street during the robbery, giving the outlaws a chance to escape in the confusion. The third group involved, the townspeople, may be the most victimized, caught as they are in the cross fire. Camera and editing work to produce the sense of fragmentation through the switching back and forth between the differing perspectives of the bunch, the law, and the townspeople by a variety of subjective techniques—shot-reverse-shots, over the shoulder shots, extreme close-ups of faces and eyes, eyeline matches—and through the use of parallel editing, which chronicles but also segments events occurring at the same time within the gunbattle. As the bunch rides into Starbuck, we see them through the perspective of children who surround two scorpions they have placed on an anthill. The subjective position derives from shot-reverse-shots, with low-angle panning shots of the bunch riding by to indicate the children's point of view. The next subjective positioning occurs from the top of the building opposite the railroad office, a bird's-eye view shot of the bunch which is the perspective of Harrigan, who asks Deke to take a look. A high-angle over the shoulder zoom-in shot of the bunch from Deke's rooftop vantage point follows. Members of the bunch are denied a subjective position until they are in the railroad office, and what we see from their perspective are rifles at the top of the building opposite. Instead of empowering them, their subjective position exposes their vulnerability as objects of an ambush. When the shooting starts, the medium divides the point of view between the two forces and the townspeople caught in the middle by shot-reverse-shots and eyeline matches for the bunch and the railroad men as they shoot at one another, and by a hand-held camera in the middle of the fracas for the confused and jostled townspeople. At one point, the cinematic apparatus subjectivizes two children's viewpoint as the editing cuts from their enraptured faces to a rider shot and crashing slow motion into a storefront window, to another rider shot and tumbling head over in the street, an example of the parallel editing which depicts actions in the street and those within the railroad office where Crazy Lee holds his hostages. The numerous cuts, parallel editing, and change of speeds create pace, tension, and excitement, but they also codify the fragmentation and chaos of the ambush and, finally, the lack of resolution. For the gunbattle is a standoff, the pathetic townspeople its real victims. Emblematic of the standoff are the extreme close-up zoom-in shot-reverse-shots of Pike and Deke measuring each other with their guns in the battle, but missing, suspending a resolution not only to the railroad's pursuit of Pike but also to the Pike-Deke conflict. As the bunch rides out of town, they again pass the children playing in the street; the children giggle and laugh as they look upon the scorpions which they smother with burning hay. An extreme close-up of the burning scorpions completes the sequence of the first gunbattle, which begins and ends with the frame of the tortured and helpless scorpions, cluing the spectator to the bunch's vulnerable position through a figurative image as well as through the cinematic apparatus's manipulation of subjective positioning.

In contrast to the presentation of the first battle, camera and editing work empower the bunch in the fight at the end. This is accomplished by the consistent positioning of members of the bunch as subjects, which reflects their control of the situation and their "wholeness" resulting from their act of integrity and honor. In Pike's, Dutch's, Lyle's, and Tector's walk to the arena, the camera centers them in the frame with medium shots from front and behind; cuts from their figures show soldiers and scenes from their viewpoint as they pass or approach. When they reach the arena, a series of shot-reverse-shots between the bunch and Mapache depicts Angel's murder followed by the killing of Mapache. The bunch's control of the arena is no more apparent than in the shots that follow. As the four hold off the soldiers from drawing their weapons, we see extreme close-ups of their faces and intent eyes, interspersed with shots of the soldiers by a straight cut or by a whirling pan. As they look at the soldiers, they hold them at bay, positioned both in the middle of the arena and as subjects of the sequence. When the fighting starts, the cinematic apparatus maintains the bunch's subjective position by initiating shot-reverse-shots with a shot of one of them shooting and then cutting to what he shoots at; or by an over the shoulder shot of a bunch member as he shoots. Such a series of shots and editing dominates the visual track until a boy kills Pike by shooting him in the back. Though a visual shot of the boy initiates the shot-reverse-shot of this act, making Pike the object of the editing, Pike nevertheless remains empowered. The cinematic apparatus eulogizes him with a close-up of his dying figure in slow motion, with silence on the sound track alternating with Dutch's cry "Pike! Pike! Pike!" ringing out before he himself succumbs.

Remythification

In his seminal article "Chinatown and Generic Transformation in Recent American Films," John Cawelti astutely categorizes *The Wild Bunch* as both a demythologization of the genre and an affirmation of myth for its own sake. After debunking the traditional western hero (for its lack of moral stature) and the conflict between civilization and the frontier (in this wasteland, no distinction exists between the two anymore), the film ultimately upholds the myth of heroism through the final act of the bunch: "The film leaves us with a sense that through their hopeless action these coarse and vicious outlaws have somehow transcended themselves and become embodiments of a myth of heroism that men need in spite of the realities of the world" (510).[8] Meanwhile, Paul Seydor supports Cawelti's claim by arguing that the power which finally mythicizes the bunch for us is the "world of art and imagination," which at the end catapults the bunch into the folklore of the people, who will forever tell the tale of the four gringos who fought for a friend and "wound up liquidating an army of oppressors and liberating a village" (135). Seydor subtly notes the distinction made between fact and art at the beginning when black and white stills alternate with moving color images. He associates the stills with photographs and with factual journalistic accounts, the moving color images with the world of art and legend which is the world of the film (33–34). I would put the emphasis, however, on the cinematic function itself, which makes the distinction. The alternation between stills and moving images is a self-conscious gesture, the film commenting upon itself as film and on its power as art to manipulate and transform its raw materials into the stuff of legends. In this way, the black and white stills are not photographs but freeze frames and fades from color to black and white, and as much a part of the world of cinematic art and imagination as the moving color images. I would argue further that the freeze frames are a part of the world of art and imagination in another way: they are signs of its preservative nature, its ability to "freeze" or capture forever a moment in time. After all, the film ends as it begins, with the use of a freeze frame during a reprise of the bunch's pastoral departure from Angel's village when it was given a farewell reserved for heroes, a parallel to and comment on its status at the end of the gunbattle of Agua Verde. The film's accomplishment as art lies in its double-barreled production of debunking then exalting its protagonists and in its preservation of that legend and the legend of its own mythmaking.

McCABE AND MRS. MILLER (1971)

The Western Hero Demythologized

With Robert Altman's *McCabe and Mrs. Miller* (1971), the demythologization of the western hero, begun as early as 1948 with *Red River*, reaches its ultimate conclusion, not countermanded as it is in *The Wild Bunch* by nostalgia or glorification of the myth for its own sake. While such films as *The Searchers*, *A Fistful of Dollars*, and *The Wild Bunch* contributed to the *decline* of the western myth, *McCabe and Mrs. Miller* explodes it entirely and represents its demise (Plecki 46). Altman, apparently, was very much aware of the anti-western nature of his enterprise: "I just wanted to take a very standard Western story with a classic line and do it real or what I felt was real, and destroy all the myths of heroism" (Atlas and Guerin 20). With such clear intentions, Altman's project demythologizes the western hero and his narrative by overturning not only his heroic status but also his relationships with society and the woman, and by replacing the traditional classic narration with a discourse that is self-conscious, idiosyncratic, ironic, and focused on producing thematic analogues.

McCabe and Mrs. Miller sustains the depiction of society evolved in the 50s and 60s westerns through *The Wild Bunch*. In *The Wild Bunch*, the traditional tension between the frontier and society dissipates in the face of an all-encompassing savagery and greed. Society mirrors the worst qualities of the frontier; the westerner himself is now an outlaw, a professional who lives by his guns and sells his talents to the highest bidder. *McCabe and Mrs. Miller* continues this demythologization in its portrayal both of a corrupt society overrun by capitalistic exploitation and of its "hero" protagonists who buy into the system. For the entrepreneurism of John McCabe (Warren Beatty) and the prostitution of Constance Miller (Julie Christie) are essential parts of the corporate landscape of the movie's America, a landscape they share with the monopolistic-minded Shee-

Pastoral idealization and the remythification of the western hero in *The Wild Bunch. Courtesy of Museum of Modern Art Film Stills Archive. Copyright Warner Brothers, 1969.*

han (Rene Auberjonois), the opportunistic double-talking lawyer and politician Samuels (William Devane), the gun-for-hire killers led by Dog Butler (Hugh Millais), and the ruthless Harrison-Shaughnessy mining company which takes over the town of Presbyterian Church by buying up its business concerns or killing those who resist. No values other than profit and power are possible in this environment. The force of an alternative community spirit is undercut by the location of this spirit in the McCabe-Miller brothel. Though a hotbed of communal activity (birthday party, hot tub bathings, and supportive caring among women), it is also where men pay for instant gratification and women sell themselves as attractive commodities. In his article *"McCabe and Mrs. Miller:* Robert Altman's Anti-Western," Gary Engle notes the film's further undermining of community spirit and cooperation by the town's nonchalant acceptance of the Dutch boy's cold-blooded murder of the naive fun-loving Cowboy (Keith Carradine) and by its acquiescence to the mining company's invasion. If corporate development represents "social progress," then inherent in that progress is also a decline of morality and humanistic values (274).

Altman's cynical depiction of the west and its people overrun by the rampant capitalism of American "civilization" plays up the lack of heroism in the modernist text of his film. However, the film eschews mere external manipulation in the production of its conscious demythologization. By positing codes of heroism within the figure of McCabe, it internalizes the drama of illusion versus reality and locates a center wherein the possibility of the myth may be tested. In this drama, McCabe is the dreamer and poet who mythicizes himself as gunfighter, gambler-businessman, and lover, only to come up against coded elements of realism that explode his role playing. At the beginning, McCabe perpetuates the baseless myth of his reputation as the gunfighter who killed Bill Roundtree by weakly denying responsibility for the killing when it is discussed in Sheehan's bar. This reputation enables him to succeed as a gambler and as a pimp, culminating in his fruitful business partnership with Constance Miller. However, when Dog Butler arrives to eliminate McCabe after McCabe had failed to strike a deal with the mining company's negotiators, he calls McCabe's bluff by goading him into a gunfight, "My best friend's best friend was called Bill Roundtree; you killed him." McCabe's timidity forces him to plead his innocence in the killing: "Bill Roundtree got caught marking a queen; he went for his gun and got shot; that's all." After McCabe's retreat out the door, Butler punctuates the implication of McCabe's admission, "That man never killed anybody."

McCabe's actions before and during the gunfight with Butler and his boys further deflate his heroic pretense. He tries to avoid the final showdown at all costs. When he realizes the intentions of the gunmen, he travels to Bear Paw to seek the company's negotiators, but they are gone. He meets instead with the calculating lawyer Samuels, who pumps him up with platitudes about taking on the monopoly in court and protecting the small businesses of the country. Samuels wants to puppet McCabe for his own political ends, knowing full well that the odds are against success. McCabe's own motives for challenging Harrison-Shaughnessy in court are self-serving as well. He does not intend to preserve the community but to protect his own skin. He says to Samuels, "Well now, I guess what you're sayin' is that if we get this thing in the papers and the courts and all that, they just can't afford to kill me, is that right?" to which Samuels replies, "You damn right that's right; they won't be able to lift one little finger against you." However, Dog Butler and his men preclude the lawyer's political circus and McCabe's sanctuary by carrying out their mission before the suit can be filed in court. In the gunbattle between McCabe and the hired killers, all pretense at heroic action ceases. Consistent with his motives for pursuing a court case, McCabe takes up guns as a matter of mere survival. Instead of calling on resources based on skill and courage to get him through the fight, he depends on calculation, luck, and "shooting 'em in the back" or unawares. In other words, McCabe shrewdly allows himself the minimum of risk in the cat-and-mouse maneuvering of the showdown. And though he succeeds in eliminating the killers, his actions accomplish nothing. He himself is killed; the mining company will move in; and the townspeople will not resist, given their already pragmatic acceptance of the takeover.

Just as McCabe's role and reputation as a gunfighter are overturned, so too is his role as the top-dog businessman in Presbyterian Church. McCabe gains his stature as a successful independent businessman through his poker game and prostitute service. However, his stature diminishes in the presence of Constance Miller. From the very beginning, Mrs. Miller shows how much more aggressive and shrewd she is when she dents McCabe's long-protected independence and makes a deal for a business partnership (McCabe had earlier responded to Sheehan's suggestion to consolidate with "Partners is what I came here to get away from"). Mrs. Miller suggests that McCabe put up the money for their house, while she handles everything else: the girls, the furniture, the business expenses, and the bookkeeping. She will pay him back, and they will split the profits in half. In part, Mrs. Miller succeeds in persuading McCabe by giving him the better end of the deal. However, in her proposition, she also plays on McCabe's lack of expertise in caring for hygiene and for the women's emotional and psychological needs. She points out to him the necessity for a proper house with proper furnishings and decorations to attract customers. In other words, she also succeeds in persuading him by exposing his incompetence. Furthermore, in relieving him of any responsibilities, she emasculates him as a business partner.

McCabe's diminishment continues when Mrs. Miller discovers later that he has difficulty with figures and that he confuses the debit and credit sides of his ledger. She lectures him on the necessity of spending money to make money, on thinking big instead of small, and, in particular, on getting the windows and doors on the house so that they can make more money. She combats McCabe's content with mediocrity by improving every area of their service and running a highly profitable house.

It is to Mrs. Miller's credit and not McCabe's that Harrison-Shaughnessy offers him a top price for his holdings, which also include his House of Fortune bar and poker casino. In his bargaining with the agents, Sears and Hollander (Michael Murphy and Antony Holland, respectively), McCabe has a chance to improve his status as a gambler-businessman. Instead, he eschews good business sense and decides to adopt a swaggering bravado in rejecting their offer. He miscalculates the patience of the negotiators when he demands the ridiculously high price of $14,000 to $15,000 after having been offered $5,500, then $6,250. Instead of being business-smart, he is just a "smart ass" to Sears and Hollander, who decide against further insult and depart, leaving McCabe to his fate with the company's hired guns.

In failing as a good businessman to strike a fair bargain with the mining company, McCabe also fails at a chance to be the lover Constance Miller may want. From the beginning of their relationship, he adopts a chivalrous attitude toward her. He accepts her prostitute's role with reluctance, winces when she goes off with a customer, and bristles when she asks whether he's had a bath and paid the kitty before making love. His soliloquy after his humiliating meeting with Dog Butler and before his journey to Bear Paw to look for Sears and Hollander is that of the man of sensitivity misunderstood by his intended, the wounded poet-lover addressing his lady in a time of crisis:

God, I never did fit in this goddamn town; God I hate when them bastards put their hands on you. When I take a look at you, I just keep lookin' an' lookin'. . . . I keep trying to tell you in a lot of different ways; just one time you could be sweet without no money around. I think I could. . . . Well, I tell you somethin', I got poetry in me. I do. I got poetry in me, but I ain't goin' to put it down on paper. I ain't no educated man; I got enough sense not to try it; can't never say nothin' to you. If you just one time let me run the show, I. . . . You just freezin' my soul, that's what you're doing, freezin' my soul.

McCabe lacks the practical realist's attitude that would make possible a viable relationship with Constance Miller in the world of the film. She herself sees the world and its relationships for what they are. Clear-eyed, she tells McCabe that Sears and Hollander would just as soon see him dead as look at him again after he rebuffs their first offer. When she

Corporate power and McCabe's miscalculated bravado and gamble. *Courtesy of Museum of Modern Art Film Stills Archive; Copyright Warner Brothers, 1971.*

hears that Dog Butler and his men are in town, she tells McCabe, who believes they're a second team of negotiators, that they get paid for one thing and that's to kill. She suggests that McCabe escape by hiding out in a covered wagon that's leaving town. McCabe chafes at her remarks, foolishly thinking he can still negotiate, then later believing he can save himself by taking Harrison-Shaughnessy to court, only to be left with the option of facing the killers alone in a gunfight. Up to the end, he mythicizes himself to Constance as chivalric businessman and lover. Before seeing Dog Butler and then going to Bear Paw, he tells her, "If a man's not going to do the business for a woman, she ain't goin' to think nothin' of him." Later, in bed the night before the gunfight, he tells her that he's tried to make her smile and that he's never been so close to anybody before. However, his confession of love is from a man doomed for not following his would-be lover's advice. In the aura of his chivalry, McCabe miscalculates the world's substance in his decision not to escape and to fight the company in court, just as he had miscalculated the agents' tolerance when he adopted a bold front to deal with Sears and the plainly annoyed Hollander. McCabe's flaw is that he isn't fully aware of the ways of the world. He is a capitalist with a romantic's heart, and therefore blind to the cynicism and ploys necessary to succeed or survive.

In the eyes of Mrs. Miller, McCabe's heroism would lie not in being chivalrous, a knight in shining armor, a swaggering ladies' man, but in salvaging a decent profit from the company's takeover, so she can realize her dream of opening a boardinghouse in San Francisco, retiring from prostitution, and living a life of comfort. In dooming himself, McCabe dooms her as well. More and more, she will take refuge from the shocks of the everyday in opium. In the early morning on the day of McCabe's showdown with the hired killers, Mrs. Miller quietly rises, dresses, leaves a sleeping McCabe, and walks over to the Chinese compound and into the opium den.

The internalization of the demythologization theme within the figure of McCabe does not even allow an existential victory, one that would enable McCabe to transcend the discrepancy between self and the world. The process of demythologization is not one of disillusionment within McCabe, not a gradual realization of the world's resistance to ideals or principles beyond its own materialistic discourse. Instead, the process takes the form of an exposure. McCabe consciously composes roles, which are then exposed by a world no longer kind to the romantic mythicist, to the image of the swaggering businessman-gunfighter-lover McCabe presents to his audience. Given this scenario, McCabe's actions at the end cannot be considered a cry of individual integrity and identity in the face of an unaccommodating world, because his mythic stature is a posture and not authentic. McCabe is merely foolish in attempting to sustain what is impossible or false. His would-be-dreamer is out of place in a realistic mise-en-scène, an anomaly in a text that works to obliterate him.[9]

Narrative Structure and Style

Just as Altman's *McCabe and Mrs. Miller* demythicizes the classic western hero, so too it undermines the classical system of narration associated with traditional westerns. It incorporates a European art cinema sensibility in its form and style to complement its nihilistic vision of modern alienated man and woman.[10] In retrospective essays on Altman, Scott Eyman and Robin Wood note the director's affinity with Continental filmmakers and their despairing vision of modern life. In "Against Altman" (1980), Eyman compares Altman with Godard, "He is the Godard of his era—gifted, contradictory, fragmented, alienated, and alienating . . ." (28), while Robin Wood, in "Smart-Ass and Cutie Pie" (1975), compares him with Antonioni: "In both Antonioni and Altman, the gestures towards a progressive viewpoint thinly conceal despair, and a sense of helplessness" (11). The theme of modern alienation in their films is not the only characteristic which links all three filmmakers. Like Godard and Antonioni, Altman reinforces the theme of modern alienation through his disruption of the classic story line, disturbing audience expectation and alienating its formed sensibilities toward narrative.[11] Altman once stated that he consciously undermines the classical system of narration because he doesn't want his audience to anticipate in the way it does when viewing a traditional narrative: "A good movie is taking the narrative out, taking the story out of it. . . . In most films so much specific information is provided that the audience is allowed to be totally uninvolved. I try to make an audience do as much work as they would do reading a novel" (Harmetz 48). In *McCabe and Mrs. Miller*, Altman disrupts the classical system of narration by his self-reflexive use of zooms, close-ups, and overlapping sound; by his limited use of verbal clues (dialogue, repetition) and visual cues (establishment shots, perspectives); by his insertion of thematic analogues through contrasting cuts, parallel scenes, and parallel editing; and by the film's lack of resolution or a satisfactory conclusion.

Both Robin Wood and John Belton note Altman's use of the zoom to deconstruct space, disorient the viewer, and call attention to the filmmaker's presence. Wood contrasts the covertness of classical mise-en-scène and deep focus to the overtness of the zoom and focus pulling techniques favored by 60s and 70s directors, the former effacing style and the filmmaker, the latter foregrounding them. For Wood, Altman's zooms are his signature, announcing his presence while also "dissolving space and undermining our sense of physical reality" ("Smart-Ass," 8–

9). In "The Bionic Eye: Zoom Esthetics" (1981), John Belton expands on Wood's observations by noting Altman's use of zooms in interiors, which "creates a very flat, dimensionless space which enhances the enclosed, claustrophobic nature of the film" (25). In my own analysis of the zoom, I would like to focus on the way Altman uses it along with close-ups not only to disorient the viewer and upset his expectations, but also to stress the entrapment of McCabe and Mrs. Miller in the prisons of the self and the world.

The claustrophobic close-ups of McCabe in Sheehan's bar at the beginning undermine his apparent success at starting a poker game and splitting the profits with Sheehan by suggesting early on his entrapment in both the fragile myth of the self and the surrounding corporate environment. Working hand in hand with this function of the close-up are the low-key available lighting, the crowded atmosphere, and the overlapping sound. Justly famous for its approximation of real life sound, Altman's overlapping dialogue also mutes a sharp realization of McCabe's newly arrived figure of attention, and its layered effect further produces the sense of McCabe's imprisonment along with the rest of the humanity within Sheehan's tomblike establishment. These techniques are repeated along with the zoom when Mrs. Miller arrives and talks business with McCabe over dinner in Sheehan's. The zoom-in of Mrs. Miller is accomplished from over her shoulder to an extreme close-up of her plate of food, with a cut to an extreme close-up of her face as she eats, followed by an extreme close-up shot-reverse-shot of McCabe watching her and then of her eating. These techniques suggest the entrapment which their business deal over dinner forecasts for them, making them vulnerable to the threat of Harrison-Shaughnessy in its greedy takeover of all the businesses in Presbyterian Church. An especially effective use of the zoom-in combined with the close-up to suggest entrapment occurs after McCabe brings his three prostitutes to Presbyterian Church, not having provided proper shelter and sanitation for their needs. In the shell of their half-built home, the youngest tells McCabe that she has "to go to the pot." As she says this, the camera zooms-in to an extreme close-up of her face, followed by a reverse cut to a zoom-in extreme close-up of McCabe's perplexed look. Here, the parallel zooms compare the exploited victim with her victimizer, himself restricted by his ill-preparedness and lack of know-how with the girls, until Mrs. Miller assumes control and "frees" him from that condition. Another use of the zoom-in occurs in the gunfight at the end. An extreme bird's-eye-view longshot of the town is followed by a stunning sudden zoom-in longshot of the three gunmen in the street from the same angle; cut to a medium shot of McCabe in bed, then a close-up of him rising. The parallel editing makes a comment, punctuating the snare McCabe is in by the cut from the three gunmen, exclaimed by the quick zoom, to the doomed figure of McCabe in close-up and in his darkened room, abandoned by Mrs. Miller.

The kind of commentary accomplished by editing in the sequence from the three gunmen in the streets to McCabe in bed occurs several times in the film and contributes to its production of analogues. Analogous figures already mentioned include Sheehan, McCabe, Mrs. Miller, the three gunmen, the lawyer Samuels, and the Harrison-Shaughnessy mining company as actors in the corporate scheme of society. Another analogy could be drawn between those who are victims in white corporate America's destruction of other ways of life: McCabe as the romantic, Mrs. Miller and the prostitutes as women-commodities, and the black couple and the Chinese as exploited minorities.[12] Yet another analogy concerns the bankrupt values associated with the unfinished church in contrast to the thriving commercial values associated with the brothel. However, editing produces the most striking analogies, revealing thematic similarities or contrasts as one scene cuts to another. The bulk of these cuts works to associate McCabe with Mrs. Miller and, at the end, the actions of the gunfight with the actions of the firefighting. A simple cut from McCabe to Mrs. Miller associates the two from the moment of her arrival in Presbyterian Church. McCabe's young prostitute again perplexes him when she attacks a customer with a knife. The episode ends with a long shot of McCabe holding the knife and restraining the young girl from further violence; cut to a long shot of the steam engine carrying Mrs. Miller into town. The juxtaposition of Mrs. Miller and McCabe in the context of McCabe's naive handling of his prostitutes "announces" McCabe's future partner and "savior" who will handle them correctly. A series of four editing cuts in the center of the film links McCabe and Mrs. Miller with the theme of destruction and foreshadows McCabe's death and Mrs. Miller's resignation in a drugged stupor. The first cut is a parallel edit. An extreme close-up of McCabe as he responds to Sears and Hollander's second offer of $6,250 with "The immediate answer to that would be *no*" is juxtaposed to an extreme close-up of Mrs. Miller's face out of focus, which slowly comes into focus as she smokes an opium pipe. McCabe's no will doom him to death as it will Mrs. Miller to the refuge of the drug. The second cut is also a parallel edit. In Mrs. Miller's room, McCabe and Constance celebrate the agents' second offer and McCabe's intended meeting with them at breakfast the next day to negotiate further. From this scene, the film cuts to the two agents in Sheehan's bar, who decide, on Hollander's insistence, that they not meet with McCabe the next day but "let Jake handle it" and turn him over to the gunmen, underlining the irony of the lovers' expectations in the previous scene. When McCabe goes to Sheehan's the next morning to meet with the agents and learns of their departure, the camera lingers on a close-

Final mise-en-scène: Mrs. Miller's withdrawal and the obliteration of the individual within the corporate landscape. *Courtesy of Museum of Modern Art Film Stills Archive; Copyright Warner Brothers, 1971.*

up of his slightly stunned look. The third parallel cut is from this close-up of McCabe's look to a close-up of the gravestone at the funeral and burial of Coyle, who died in a fight the night before. The parallel editing suggests McCabe's death sentence by virtue of the agents' decision to let "Jake handle it." The fourth and final cut is from the mock gunfight of McCabe and the cowboy, who arrives in town during the funeral, to the real gunfighters crossing a stream on horseback on their way to Presbyterian Church. The out of focus zoom-out into focus shot of the horses' hooves and then of the three killers on horseback in a low-angle shot, the sun striking the lens of the camera, compares with the quick zoom-in shot of the gunmen on the morning of the gunfight. Each zoom is a highly self-conscious emphasis on the killers and the way they stand in relation to McCabe. The cut to the killers on horseback gives the lie to McCabe's relief on learning that the cowboy is not there to kill him but to find the whorehouse.

The most striking use of parallel editing occurs at the end of the film, where we see a series of cuts between McCabe's struggle with the gunmen and the townspeople's struggle to extinguish the fire in the church, followed by a series of cuts between a fatally wounded McCabe half-buried in the snow and Mrs. Miller entombed in the opium den. In the first case, the parallel editing underscores the irony of the townspeople's actions to save a church they paid little attention to before and have no stake in, while remaining oblivious to McCabe's plight as he faces three gunmen alone. Furthermore, the hollow actions of the townspeople reinforce the futility of McCabe's actions. Though the townspeople succeed in putting out the fire in a show of community spirit, they will disperse into their separate realms, and the rebuilt church will be the empty figurehead it was before the fire. Likewise, though McCabe kills the gunmen, he fails to divert the long tentacles of the mining company from Presbyterian Church, and, besides, he had already lost Mrs. Miller her chance to be free of a prostitute's existence and doomed himself in the process as well.

Consistent with the principle of art cinema narration, the conscious use of parallel editing, close-ups, zooms, and overlapping sound in *McCabe and Mrs. Miller* cues the viewer not only to the film as film, but also to the workings of the apparatus to produce thematic commentaries. The viewer herself works in concert with the apparatus to realize the analogies, so that the true experience of the film is not a syntagmatic one that pursues its story line, but a paradigmatic one that attends to its deep analogous structures. It is appropriate then that the film conclude with another analogy formulated through the workings of the apparatus, a profound commentary on the doomed status of McCabe and Mrs. Miller. As the camera zooms into a close-up of Mrs. Miller's face in the opium den, a parallel edit cuts to a zoom-in close-up shot of McCabe, buried up to his chest in a drift, the wind-whipped snow shrouding his figure in a white blur. White, the absence of all color, suggests the idea of "nada" underpinning the image. McCabe is obliterated not only by the corporate landscape, but by the natural one as well. Finally, the apparatus erases him from the film itself as it cuts back to Mrs. Miller. An extreme close-up of Mrs. Miller's face cuts to an extreme close-up of the opium jar she gazes at and turns in her hand, which cuts to an extreme close-up of her dazed eyes, the camera zooming in to the dark pupil of her right eye. The dazed pupil acts as a metonymy for Mrs. Miller in her state of forgetfulness, which she induces to counteract the travail of the actual. Furthermore, the darkness of the pupil contrasts with the blurred whiteness of the snow which enshrouds McCabe. The community of all colors which produces black, ironically, produces the color of death, of dissolution. The film ends with a reverse shot of an extreme close-up of the dark surface of the opium jar, its cold lifelessness reflecting, to the numbed eye of its beholder, the emptiness both object and subject share. As the apparatus erased McCabe through a parallel edit, so too it erases Mrs. Miller from its spectacle by the reverse edit to the jar's surface.

As the end credits roll up over the jar's surface, the sound track overlays the sense of nihilism suggested by the analogous images at the end. The Leonard Cohen song intones the loss of what could have been, "I'm just a station on the way, I know I'm not your lover." After the song, the final sound of the wind-swept snow recalls the sound of the wind-swept trees at the start as McCabe traveled to Presbyterian Church, implicitly inscribing, in retrospect, the doomed nature of McCabe's American adventure from the very beginning.

CHAPTER FOUR

Counterculture: *Midnight Cowboy, Five Easy Pieces, Carnal Knowledge, American Graffiti, Lenny*

"Counterculture" is a term associated with the youth movement of the late 1960s—the rebellion against a mainstream America dominated by corporate values, middle-class suburban conventions, and redneck attitudes. The movement was symbolized most effectively by the protest against the Vietnam War and its most powerful supporters, the military-industrial complex and President Lyndon Johnson. But the movement also spilled over into a rebellion against an environment created by parents and their middle-class mores. Overnight arose a hippie culture with its anthems of sexual freedom, open relationships, drug experimentation, and communal living. The impact of *Bonnie and Clyde, The Graduate*, and *2001: A Space Odyssey* is explained in part by their embodiment of counterculture themes and creation of new myths for an audience in desperate need of them. The overwhelming response to these films influenced the industry to produce more films with counterculture subjects. Films such as *Medium Cool* (1969), *M*A*S*H* (1970), *Getting Straight* (1970), *The Strawberry Statement* (1970), *Move* (1970), *Zabriskie Point* (1970), and *Billy Jack* (1971) deal with the radicalization process of their white male subjects. Meanwhile, *Easy Rider* (1969), *Bob & Carol & Ted & Alice* (1969), *Alice's Restaurant* (1969), *Joe* (1970), *The Magic Garden of Stanley Sweetheart* (1970), and *Woodstock* (1970) set their narratives within a liberated hippie culture.

Ironically, the second group of films was significant not so much for its counterculture outlook as for its deconstruction of such an outlook. The counterculture movies of 1969 and 1970 (the height of the hippie movement) revealed that the counterculture carried within it the seeds of its own destruction and prepared for the reactionary films later in the decade.[1] For example, Wyatt (Peter Fonda) and Billy (Dennis Hopper), the anti-establishment heroes of *Easy Rider* who are killed at the end by southern rednecks, self-destruct from the beginning as they buy into the corporate values and chauvinist attitudes of mainstream culture. They wheel and deal in hard drugs to finance their trip; they travel east (not west to a new land as their mythic forbears) to a decadent New Orleans, where they engage in a Sodom and Gomorrah debauchery with women they view as objects. Meanwhile, *Bob & Carol & Ted & Alice* depicts the false promise that "liberation" holds out to its adult middlebrow characters, who, in the end, cannot go all the way toward sexual liberation, settling back instead into a comfortable, nonthreatening conventional morality. *Alice's Restaurant* illustrates the failure of the hippie movement to sustain itself beyond its experiments in sex and drugs and Vietnam protest. The film finally centers on the lack of responsibility as the distinguishing feature of individuals in the movement, a lack that leads to betrayal, death, and the loss of community. *Joe* purportedly revealed the prejudices of a redneck and a businessman against hippies, but in the process exposed the drug dependency and the uncommitted lives of those in the counterculture.

Other films illustrated the influence of *Bonnie and Clyde*, *The Graduate*, *2001*, and the counterculture in other ways. *Midnight Cowboy* (1969), *The Last Picture Show* (1971), and *Carnal Knowledge* (1972) took advantage of the permissiveness of the times and within the industry to examine frankly and honestly the sexual attitudes and practices within American culture. *Five Easy Pieces* (1970) followed the adventures of a dropout from an elite middle-class environment; *A Clockwork Orange* (1971) depicted the extremes of both individual freedom and government control; *American Graffiti* (1973) mirrored the disillusionment of 1960 graduates in their post–high school lives through the Vietnam War; and *Lenny* (1974) was a modernist biopic of an anti-establishment figure who broke down sexual taboos, defied harassment and arrests by authorities, and died through an overdose of drugs.

THE SEARCH FOR NEW MYTHS

A common theme of the counterculture films was the passing away of traditional myths or their inadequacy to fulfill the needs of contemporary society. During a period of cinematic experimentation, *The Last Picture Show* uses traditional black and white cinematography and a neoclassical style to project a nostalgia for a more innocent time. Meanwhile, its reflexive use of films within a film contrasts staunchly conservative movies, such as *The Father of the Bride*, *The Sands of Iwo Jima*, and *Wagonmaster*, to those that begin to break down prosocial myths, such as *Red River*, in which a hardbitten John Wayne westerner threatens rather than protects the community in contrast to the classic westerners of the past. The narrative itself illustrates the collapse of the traditional family and community rituals, the search for personal fulfillment, and the disillusionment process in the postwar period, a time of transition symbolized by the passing of the picture show and the rise of television. Sam the Lion (Ben Johnson) represents the mythic hero of the past. He operates the picture show and the pool hall, last of the gathering places for the community, and he is remembered as a romantic icon by Lois Farrow (Ellen Burstyn), whose miserable married life was brightened only once by an affair with him: "I guess if it wasn't for Sam, I would have missed it, whatever it is. I'd a been one of those Amity Types who thinks that playing bridge is the best thing that life has to offer." When Sam dies, the myth of the romantic hero and of the community die with him.

Five Easy Pieces depicts an individual searching for a new myth as a reflex of his rejection of conventional ones. A rootless Bobby Dupea (Jack Nicholson) searches for a new frontier, a new innocence, a place to be himself, and at the same time struggles against a confusion and fear of any commitment other than to his own feelings. He rejects a career as a concert pianist and a cushioned life of culture and wealth, opting instead for a blue-collar job in the California oil fields, bowling and beering for pleasure and coupling with the dim-witted but warm-hearted country woman, Rayette (Karen Black). After failed attempts to connect with Catherine (Susan Anspach), another musician, who, like him, sees through the hypocrisy of upper-middle-class society but is unable to escape from its security, and with his father, whose stroke-stricken body prevents an understanding of the son's apology and confession of guilt, Bobby abandons Rayette and hitches a ride to Alaska in hopes of finding something "cleaner." Ironically, in running from the old myths, Bobby Dupea can't find any substitute except the myth of a solipsistic self. He says to his uncomprehending father, "I move around a lot, not because I'm looking for anything really, but because I'm getting away from things that get bad if I stay."

Both *Midnight Cowboy* and *Carnal Knowledge* expose the bankruptcy of two cherished American myths, the myth of the American dream of success and the myth of male sexuality. In John Schlesinger's *Midnight Cowboy*, Joe Buck (Jon Voight) is a modern would-be John Wayne figure from Texas who journeys to New York in order to make a big score, but his dream is skewed and doomed from the start. Its fulfillment depends on the successful marketing of an all-American virile cowboy image to sell his body. His pursuit of the dream ends in the loss of innocence and self-respect. Prostitution is an apt parallel to the American dream's selling out to a laissez-faire materialism that co-opts the values of fair play, tolerance, generosity, and community. In his wanderings, Joe Buck discovers the dark underside of the American pursuit of happiness—greed, deceit, fraud, and self-absorption. He discovers the inevitable decadence

Jack Nicholson's Bobby Dupea in *Five Easy Pieces*—alienated between two cultures. *Courtesy of Museum of Modern Art Film Stills Archive. Copyright Columbia, 1970.*

at the end of the long process of American history, a discovery prefigured in his journey east, not west. No frontier exists anymore except the
frontier of decadence, as Billy and Wyatt found in New Orleans on their
odyssey from California in *Easy Rider*. The quests of Joe Buck and of
Billy and Wyatt recall, of course, the mythic quests of American legendary heroes from Leatherstocking to Ford's classic westerner. These journeys eastward, however, parody those of the traditional mythic hero.
Rather, they portray more accurately the disillusioning experiences of
Huck Finn and those Jamesian Americans who cross the Atlantic from
the new land and travel east to Europe only to find an entrenched, de-
cayed, moralistic culture that stifles their American sense of individuality
and their great expectations for an authentic experience. Joe Buck's adoption of the myth of the cowboy is played out against a contemporary
setting that doesn't allow it to flourish. On a New York talk show, to
which Joe listens on the radio as he rides the bus from Texas to New
York, an interviewer asks a woman, "What's your idea of a man?" to
which she answers, "My idea of a man is Gary Cooper, but he's dead."
At the end, Joe Buck realizes the full implications of this answer—the
myth of Gary Cooper, guardian of cherished traditional values in such
Hollywood films as *The Virginian*, *The Westerner*, *Sergeant York*, and *High
Noon*, is gone.

Midnight Cowboy challenges also the myth of male sexuality by undermining the heterosexuality of its protagonist. After failing to pick up the
middle-aged women he intended, Joe Buck turns to homosexual prostitution. Furthermore, his relationship with Ratso Rizzo (Dustin Hoffman)
turns out to be his most intimate and lasting one. Like all male bonds
in the buddy film genre, the relationship between Joe and Ratso betrays
a homoeroticism that is displaced in cameraderie, ironic put-ons, clown-
ing, and deep caring for one another. Joe's second female pickup, Shirley
(Brenda Vaccaro), chides him for his impotency, "Fay and gay, is that
your problem?" a latent possibility and fear he overcomes by making
love to her. Joe's "feminine" qualities of tenderness and generosity undercut the masculinity he wishes to project and come to the fore by the
end of the film. His sensitivity is displayed in the painful memories of
his life as an orphan with his grandmother and of the gang rape of his
former girlfriend, a brutality fostered by the myth of an aggressive male
sexuality that he was forced to witness and suffer. Joe's generous soft-
heartedness betrays him into giving his first pick-up, Cass (Sylvia Miles),
twenty dollars for "cab fare" and relinquishing his own fee from her
when she begs off for lack of cash. Similarly, after oral sex with a male
date in a movie theater, Joe foregoes taking the pleading boy's watch
after he couldn't pay the agreed upon fee for the session. Joe's nonag-
gressive nature belies the macho image he projects. His most accomplished action is a selflessness that results in a lateral relationship with

Rizzo in contrast to the vertical relationship usually prescribed for men in a competitive society.[2] Joe acts aggressively only once, when he steals money from a male pickup to take a sick Rizzo to the warm climate of Florida. In the bus to Florida, Joe nurtures Rizzo as a mother would her child, wrapping him in a warm blanket, changing his wet clothes, and cradling him in his arms when he dies. Appropriately, once Joe reaches Florida, he discards the macho cowboy outfit associated with the myth of a male sexuality to which he can no longer subscribe.

Mike Nichols's and Jules Feiffer's *Carnal Knowledge* exposes the myth of male sexuality as a self-interest that refuses to see the other as anything but an object, as a compulsive need to dominate, and as a brutality that victimizes both physically and psychologically. The film follows the sexual careers of two men from their Amherst College days in the fifties to the Vietnam era. Jonathan (Jack Nicholson) and Sandy (Art Garfunkel) typify the sexual hangups of the mainstream American male. Aggressive Jonathan uses sex to dominate women and to stroke his ego, so he engages compulsively in a career of sexual conquests; meanwhile sexually timid Sandy idealizes women and marries his first love. Each buys into a myth that distorts his perception of the individual person—Jonathan into the Eve/Temptress myth and Sandy into the Mary/Madonna myth. The recurring female skater in white upon whom they gaze is a blank slate on which they would write their own desires: "Do you want her?" "I wouldn't kick her out of bed." Jonathan shops for women as he would for a good piece of steak: "I knew a girl that had a good pair of tits on her, not a great pair; almost no ass at all, and that bothered me; sensational legs. I would of settled for those legs if she had just two more inches here and three more there."

The film centers on Jonathan's attitude as typical in defining one-way relationships between males and females. The relationship "works" for him only if it means domination, ego enhancement, orgasmic pleasure, and lack of commitment—in other words, masturbation with another. When Jonathan betrays Sandy at Amherst by sleeping with his girlfriend Susan (Candice Bergen), he chooses not to tell Sandy out of fear that, if everything were brought out into the open, Susan would choose Sandy over him. In his affair with Bobbie (Ann-Margret), Jonathan persuades her to quit her job, preferring availability over extra cash as long as she services him without the pressure of commitment. Jonathan persistently undermines Bobbie's attempts to break down his protective shell. At one point, he selfishly demands his beer at dinner, even though it means that Bobbie must go out to the store to get it. Later, when Bobbie gives him an ultimatum, indicating her desire for a deeper relationship, he deflects her pain by ignoring it and impishly negotiating a one night partner swap with Sandy, which leads to Bobbie's suicide attempt. Jonathan's self-serving consumer attitude toward women is summed up by his

"Ballbusters on Parade" home movie, which constitutes his sexual history. In his commentary, the women become more and more depersonalized:

Here's a real cunt; I forget her name . . . Nancy; I banged her in Berlin. Here's something I went with a couple of months; first time I banged her was on a yacht race to Nassau. This slob I went with for a year until I got so sick of her ballbustin', I couldn't get it up anymore. This was my Jap in the sack.

In the end, Jonathan can only "get it up" by way of an elaborate ritual developed with a prostitute, Louise (Rita Moreno). The ritual includes his payment of a hundred dollars and her enticement to his male ego as prelude to oral sex:

Women love a man who inspires worship, because he has no need for any woman, because he has himself; more beautiful, more powerful, more perfect—you're getting hard—more strong, more masculine, extraordinary, more robust—it's rising, it's rising—virile, domineering, more irresistable—it's up, it's in the air.

The myth of an aggressive domineering male sexuality leads Jonathan to a dead end, to an emotional and, ironically, physical sterility. The other alternative is the development of a new myth, predicated not on a vertical transcendent relationship but on a horizontal one. Sandy attempts to work out such a relationship in his highly conventional marriage with Susan and then later in his unconventional union with Jennifer (Carol Kane), a hippie love child. He tells Jonathan that he and Susan work to establish a caring reciprocity: "We're considerate of each other's feelings; I had a tendency, men I guess have, to be selfish, but I stopped. I don't do that now." Later, Sandy recognizes the many roles people are forced to play in relationships, and he reaches out for a more authentic experience with Jennifer, who "doesn't believe in all that, believes in just life, just love." Though Sandy's efforts with Susan fail (he was also cheating on her at the time) and though his affair with Jennifer may be yet another pose, another instance of role playing, his sentiments are not insignificant. The counterculture values he professes look forward to possibilities within male-female relations undreamt of in Jonathan's narrow sphere.

COUNTERCULTURE AESTHETICS

The aesthetics of the counterculture movie takes its cue from the examples of *Bonnie and Clyde* and *The Graduate*. It combines in an eclectic way the codes of expressionism and realism, fusing new wave and neo-

Jonathan with the prostitute Louise—narcissistic sexual ritual in *Carnal Knowledge. Courtesy of Museum of Modern Art Film Stills Archive; Copyright Avco Embassy, 1971.*

realistic techniques: on the one hand, disjunctive editing, ellipses, fragmented structure, rapid collage montage, closed subjective framing, soft
focus, distorted angles, hand-held camera, flashbacks, flashforwards, and
mixed genres; on the other hand, long takes, deep focus, wide-screen
compositions, tracking/panning camera, grainy cinematography, actual
locales, episodic structure, open framing, overhead mike and actual
sounds, and a montage of songs and music from the time and setting of
the film. Not every counterculture movie combined these characteristics
to the high degree or with the great success that *Bonnie and Clyde* and
The Graduate did; however, we see a mixture of these techniques with
varying degrees of emphasis in such films as *Alice's Restaurant*, *Easy
Rider*, *Midnight Cowboy*, *M*A*S*H*, *Five Easy Pieces*, *Carnal Knowledge*,
American Graffiti, and *Lenny*.

   Alice's Restaurant, *M*A*S*H*, *Five Easy Pieces*, and *American Graffiti*
achieve a naturalistic, documentary effect. Episodic construction, grainy
cinematography, actual locations, and mise-en-scène compositions appropriate a slice of life, sign-of-the-times look of characters caught in and
living out the history of America in the 60s and early 70s. The result,
however, is double-edged. The films complicate our relationship with
the characters—we recognize ourselves in them as they live out the turmoil and emotions of the time, and we are also distanced from them by
the documentarylike approach. The narration reveals moments lived
within an authentically cluttered, localized, and historical environment
at the same time that it provides commentaries on the characters and
situations that make up those moments. The effect is a variation upon
that of Italian neorealism, which in theory sought to offer *no* commentary
in its development of a new naturalism. Its purpose was to foster the
illusion of a dispassionate look at beings caught in the complex web of
social and economic forces through the conventions of episodic structure,
natural lighting, actual locales, nonprofessional actors, and revelation of
ordinary everyday events. Often, however, the dynamics of neorealism
presented a worldview of overwhelming authoritarian forces, as in *Open
City* (1944), or of economic forces, as in *The Bicycle Thief* (1949), so that
commentary was inevitable in the form of compassion for the common
folk whose lives were seen as struggles to maintain a humanity and
dignity in the face of life's necessary hardships. In the counterculture
movies of the Vietnam War era, the neorealistic style works both to involve and to detach the audience, to discover the oppressive forces that
bind, and to reflect upon the alienation, moral confusion, and false myths
within.

   The neorealistic codes of *Five Easy Pieces* are actual locales, a Tammy
Wynette/classical piano music sound track, tracking and panning camera, hand-held camera, long takes, grainy cinematography, and wide-
screen composition. Combined with the classical narrative style, *Five Easy*

Pieces' neorealism effectively portrays the 60s alienation and confusion of Bobby Dupea, played out against the blue-collar working-class environment of Southern California and the upper-class cultural scene in upstate Washington. The opening montage establishes the setting and atmosphere of the L.A. oil fields through detailed shots of equipment and work activity. In the first part of the film, the apparatus explores routine activities of Bobby and his friends to capture the ordinary flow of life within this particular social milieu, delineating character and personal relationships. Bobby comes home from work, opens a can of beer, greets Rayette, who pouts when Bobby evades her request for a declaration of love. They go bowling with their friends, where Bobby expresses dissatisfaction with Rayette's klutzy play. Rayette and Bobby make up in the car afterward. Another montage of work activity in the oil fields is followed by a poker game in the locker room. The focus here is on personal relationships that evolve out of ordinary everyday activities. When Bobby hears that his father is ill, he quits his job and drives up to Washington for a visit. The apparatus does not make an elliptical cut from Southern California to Washington, but follows Bobby and Rayette as they make their way up the coast, picking up a pair of lesbians, conversing in the car, and eating in a roadside restaurant. The conversation with the lesbian Palm Apodaca (Helena Kallianiotes) and her friend, Terri, introduces counterculture sentiment in comic relief form. Palm cannot stop talking about the filth in America, to everyone's amusement, then boredom, then exasperation. The justly celebrated confrontation with the waitress in the restaurant extends the counterculture rhetoric in Bobby's frustration with established, inflexible rules and attitudes. The filmic apparatus constructs the road trip to Washington as episodic, but in doing so, it turns an ordinary event into a revelation of character and theme. The sequences with Palm Apodaca and the waitress are the "found moments" of the film that approximate the "privileged moments" of Italian neorealism and the French New Wave.[3]

Neorealistic techniques also come into play in the last part of the film. When Bobby arrives at his family's estate on an island in Puget Sound, a tracking, panning camera follows him around the house in a long take, revealing the elegant, cushioned surroundings; as he plays the piano for Catherine, the camera pans the walls of the entire room full circle to reveal the family's background and accomplishments in its photographs. With an extended long shot of the service station, the film's end captures the double dramas of Bobby's escape from Rayette as the truck he's in moves out onto the highway heading north, and of Rayette's abandonment as she stands by the car waiting and wondering where he is. Though the narrative is filtered through Bobby's subjectivity, the aesthetics of neorealism distances us from his character and allows us to see him for the complex person he is. It enables us finally to judge this man, who, as Catherine says, is "a person who has no love for himself, no respect for himself, no love of his friends, family, work . . . *something*." The last scene amply demonstrates how this aesthetics works. Bobby's abandonment of Rayette is captured in all its nakedness by the extended long shot that includes the entire mise-en-scène so that we see both his escape and the beginning of its consequence in Rayette's bewilderment.

The neorealism of *American Graffiti* achieves an even greater naturalism than the one we find in *Five Easy Pieces*. The episodic construction, grainy cinematography, "found moments" are more pronounced. The story takes place over the course of the last evening of summer in Modesto, California, before two high school friends leave for eastern colleges in 1962. The movement from one group of teenagers to another is random-like, and each scene portrays ordinary teenage activities: cruising, dancing, talking, eating at the drive-in, drag racing, making out, minor scuffles, and so on. The apparatus produces wide-screen compositions and open frames to situate the characters in the context of their environment. It concretizes details in the foreground, periphery, and background surrounding the privileged action. For example, as Laurie (Cindy Williams) and Steve (Ron Howard) dance at the sock hop in a medium shot, other dancers surround them in the foreground and background; the frame is fluid as dancers move in and out of it; other teens line the walls on the side and in the back. When Bob Falfa (Harrison Ford) and John (Paul Le Mat) cruise down the street in separate cars challenging each other to a drag race, they are on screen left, the camera backtracking in front of them, while on screen right, other cars pass them going the other way in a long take.

The density of environmental details in wide-screen mise-en-scènes works toward the marvelous naturalistic style of *American Graffiti*, one responsible, along with the fifties and early sixties rock sound track, for the re-creation of the atmosphere and tone of the early 1960s, producing a nostalgia of high school charm and innocence that draws the audience into an identification with the characters. However, the neorealism also produces a documentarylike distance and prepares for the commentary at the end when pictures of the main characters appear with captions reporting what happened to them in the future. The future status of each character contrasts with the innocence and promise of the high school graduate figured in each picture: "John Milner [Paul Le Mat] was killed by a drunk driver in June 1964"; "Terry Fields [Charles Martin Smith] was reported missing in action near An Loc in December 1965"; "Steve Bolander [Ron Howard] is an insurance agent in Modesto, California"; "Curt Henderson [Richard Dreyfuss] is a writer living in Canada." A counterculture commentary is especially significant here. Vietnam de-

Wide-screen mise-en-scène and the neorealistic style of American Graffiti. *Courtesy of Museum of Modern Art Film Stills Archive; Copyright Universal, 1973.*

stroyed Terry Fields and forced Curt Henderson to flee to Canada to avoid the draft, while Steve Bolander succumbed to materialism at a time when idealism motivated many other college students.

The naturalism of *American Graffiti* is seemingly unself-conscious, a felicitous achievement, what we would call "refreshing." In contrast, *Carnal Knowledge* constructs its neorealistic elements in a self-conscious manner, which results in a naturalism that is highly stylized. As a consequence, the neorealism of the film doesn't engage: it distances as it objectifies the characters to the point of putting them under a microscope. The film lays bare the distortion of male-female relationships precipitated by the sexual hang-ups of its male characters.

Carnal Knowledge explodes the myth of romance between the sexes from the beginning. During the credits, a voiceover conversation takes place between Jonathan and Sandy along with the music of "Moonlight Serenade." The unrelenting reduction of male-female relations to sexual considerations in their talk ("As long as she's tall and has big tits, I don't care if she's a little ahead of me") undercuts the romanticism of "love" supplied by the music. The first sequence is shot in a highly self-conscious neorealistic style—panning and tracking camera, open framing, deep focus, and long takes—a style compatible with the exposure of the awkwardness and alienation that typify the relations between the sexes in the film. In a long take, the camera follows Susan by tracking and panning as she arrives at a college social, walks into the building, stops at the entrance to a room, the room in deep focus with Susan in the foreground; the camera tracks right to left as she continues down the hallway; she passes Jonathan and Sandy, who are standing at the entrance to another room, the camera stopping on the two men; Susan continues walking into the room and leaves the frame. The camera remains on the men in a medium shot as they talk about making it with Susan; Sandy then walks into the room, the camera panning to reveal the room and Susan sitting on a window ledge; the camera remains in position at the entrance in a deep focus shot of Sandy moving toward Susan, standing before her for a few excruciating seconds, then turning to walk back toward the camera and Jonathan, the two men now in a medium shot. Sandy decides to go back in and walks out of the frame, leaving Jonathan in the frame looking off screen toward Sandy and Susan, as the camera zooms in to an extreme close-up of his face. The apparatus makes its first edit in the sequence, cutting to a deep focus shot of Susan in the foreground left, Sandy walking toward her in the middle ground, and Jonathan standing against the door in the background right. As Sandy and Susan talk, Jonathan looks on, reacting to laughter off screen right and to people walking into the frame from the right; he then walks out of the frame right. The apparatus then makes its second cut of the sequence, from the deep focus shot to a two shot of Susan and Sandy against the window ledge.

The fluidity of movement, the liquidity of the frame, and the spatial depth of the compositions expose the mating rituals of America's campuses: the artificial social setting, the voyeuristic measurement of the woman by the man, the awkward attempt at contact, the superficial chit-chat, the lack of real communication, and the lonely travail of those who stand around and gaze with desire. In the first sequences of Jonathan and Bobbie together, the apparatus adopts a fluid movement to define the purely sexual nature of their relationship. In a long take, the camera tracks around Bobbie and Jonathan as they sit in a restaurant, revealing the sexual innuendoes of their conversation; in another long take, the camera tracks through Jonathan's apartment and into the bedroom, accompanied by sounds of intense lovemaking on the sound track, coming to a stop in front of the bed as Jonathan and Bobbie reach orgasm. In later sequences, the apparatus exposes through a series of facial close-ups the sexual bias of Jonathan's "love" for Bobbie and Bobbie's increasing frustration over his lack of commitment—his obliviousness to her demands and her exasperation over his evasions. The close-ups contrast to the fluidity and openness of the neorealistic techniques, but they work in concert with them to emphasize Jonathan's entrapment within his own self-interest and Bobbie's gradual realization that she has just been a "piece of meat."

In *Carnal Knowledge*, close-ups function also to create segments of confession scenes in the style of Ingmar Bergman. At times, Jonathan, Sandy, and Bobbie each talk to the other isolated within the frame and in close-up, giving the illusion of addressing the camera and the audience. Bergman developed this device in *Winter Light* (1963), perfecting it in *Persona* (1966). In the latter film, the isolated close-up of Alma (Bibi Andersson) as she reveals a past orgy and abortion begins as a conversation with Elisabeth (Liv Ullmann) but turns into a vivid self-confession to the camera and the audience. As the women's identities merge in the course of the film, Alma's conversations with Elisabeth take on the nature of soliloquies, reflecting off her double and onto the self as she probes the depths of her own personality. She talks literally to herself, isolated within the frame, with only the apparatus as witness. In later films such as *The Passion of Anna* (1969) and *Autumn Sonata* (1978), Bergman dispenses with the illusion of conversation altogether; his characters address the camera directly in close-ups and talk to the audience in the theater about their most private feelings and thoughts. In *Carnal Knowledge*, Nichols stops short of direct address to the camera, and he doesn't use the illusion of direct camera address in the complex expressionistic manner of *Persona*. After all, Nichols's text, though self-conscious in its style, is realistic, and his isolated close-ups of figures talking are grounded in an implied shot-reverse-shot sequence. At the same time, however, they operate as direct addresses to the camera and the audience in their function as admissions of lost souls. In one such "address," Jonathan confesses the nature of his relationship with Bobbie:

Just between the two of us—been having, oh, I don't know, a little trouble; I wasn't worried, but still and all, a little trouble with, well, myself, you know, getting hard. Took a long time. . . . As I say, I wasn't too worried, but . . . I won't lie to you, I was a little worried. Then along comes this Bobbie. I get one look at the size of the pair on her, and I never had a doubt I would ever be anything but ok again. I was, I was.

In her book on masculinity in the American film, *Big Bad Wolves* (1977), Joan Mellen says that Jonathan's subjectivity controls the narration to the extent that it becomes the dominant attitude in the film and therefore subverts the intended critique of his self-centered sexuality. Mellen argues that Jonathan's hatred of women is justified because all the women in the film *are* "ballbusters," as Jonathan claims, and none of them is around long enough to disprove his perspective (315–317). However, though Jonathan's perspective remains at the center of the film, his is not the central intelligence that controls the narration. The point of view of the filmic apparatus is objective rather than subjective. Events are not filtered through Jonathan's perspective. The film's neorealistic style and the confessional nature of the close-ups objectify the characters and place them under scrutiny. Jonathan's attitude looms large because it is the one most fully microscoped, the apparatus's true foil. It may dominate the film, but it never undercuts the film's intention. Men in the audience may recognize themselves in Jonathan with rue, but they would never want to think themselves like him, reduced to a friendless automaton of self-gratification and male thumping at the end. And it is the film's objective style that exposes Jonathan's monstrosity and keeps the audience at arm's length from him.

Midnight Cowboy achieves the compatibility of style and its intended effect that we find in *Carnal Knowledge*. Schlesinger's film employs an expressionistic narration to capture both the nervous, decadent energy of New York's underside and Joe Buck's sensitive subjectivity. Its use of zooms, distorted angles, flashbacks, flashforwards, hand-held camera, collage montage, and other pyrotechnics contrasts sharply with the objective and neorealistic discipline of *Carnal Knowledge*. Instead of keeping us at arm's length, *Midnight Cowboy*'s narration immerses us in Joe Buck's interior life, revealing a wincing, alienated soul, tortured by memories of a lonely childhood and an ill-fated love: abandoned by his mother, scorned by his grandmother's lovers, and shattered by his true love's gang rape and consequent madness.

Joe's memories of this painful past flash onto the screen during the first part of his odyssey. They parallel his departure from Texas and his initial experiences in New York. On the bus ride to New York, Joe experiences glimpses of his past life with his grandmother and girlfriend. Later, those memories expand. Most of the time, the apparatus is in sync with Joe's consciousness during the flashback scenes. For example, Joe remembers making love to his girlfriend in a movie theater during his first sexual encounter with a male in a Times Square porno theater, and he remembers his baptism by immersion during his encounter with a Jesus freak. Later, a dream turned nightmare will reveal the full horror of the rape experience. However, one flashback of the rape seems to be motivated by the choric intentions of the apparatus. After Joe discovers that Ratso tricked him out of twenty dollars, supposedly tipping him off to a pimp who turns out to be a religious fanatic homosexual, he fantasizes catching Ratso in various places in the city. Interspersed with this fantasy are brief shots of the gang rape. This can't be coming from Joe's consciousness because all his attention is focused on his anger over Ratso's betrayal. Instead, the flashbacks act as commentary on Joe's victimization in the present by juxtaposing it to Joe's and his girlfriend's victimization in the past. Ultimately, all of the flashbacks perform this choric function, since they parallel the period of Joe's misfortunes with Cass, who gypped him out of twenty dollars when she should have paid him; with his first male john, who couldn't pay him after their session; and with Ratso.

One flashback also functions to mark a turning point in Joe's sojourn in the city—Joe's dream and consequent nightmare of the rape. When Joe finally finds Ratso, his loneliness and lack of success have created in him such a need for human companionship and support that he reaches out to Ratso instead of administering the beating he had planned. Ratso accommodates him by giving him a place to stay. Joe's nightmare occurs during his first night in Ratso's hovel. Scenes of the rape and his separation from his girlfriend alternate with the image of Ratso jabbing him with a broken bottle and a building collapsing. Joe wakes up in a sweat. The nightmare is a cathartic experience, for Joe will no longer be haunted by memories of the pain and alienation he suffered in the past. The exorcism of his demons parallels his success and his deepening friendship with Ratso in the second half of the movie. His more positive experience in New York allows him respite from memories of his earlier victimization.

Though the filmic apparatus stops producing images of what is going on in Joe Buck's mind in the second half (one sequence taps *Ratso*'s subjectivity when he fantasizes life in the Florida sun), the effect of our glimpse into Joe Buck's consciousness ripple through to the end. We have shared Joe's sense of alienation and wounded sensitivity; we have detected his vulnerability but also his strength, which is his insight into and understanding of society's victims and outcasts. It comes as no surprise to us that Joe has the capacity to see through the macho myth of a male sexuality that brutalized him in the past and deceives him in his self-assumed role as hustler in the present. The film's subjective narration empowers the main character for us, making our sympathies consistent with its own. Joe's compassion for and care of Ratso are the culmination of the process of his discovery of the lie at the center of the John Wayne myth. One need not fear that gentleness precludes being a real man, a fuller human being denuded of popular myths of manhood. Instead of hardening in traditional male roles as Jonathan does in *Carnal Knowledge*, Joe and Ratso both break down the stereotypes, even tapping into an unconscious homosexuality as they approach a fuller humanity. At the end, the apparatus can afford to peer at Joe Buck from outside the bus looking in as he cradles a dead Ratso in his arms. Though it separates us from him by the bus window, the narrative remains energized by his point of view, so that we still feel his pain, embarrassment, and disappointment, but also his expectations for a new life in Miami, different from those rife with distortions when he started out in quest of the big score in the Big Apple.

LENNY: CULMINATION AND DEAD END

Bob Fosse's *Lenny*, coming as it did in 1974, may be viewed as the culmination of the counterculture film—both a propaganda statement of Lenny Bruce as a moralizing comic persecuted by the forces of a backwater conservatism and a textbook illustration of realist and expressionist techniques.[4] If it is a culmination, however, it is also a dead end, for it chronicles the ultimate annihilation of the counterculture hero by external and internal factors—by a society bent on conserving its traditional morality and by the counterculture figure's own self-destructive tendencies. *Lenny*'s terminus quality is marked by its reflexivity. The presentation of the filmic apparatus is so apparent and self-conscious that the film's style almost slips into self-parody. The movie seems to function mechanically rather than inspirationally. Be that as it may, Fosse's film is an admirable melding of cinematic technique and content, even though the precise, elaborate enunciation puts on a show of its own and steals the spotlight at times.

The counterculture theme in *Lenny* occurs in three distinct but related ways. First, the film focuses on the rebellious decisions and actions of Bruce (Dustin Hoffman): his decision to marry Honey (Valerie Perrine) against the advice of his agent (Stanley Beck), his break with mentor Sherman Hart (Gary Morton) when he decides to talk dirty in his routines against Hart's stricture, his drug taking, his sexual experiments,

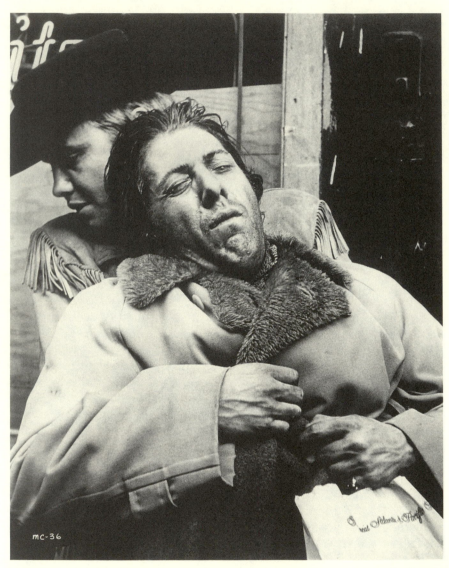

Joe Buck and Ratso Rizzo: compassion and care versus the macho myth of male sexuality. *Courtesy of the Wisconsin Center for Film and Theater Research; Copyright United Artists, 1969.*

Counterculture anti-hero and the self-conscious aesthetics of *Lenny. Courtesy of Museum of Modern Art Film Stills Archive; Copyright United Artists, 1974.*

and his run-ins with the law over his "obscene" language. Second, it highlights Bruce's comic routines that satirize repressive conventions and myths: on "dirty" language (the "clap," "cocksucking," and "tits and ass" routines), on racial myths (the "nigger, spick, mick, kike" and "integration" routines), on homosexuality (the "dike" and "cocksucking" routines), on pornography (the "*King of Kings*' violence vs. stag movies' hugs and kisses" routine), and on the systematizing of justice (the "law" and "trials" routines). And third, it inserts references to those two time-honored counterculture emblems, the Vietnam War and the Kennedy assassination, in the "Jackie Kennedy" routine and in the pathetic Chicago act. In the Chicago act, a drugged Bruce inveighs against harassment, repression, and the Vietnam War:

It's harassment, man; its repression; it's club owners being called up in the middle of the night and being told not to hire me or they're gonna lose their liquor license; it's Vietnam; it's atrocities here and there!

The film's double-edged perspective is sharply etched throughout the narrative. Lenny's actions are rebellious and obsessive at the same time. His defiance of the law in his irreverent nightclub acts and in his studied challenge in the courts is balanced against his stubborn rejection of the advice of agent, mentor, and attorneys. His experiments with sex and drugs turn out to be self-indulgent rather than liberating. His relationship with Honey allows him to experience the sensuality and emotional high of true love as it gives him the opportunity to betray her by his affairs. Honey also functions as a sounding board for Lenny's own moral hypocrisy. He introduces her to lesbian sexuality against her wishes, then jealously accuses her of liking it and condemns her for being perverted.

Lenny's realist/expressionist mode of discourse punctuates its two-sided view. Its grainy black and white cinematography, hand held camera, and occasional long takes create a documentarylike style that underlines its neorealistic impulse to depict its characters as victims of social forces. The black and white cinematography is also used for pictorial effects to project tableaux that eulogize its characters: Honey in a nude pose on a bed surrounded by flowers, suffused in white light, and Lenny at the height of his fame in a pose on stage leaning against the microphone stand, back to the camera, silhouetted against the spotlight. On the other hand, the grainy black and white, hand-held camera, and long takes project a gritty realism that levels the characters and reveals their vulnerability and flaws. This is especially true when the cinematography combines with the disjointed movement and glaring close-ups of the hand-held camera to capture the smoke-lit shabbiness of the backstage and cheap hotels; the alienated desperation and ennui of the alcohol, drug, and sex parties; and the quiet horror of the death scene at the end. One long take stands out in its relentless naked look at the drugged Lenny's Chicago performance that led to his second arrest for obscenity. The take is a high-angle shot of the stage from behind the audience. It dwarfs the figure of Lenny and exposes his hesitant, broken, and dazed delivery, cutting away only after it records his stumbling exit from the stage.

Another technique that the apparatus uses to present its ambivalent perspective is its editing. The editing builds layers within the film's structure that play off against one another, contributing to the fractured view of the main character. The film's structure is a fusion of interviews, flashbacks, and a choriclike commentary by a bearded middle-aged Bruce figure. The apparatus combines these elements by cutting back and forth between them, at times very rapidly; but the arrangement is always logical and precise—interviews with Honey, Lenny's mother Sally Marr (Jan Miner), and Lenny's agent Artie Silver (Stanley Beck), accompanied by flashbacks and by Brucean commentary. The content of the interviews and the accompanying flashbacks are always strictly chronological. The images may be fractured by the multilayered structure, but time is not, except for that bearded Lenny figure who is located in the time of Bruce's life just before his third and last arrest for obscenity in New York. As such, the discourse jumps forward into time when it cuts to this figure. However, he may as well be located outside the time of the narrative in his function as a choric figure commenting on the action from beginning to end.

Along with editing, the apparatus also utilizes voice-overs to link the interviews, flashbacks, and commentary. The credit sequence is a good illustration of this. After the "Dustin Hoffman" and *Lenny* credits, the black background fades into an extreme close-up freeze frame of a pair of lips. The camera pulls back to reveal Honey's face and she begins to talk about Lenny's arrests for obscenity and drugs; a voice-over announces, "Ladies and gentlemen, Lenny Bruce!" The sequence cuts to the bearded Lenny in a nightclub doing his bit on the suppression of words and his "clap" routine ("Eleanor Roosevelt gave Lou Gehrig the clap"); cut back to the rest of the credits accompanied by a voice-over of Lenny's routine and lyrical background music. After the credits, the sequence ends with a fade to a closeup of a tape recorder, cut to the back of Honey's head as she talks about her first meeting with Lenny when she was working a strip joint in Baltimore; cut to a flashback of her strip act. The sequence presents an ambivalent view of Lenny. It mixes Brucean heroics (his satiric routine, Honey's references to his obscenity arrests) and elegiac music with Brucean self-destructiveness (Honey's references to his drug arrests).

Other layered sequences follow in which the bearded Lenny figure does routines as commentary on the interviews and flashbacks. For example, interviews with Lenny's agent and mother on Lenny's marriage to Honey are interspersed with flashbacks of Lenny's decision to marry Honey against his agent's advice and the couple's visit to his mother and aunt, followed by a cut to the bearded Lenny on stage doing a bit on how husbands get jealous about their wives after they get married; cut to Lenny telling Honey he doesn't want her to strip anymore, cut to the bearded Lenny finishing his bit on the hypocrisy of such a husband who was attracted to her "jugs" in the first place: "That's where all the conflict starts; we all want a wife to be a combination Sunday school teacher and a $500 a night hooker." Here, the layered images and sounds work to express both Lenny's integrity (his decision to marry Honey) and his hypocrisy (his moralistic attitude toward Honey's stripping). Other ambivalent layered sequences that contain the Brucean commentary include Lenny's cheating on Honey ("If they got pictures, deny it; if they walk in, deny it") and his sexual experiments with lesbians and menage-à-trois ("And now a word about dikes, I like dikes"), followed by his jealous reaction to Honey's sexual proclivities.

Later, the Brucean commentary will accompany interviews about Lenny's trials with the appropriate flashbacks. In this case, society's persecution of Lenny and his resistance contrast to the obsessive inclusion in his act of his trial proceedings that dulls his routines, and his foolish dismissal of his attorneys that leads to his suicide. By the end of the film, the apparatus is layering in subliminal fashion Lenny's counterculture image shadowed by images of his self-destruction. The apparatus flash-forwards from Lenny's final trial in New York ("Then sentence me; I have no money left. . . . I can't afford a trial. . . . Please sentence me") to the scene of his death, then rapidly cuts from interviews with Honey, agent, and mother to brief flashbacks of Lenny's last days and the arrival of police at the death scene. The film ends with a lingering take on Lenny's naked body lying on the tiled floor of his bathroom as the camera slowly zooms back, accompanied by a voice-over of Lenny, "Into the shithouse for good; forget it, forget it."

CONCLUSION

Although *Lenny*'s counterculture posture played to the sensibilities of the time, not many people embraced it as an anthem to rally around. The movie failed to elicit audience empathy for this persecuted figure. The film's reflexivity and its cinematic pyrotechnics override the drama of characterization and human relationships. Moreover, the apparatus manipulates the action according to its double-barreled intentions, reducing the narrative to vignettes and the characters to cardboard figures against staged backgrounds. *Lenny* lacks the character depth, dynamics, and development that we find in earlier counterculture films, such as

Five Easy Pieces, Midnight Cowboy, and even *Carnal Knowledge*, in which the challenge to traditional myths emerges from the internal drama of character and character relationships and not from the external imposition of counterculture themes by the discourse. In fact, none of these three films deals with pointed counterculture events. Rather, they present characters living with myths that distort their perception and relationships and their consequent rebellion, change, or stagnation. In other words, the counterculture idea is embedded within a drama of character, not inscribed by repeated inclusion of counterculture ideas by the discourse. The result is that the earlier films possess a conviction and audience appeal that *Lenny* lacks.

However, thanks to *Lenny's* dazzling display of editing, grainy black and white cinematography, and tiered surface, it offers us a multivalanced figure that sums up the counterculture and suggests its doom at the same time. It takes the counterculture film to its inevitable conclusion, to which it has been pointing all along. Its heroes cannot elude their alienation, their isolation, their inability to change society's course. They may triumph within the realm of their personal conflicts as in the case of Joe Buck, but they remain surrounded by myths that prove too entrenched to budge. For examples, one turns to the disillusioned commune dwellers in *Alice's Restaurant*, the slain martyrs of *Easy Rider*, the failed experiment of the middle class in *Bob & Carol & Ted & Alice*, Bobby Dupea's pathetic escape to Alaska in *Five Easy Pieces*, and the indomitable but contained Alex in *A Clockwork Orange*. The final image of a pumped up inert Lenny says that counterculture heroes end up dead and gone, while society remains with its myths and restraints. It is no wonder that the discourse and aesthetics of the counterculture film hold court over narrative and characterization by the time of *Lenny*. The aesthetics trumpets a self-reflexive critique that jars the transparency of a classical narrative system responsible for naturalizing conservative myths, as it elegizes the passing of a bright but brief spirit, seemingly no longer viable in the midseventies.

CHAPTER FIVE

Gangsters and Private Eyes: *The Godfather* Films and *Chinatown*

In 1969, movies like *The Wild Bunch* and *Butch Cassidy and the Sundance Kid* could still depict a need for heroes even in a time of moral confusion over the Vietnam War, the civil rights movement, and the sexual revolution, perhaps *because* of the moral confusion. However, by 1971, the mood of America had darkened, and movies released in that year reflected this change. Along with *McCabe and Mrs. Miller*, such movies as *Carnal Knowledge*, *A Clockwork Orange*, *Dirty Harry*, *Klute*, and *Straw Dogs* depicted a society excessively violent and morally bankrupt. Its "heroes," like Alex in *A Clockwork Orange*, or Harry, or David in *Straw Dogs*, answer to the most brutal instincts in us all, cancelling the traditional qualities we associate with heroism. The mood of the nation reflected in these films prefigured the disillusionment and despair which would follow upon the events which later became known as Watergate, revealing corruption in the highest places in the American government. No better Geiger counter exists to measure the temper of the times than the initial cynicism of *The Godfather* in 1972 and its culmination in the scathing critique of American capitalist society in *The Godfather, Part II*, and *Chinatown* in 1974.

The critique of America in the *Godfather* films and *Chinatown* exists on the level of both genre and narration—in the transformation of the traditional gangster and detective films, inscribed through the modern sensibilities of an art cinema narration. For example, the *Godfather* films transform their genre by varying the subversion of the prosocial myth we find in *Bonnie and Clyde*. While the 1967 film overturns the prosocial myth of the traditional gangster film in favor of the myth of the rebel figure, the *Godfather* films shatter the myth by depicting criminality as the norm everywhere, implicating society at large as a reflection of the gangster world, and vice versa. Given this scenario, the Corleones pursue the ruthless but accepted ways of American capitalist society. Meanwhile, *Chinatown* transforms the detective genre by upsetting the moral code of the detective hero and by rendering prosocial forces helpless in the face of the overwhelming corruption in the corporate network of 1937 Los Angeles. The morally compromised maneuverings of both criminals and such "prosocial" figures as Sergeant McCluskey, Senator Geary, and Jake Gittes within a wasteland environment link the *Godfather* films and *Chinatown* to the westerns of the period, which themselves subvert the prosocial myth in their depiction of entrepreneurial lawmen and gunfighters engaged in brutal enterprises within a landscape that offers no distinction between its villains and its "heroes."

Just as *The Wild Bunch* and *McCabe and Mrs. Miller* reflect the disposition of the times toward disillusionment and sedition on the level of both content and form—through the cynical portrayal of "heroes" and society achieved by the subversion of genre and classical narration—so too the *Godfather* films and *Chinatown* accomplish their respective visions through generic and narrative subterfuge.

THE GODFATHER FILMS: 1972, 1974, AND 1990

The Rise and Moral Downfall of Michael Corleone: *Parts I and II*

The Godfather and *The Godfather, Part II* ape their genre's classic pattern of rise and fall, presented in part through spectacular set pieces that highlight stages in the criminal careers of Vito Corleone (Marlon Brando) and his son Michael (Al Pacino). *The Godfather* features such set pieces as the garroting of Luca Brasi in a bar; the attempted assassination of Vito on the streets of New York; Michael's shooting of Sollozzo and McCluskey in Louis's, which initiates him into the family business; the slaughter of Sonny (James Caan) on the causeway; the explosion of Apollonia in Sicily; and the assassinations of the heads of the Five Families that reestablishes the Corleones' power in the underworld. Meanwhile, *Part II* features the shotgunning of Vito's mother from point blank range on Don Ciccio's estate; the attempted assassination of Michael in his bedroom on Lake Tahoe; Vito's hit on Fanucci during the Festa San Gennaro in Little Italy, which catapults him to the leadership of his gang; Vito's vengeful disembowelment of Don Ciccio; and the simultaneous actions of Pentangeli's bathtub suicide, Hyman Roth's assassination in the airport, and Fredo's execution on Lake Tahoe that consolidate Michael's power within his own family and within the world of the Mafia.

The classic pattern of rise and fall in *Part I* and *Part II* centers specifically on Michael. The first film traces Michael's rise to godfather status, while the second depicts his consolidation and maintenance of power, but also his increasing isolation, his moral failure, and the destruction of the family. Michael's fall resists comparison with those of gangsters past. The customary punishment meted out includes both a fall from power and a violent death. And it doesn't matter whether the gangster is done in by social authorities, a rival gang, or a member of his own organization. Each force carries out the prosocial will underlying the classical paradigm. Coppola's version spares both Michael and Vito Corleone, the first godfather, from the gangster's traditional fate. Firmly entrenched and plotting a series of assassinations to ensure the family's domination, Vito dies an "unnatural" gangster's death, flush with power and not done in by authorities or a rival gang, of a heart attack while playing in the garden with his grandson Anthony. Though Vito's end mocks by contrast the usual generic fall, he nevertheless suffers for his crimes in the attempt on his life, his long recuperation, and the brutal murder of his eldest son, Sonny ("Look how they massacred my boy"). And if the godfathers, Vito and Michael, escape the conventional fate accorded to characters of their ilk, other family members such as Sonny, Apollonia, and Fredo share in the traditionally violent, brutal consequence of crime.

Michael's end represents a personal and moral punishment, a transformation of the genre's customary social and physical one; or it may be more accurate to say that it represents the realization or expression of a potential within the gangster film—the potential for a shift from an external punishment to an internal one as grounds for the protagonist's downfall. Michael gains and retains absolute power, but this means destroying anyone who gets in his way, even immediate family members. Ironically, in securing the sovereignty of the family, Michael must betray those closest to him. He orders the murder of Carlo, Connie's husband, for his part in Sonny's killing, and the murder of his brother Fredo (John Cazale) for Fredo's unwitting role in the attempted assassination on his life. He ostracizes Kay (Diane Keaton) because of her criticism and bitter disillusionment over his violent life-style and failure to legitimatize the family business. And he betrays Tom Hagen (Robert Duvall) by questioning Tom's loyalty and cruelly suggesting that Tom accept other offers for his services if he can't agree with Michael's decisions. The business side of the Corleone operation may be firmly entrenched in the end, but Michael's personal life and the family community lie shattered.

Kay as Moral Chorus

When speaking of the end of The Godfather, Part II, Coppola said that he meant to subvert the romanticization of Michael and the family in the first film:

This time I really set out to destroy the family. Yet I wanted to destroy it in the way that I think is most profound—from the inside. And I wanted to punish Michael, but not in the obvious ways. At the end, he's prematurely old, almost syphilitic, like Dorian Gray. I don't think anyone in the theater can envy him. (Farber, "They Made Him" 19)

However, Michael's deromanticization really starts at the end of *Part I* when he comes under the scrutiny of Kay, who begins to act as a chorus to the lies and betrayals of the Mafia family. Kay witnesses the scene in Michael's den when Connie (Talia Shire) bursts in and accuses Michael of ordering Carlo killed. After Connie leaves, Kay asks Michael whether this is true, and he says no. However, after she leaves the room and looks back from the vantage point of the kitchen opposite Michael's den, she observes a ritual honoring Michael as the new godfather; Clemenza, Al Neri, and Rocco Lampone pay tribute to him by kissing his hand and calling him "Don Corleone." As Kay beholds the scene revealed before her with a look of doubt, Al Neri comes forward, closes the door, and shuts her out from the inner sanctum of Michael's "business dealings." In this way, *Part I* ends on Kay's scrutiny of Michael's hypocrisy and prepares for the even greater scrutiny in *Part II*, which begins with a reprise of the last scene in *Part I*—Michael looking down at Rocco, who is kissing his hand (Rocco was kissing Michael's hand when Al Neri closed the door in the previous film).

In *Part II*, Kay's role as chorus to Michael's moral status takes on greater dimensions. While dancing with Michael at Anthony's first communion party at their Lake Tahoe estate, Kay reminds him of his promise to her seven years ago that the family business would be legitimate in five years. After the attempt on Michael's life in their bedroom, Kay's silence indicates her anger now that Michael's business endangers the family in its own home. While Michael is away on business in Miami and Cuba, Kay aborts their son, because she doesn't want it involved in Michael's world. Later, after the Senate hearings, Kay tells Michael she is leaving him and taking the children. Misperceiving her motives, he tells her he's sorry he couldn't be with her during her "miscarriage," and that things will change. Kay's response articulates her moral position, revealed in the past only through her looks: "Michael, you are blind; it wasn't a miscarriage; it was an abortion; just like our marriage is an abortion. I didn't want your son, Michael. This must all end." When Kay clandestinely visits her children after their divorce, Michael catches her saying goodbye to Anthony and closes the door on her, crowning her movement from family member to outcast and solidifying her role as choral conscience begun at the end of *Part I*, when another door closed on her.

Kay's removal from the family parallels Michael's increasing isolation from those around him and signals the end of the family as a warm, protective unit. Signs of the family's disintegration were apparent at the very beginning of *Part II*. Connie arrives at the first communion party with yet another fiance in tow to ask Michael for more money to bankroll her loose life-style; her mother scolds her for neglecting her children. The orchestra puzzles over Pentangeli's request for the traditional Italian tarantella played at Connie's wedding in *Part I*; instead, it plays the frivolous "Pop Goes the Weasel." Fredo can't prevent his alcoholic wife from making a scene on the dance floor and needs one of Michael's men to take care of the situation. Pentangeli, who runs the Corleone family business in New York, disagrees with Michael over sharing their turf with the Rosato brothers and with doing business with Hyman Roth; and finally, Johnny Ola's and Hyman Roth's opportunity to assassinate Michael stems from Fredo's dissatisfaction over his secondary position in the family, having been passed over in favor of Michael.

Parallel Structure as Moral Commentary

Part II employs a parallel structure to critique Michael's moral fall and the family's destruction further. Unlike the classic chronological narration of the first film, *Part II* cuts back and forth between Michael's story in 1958–1959, from the time of Anthony's first communion to Fredo's killing, and Vito's story, from the time of his immigration to America at the age of nine in 1901 to his return to Sicily to kill Don Ciccio in 1925. Through the insertion of the young Vito's story, the apparatus produces an analogous structure in the juxtaposition of the two generations. The secondary story enhances the critique of the primary story by contrasting the degeneration of the family under Michael to the rise of the family under Vito, the cold atmosphere and hollow relationships of the one to the warm, strong bonds of the other. In *"Godfather II*: A Deal Coppola Couldn't Refuse," John Hess explores how the transitions which link the Michael and Vito sequences work to juxtapose the state of Michael and his family to that of Vito and his. For example, through a slow dissolve, the first transition links the nine-year-old Vito, singing in his quarantine cell on Ellis Island, with his grandson, Michael Anthony, who is walking down the aisle for his first communion. On the one hand, the juxtaposition implies the fulfillment of the boy Vito's immigrant dream; on the other, it leads into a presentation of that fulfillment as hollow since the lawn party which follows is "garish, hectic, repulsive." Another transition juxtaposes Vito's warm family gathering on the stoop in Little Italy, after the killing of Fanucci has ensured his ascendancy to the head of his gang, with Michael's return to the cold rooms of his estate and Kay's turned back, after the Cuban revolution shattered his business deal with the Batista regime. Yet another transition contrasts Michael's argument with Kay and the breakup of his marriage to Vito's triumphant arrival in Sicily to meet with his Genco olive oil business associates and participate in a Corleone (Andolini) family reunion (Hess 10).

Control of Subjectivity as Moral Commentary

Another way in which the cinematic apparatus critiques Michael is through its control of subjectivity in both *Part I* and *Part II*. The classic narration of *Part I* subjectivizes the characters of Vito and Michael, drawing the viewer into the story through an identification with them. However, the privileging of Michael through point of view positioning in the greater part of *Part I* gives way to his disenfranchisement at the end when he becomes the object of Kay's scrutiny. In *Part I*, two sequences subjectivize Michael in particularly effective ways to produce audience identification: the family meeting in which Michael suggests a plan to kill Sollozzo and McCluskey and Michael's assassination of Sollozzo and McCluskey. In the family meeting, a dramatic take switches the attention and subject of the sequence from Sonny and Tom to Michael, empowering Michael not only as subject of the sequence but also of the greater part of the film to follow. The camera frames Michael in the center, sitting in an armchair in a long medium shot, with Sonny and Tessio on the sides in the foreground and Tom sitting at the desk behind him in the background. The room is hushed as Michael begins to intone in a calm voice, "They want to have a meeting with me, right?" As he continues to speak, the camera slowly zooms forward into a close-up of his face at the point where he says, "But if Clemenza can figure a way to have a weapon planted there for me. . . ." As Michael pauses, the camera itself stops its zoom, punctuating the taut silence and dramatically setting up Michael's punch line, "Then I'll kill them both." The apparatus then reveals that Michael has become the subject of the sequence during this take in the following reverse shot of Sonny, which is from Michael's point of view. Meanwhile, the apparatus subjectivizes Michael in three ways during his meeting with Sollozzo and McCluskey in Louis's restaurant. At the beginning of the meeting, the first shot is an over-the-shoulder shot from Michael's point of view, with Sollozzo as its object in a medium shot in the background. Later, after Michael has found the gun in the restroom, he pauses before coming out. The camera catches a glimpse of the back of his head in a long medium shot from behind the stall's door as he cradles the sides of his head with his hands. This technique of giving the illusion of peering in on a very private moment by capturing Michael's figure from behind as he pauses before emerging to carry out the execution of Sollozzo and McCluskey subjectivizes the pressure he feels and intensifies the moment. The third technique emphasizing Michael's subjectivity is an over the shoulder zoom-in shot from Sollozzo's position with Michael sitting at the table in the background in medium shot. As Sollozzo talks, the camera slowly zooms into a close-up of Michael's face as he waits for the propitious moment to gun down his two enemies. The zooming close-up here functions in the same way it did in the previous sequence when Michael outlined the plan of execution, subjectivizing Michael and intensifying our involvement with him.

The subjectivizing techniques in these two sequences work to involve the audience with Michael, so that we sympathize with his maneuverings to retain the family's power by eliminating its enemies. However, after the killings of the heads of the Five Families, the apparatus turns on Michael, relegating him to the position of an object, while subjectivizing Kay's moral perspective. When Connie bursts into Michael's den, the point of view is from her perspective as the camera is behind her with Michael sitting at his desk in the background as she confronts him about Carlo's killing. After Connie leaves the room, Kay gains the subject position as we see Michael from an over the shoulder shot from her point of view; this is followed by a reverse shot of Kay in close-up looking intently on Michael. When Kay asks the crucial question, "Is it true?" for the third time, it comes as the camera scrutinizes Michael in a medium over the shoulder shot from her perspective. He says, "No." Though Kay is unsuspecting at this moment, Michael cannot hide his hypocrisy from the movie audience, which now visualizes Michael as an object under investigation. Kay leaves the room relieved and walks to the kitchen opposite Michael's den. In a breathtaking deep focus shot from Kay's perspective in the kitchen, we see Michael in his room opposite in a long shot, joined by Clemenza, Rocco, and Al Neri, who honor him as godfather. In the foreground left, Kay turns and sees this ritual; the apparatus then cuts to a medium shot of the scene, still from Kay's perspective. Al Neri comes to the door and begins to close it; the scene cuts to a medium close-up of Kay's face looking wonderingly as the door closes on her.

As *Part II* continues Kay's scrutiny of Michael begun at the end of *Part I*, so too it continues to objectivize Michael. When we first see Michael at Anthony's first communion party, it is in a medium long shot as he sits with Kay, listening to Senator Geary's speech honoring the Corleones for their generous gift to the state university. In his first business meeting, the editing is shot-reverse-shot between him and Senator Geary, none of them an over the shoulder shot to establish a particular subject position. This is in direct contrast to the stunning opening shot of *Part I*, the over the shoulder shot from Vito's point of view, revealed by the slow zoom of the camera from the extreme close-up of Bonasera's face to a medium shot of his whole figure.

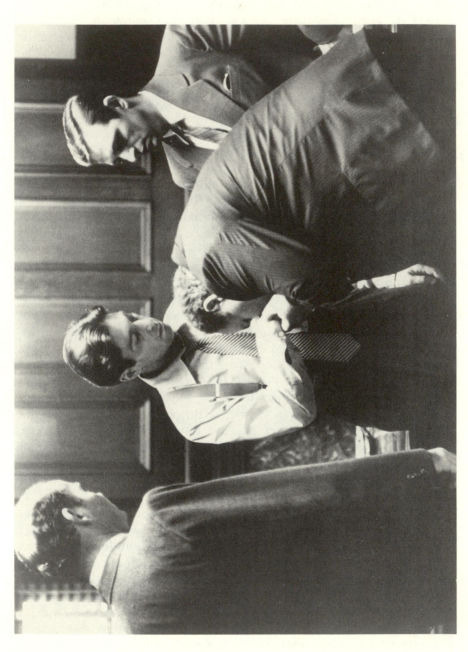

After Michael's lie, Kay's privileged view before its cancellation. *Courtesy of Museum of Modern Art Film Stills Archive. Copyright Paramount, 1972.*

Retrospective Moral Commentary

I don't want to suggest from the preceding that the critique of Michael occurs only in *Part II* and at the end of *Part I*. The critique and reflexivity of *Part II* throw the figure of Michael in *Part I* into greater relief. In retrospect, *Part II* helps us see more clearly signs of Michael's dark side in *Part I*, complicating his character and our identification with him. *Part I* provides us with glimpses of Michael's egocentric nature, steely temperament, and perfunctory treatment of others, characteristics that eventually lead to his moral downfall. For example, at Connie's wedding, Michael reveals to Kay a stubborn independence, one which he has used to isolate himself from the family's illegal business: "That's my family, Kay; that's not me." The coda at the end of *Part II* highlights this dogged autonomy through Michael's independent decision to join the marines after the Japanese bombing of Pearl Harbor, against the wishes of his family. He rebuffs all of his brothers' objections, telling them that *he*, not his father, will decide what course his life will take. As everyone leaves the dining room to greet Vito, who has just arrived home and whose birthday it is, Michael remains in his chair, alone and unwilling to share in his father's celebration. The coda at the end of *Part II* retrospectively foreshadows the intractibility of Michael's ruthless decisions in *Part II*, which lead to his moral and physical insulation after the killing of Fredo. The picture of the young rebellious Michael alone in the dining room parallels the image of the older Michael which follows the coda: alone on a bench on his Nevada estate, surrounded by bare trees, emotionally and spiritually defunct.

In addition to revealing Michael's independence and intractibility, the first film also provides a glimpse of Michael's coolness under fire in the hospital sequence, a premonition of the steely temperament which will harden him to Kay, Fredo, and Tom later. When Michael and Enzo are stationed on the hospital steps to foil the second attempt on Vito's life, Enzo's hands shake so much he can't light his cigarette; Michael takes the lighter, strikes it, and lights Enzo's cigarette, noting that his hands are calm and steady. *Part I* also reveals the moment Michael seizes on revenge as both a business and a personal proposition, a solution that he will follow throughout his criminal career. The moment occurs when he suggests killing Sollozzo and his protection, the corrupt cop McCluskey. Even though he assures Tom and Sonny that it is just "good business" and "nothing personal," everyone knows that the rhetoric disguises what is very personal—Sollozzo must die for masterminding the hit on their father, while McCluskey must pay not only for his role in the second attempted assassination at the hospital, but also for insulting and slugging Michael.

Part I also highlights Michael's cool, businesslike treatment of his family and associates by contrasting it to his father's warm, caring relationships. Vito's familial attitude and warm gestures dominate the interviews he conducts during Connie's wedding ("A don can never refuse a request on the day of his daughter's wedding"). In his first interview with Bonasera, the don expresses disappointment over the undertaker's unwillingness to do things in the "family way," which is to ask a favor in return for a future favor. Instead, Bonasera requests that Vito kill the men who raped and beat up his daughter for whatever price the don will name. Vito chides Bonasera for never wanting his friendship, for not exchanging visits, "even though my wife is godmother to your only child." He refuses the formal business arrangement proposed by the undertaker. Only after Bonasera asks him to "be my friend" and calls him "Godfather" does Vito assent to his request. In the interview with his godson, Johnny Fontaine, Vito's strong paternal feelings come into play in several ways. When Johnny cries and says, "I don't know what to do," because the Hollywood magnate Wolz refuses to give him a role that would boost his flagging career, Vito reacts with paternal anger, slaps Johnny, and encourages him, "You can act like a man!" Vito then asks him whether he spends time with his family, "because a man who doesn't spend time with his family, he can never be a real man." Vito says this as much for his eldest son's sake as for Johnny's, for, after expressing this sentiment, he turns to look at Sonny, who had entered the room moments before, flustered from his tryst upstairs with the bridesmaid, Teresa Mancini. Vito then comforts Johnny ("Rest now"), reassures him about the role from Wolz ("I'm going to make him an offer he can't refuse"), and hugs and kisses him as he leaves.

Vito's paternal affection and keen family sense as he conducts business at the beginning of *Part I* contrast to Michael's cool, professional, and bossy attitude in *his* business meetings at the beginning of *Part II*. Michael's meeting with Senator Geary turns into an ugly confrontation, each extorting the other; Michael and Pentangeli argue over the Corleone business relationship with the Rosato brothers and Hyman Roth; Michael tries to persuade Connie to give up her loose and lavish life-style and orders her to break the engagement with Merle (Michael is, of course, responsible for Connie's dissipation after Carlo's murder). The only agreeable meeting is with Johnny Ola, representative of Hyman Roth, with whom Michael desires a partnership. However, the meeting is laced with betrayal, since it is Johnny Ola, with Roth's approval, who has masterminded the upcoming attempt on Michael's life later that evening.

The contrast between Vito's and Michael's styles of conducting business and handling family members and associates is apparent in *Part I* after Michael takes over as head after his return from Sicily. Without prior consultation, Michael announces to Tom Hagen (Robert Duvall) that he is no longer consigliere but in charge of the family's Las Vegas operation. With no regard for Tom's feelings, Michael tells him, "You're out, Tom" in a definitive manner after Tom protests. In contrast, Vito, sensing Tom's hurt, puts his hand on Tom's arm and, in a concerned tone, reassures him that the family still has confidence in him, that the change is not due to poor performance ("I never thought you were a bad consigliere"), and that the move is for his own good because things may get rough. Michael's blunt, no-nonsense air, his lack of concern and appreciation are also apparent in his treatment of Fredo when he arrives in Las Vegas to buy out Moe Green. Annoyed, Michael ungraciously undercuts Fredo's hospitality by ordering him to get rid of the band and women on his entrance to his suite. After Michael's confrontation with Moe Green, in which he demands a takeover of Moe's Vegas operation, Fredo tells his brother, "Mike, you don't come to Las Vegas and talk to a man like Moe Green like that." Michael warns Fredo, "Fredo, you're my older brother and I love you; but don't ever take sides against the family again, ever." The Las Vegas sequence foreshadows Michael's treatment of his older brother in *Part II*, in which Michael's wounded feelings, after his discovery of Fredo's betrayal, overcome any thought of forgiveness or softening. Instead, Michael uses Fredo to gain information that helps him in the Senate hearings, then casts him aside:

"Fredo, you're nothing to me now; you're not a brother; you're not a friend. I don't want to know you or what you do. I don't want to see you at the hotels; I don't want you near my house. When you see our mother, I want to know a day in advance so I won't be there. You understand?"

Michael's heartless obsession with vengeance is nowhere more apparent than in his confrontation with Tom before the three-pronged killings of Roth, Pentangeli, and Fredo. Michael has beaten the Senate rap after Pentangeli reneged on his testimony. Tom reminds Michael that he is stronger now and that Roth and the Rosato brothers are on the run. He asks him, "Is it worth it? Do you want to wipe everybody out?" Michael replies, "I don't want to wipe everybody out, just my enemies." He then hurts the one person in his immediate family who has been staunchly loyal to him without interruption, forcing Tom into concurrence: "You gonna come along with me in these things I have to do or what? Because if you don't, you can take your wife, your family, and your mistress, and move them all to Las Vegas."

In the end, Michael attains absolute power, but at the cost of his own soul and the lives and happiness of his family and associates. His hubris blinds him to the awful consequences of his inflexible actions. Michael's moral downfall may be a significant departure from the traditional social and physical collapse of the classic gangster figure, but the personal tragedy of Michael and, say, Tony Camonte (Paul Muni) or Rico (Edward

G. Robinson) of *Scarface* (1932) and *Little Caesar* (1930), respectively, follows from the same hubris, the same drive to overreach and become absolute. Tony and Rico reach the top, crave more, stumble, and die; Michael reaches the top, stays there, and remains alive, but he might as well be dead.[1]

Indictment of Capitalism and the American Family

Though Michael's fate represents an important change in the way the gangster protagonist is disposed of, the most significant generic transformation in the *Godfather* films has to do with the dominant prosocial bias of the genre. While *Bonnie and Clyde* overturns the genre's prosocial myth in favor of the myth of the individual, the *Godfather* films upset the prosocial bias by erasing the traditional division between criminal and prosocial forces and indicting the whole economic, political, and social system as the primary accomplice in the criminal career of the Corleone family. In other words, the *Godfather* films depict the corruption of the gangster as part of a larger corruption, stemming from the abuses within a system of free enterprise.

In the classic gangster film, the genre's ideological bias is deflected from the capitalist basis of the gangster's drive for power by focusing on the protagonist's hubris. His arrogant drive toward success catapults him to a destruction for which he is solely responsible. His personal tragedy cancels an ever potential indictment of the society which spawned him. Instead, society plays a positive role in eliminating the criminal element and restoring balance and order, not only within the world of the film, but also within a movie audience attracted by the gangster's bold strike for a freedom without responsibility.[2] In *The Godfather* films, however, the personal tragedy of Michael's moral downfall does not deflect from the capitalist basis of his actions. Instead, it *reflects* the moral tragedy of a society commodified and grounded on the desire for success at any cost. Michael's tragedy is not merely his own; it is America's tragedy as well.

The claim that organized crime reflects American capitalist society in the *Godfather* films is not a new one. Coppola himself said that he made conscious use of the Mafia as a "metaphor for America":

I always wanted to use the Mafia as a metaphor for America. If you look at the film, you see that it's focused that way. The first line is "I believe in America." I feel that the Mafia is an incredible metaphor for this country. . . . Both are totally capitalistic phenomena and basically have a profit motive. (Farber, "Coppola and *The Godfather*" 223)

The profit motive pervades all levels of society in the world of the *Godfather* films. It links public officials, legitimate businessmen, common hoods, and high-level Mafiosi. The Corleone payroll includes politicians, lawyers, judges, journalists, and policemen. Michael reminds Senator Geary, "We're all part of the same hypocrisy, Senator." In the business deal with the Cuban dictator Batista, Michael and Hyman Roth are only two of many partners, who include U.S. senators, congressmen, and the heads of American conglomerates on the order of AT&T and U.S. Steel.

The correlation made between the gangster and society in the capitalist web of corruption is nowhere more apparent than in the films' generic transformation of the family. In "Keeping Up with the Corleones," William Pechter says that the treatment of the family in *The Godfather* is new to the genre because it domesticates the gangster to such a degree as to make him a family man who amasses power in order to provide for his dependents (90). In other words, the Corleone family is like any other family striving to attain the American dream of material success. Conformist in their attitude, the Corleones fit into the mainstream of middle-class America and its capitalist values. In contrast, poverty marginalizes the family of the classic gangster and motivates him to rebel against economic inequities through a life of crime, pitting him *against* society. Furthermore, the classic gangster's animallike qualities and the pathological nature of his familial relationships underscore his anomalous position. One recalls the apelike Tony Camonte's incestuous liaison with his sister, Cesca, in *Scarface*; Rico's childish mother love and worship in *Little Caesar*; Tom Powers's misogyny in the grapefruit scene in *Public Enemy* (1931); Roy Earle's fetishistic love for the crippled Velma, daughter of the Okie family he "adopts," in *High Sierra* (1941); and the epileptic Cody Jarrett's oedipal obsession with Ma in *White Heat* (1949). By contrast, the Corleones appear "normal."

However, the normality of the Corleones, their blending into the very fabric of American society only means that they share in its bourgeois hypocrisy; success can only be achieved through a series of compromises that destroys the integrity of the family and its individuals. The dangers inherent in the capitalist impulse surface in Michael's paranoid vengeance, exposing the worm at the heart of American society. Vito's "successful" separation of a personal family life of affectionate generosity and a professional life of criminal violence gives way to the inevitable collapsing of the personal and the professional in Michael's harsh treatment of the family in the name of economic power. The example of Michael gives the lie to the bourgeois notion that one can be virtuous in one's personal life yet ruthless in one's professional life, that the "goodness" of the one remains untouched by the viciousness of the other, all because ruthlessness is an accepted trait of the business ethic.[3]

The destruction of humane values in the world of the Corleones reflects the destruction of those values in the larger world of which it is a part. In his Marxist analysis of the *Godfather* films, John Hess observes

how business in *Part II* destroys the family and, with it, such basic values
as community, love, respect, support, and appreciation, since the main
goal of capitalism is profit, not the meeting of human needs. Business
relations destroy four levels of familial affiliations: the nuclear family,
the Mafia family, the ethnic community, and the Catholic Church. In the
first, Michael not only destroys his own family but Connie's as well; in
the second, Michael pushes aside Pentangeli's objections to do business
with outsiders Roth and Ola, who, along with Fredo, betray him; in the
third, the family moves to Nevada, incorporates outside the Italian community by doing business with the Jew Roth, and begins to lose its eth-
nicity in its efforts to become more "American"; in the fourth, the various
murders which take place during religious ceremonies underline the
church's impotence in the face of its members' transgressions and hypocrisy (10–11).[4]

Though the *Godfather* films dramatize the erosion of values within various familial institutions largely in Michael's generation, they locate the
source of that corruption in Vito's early life, revealing that the diseases
of a rampant capitalism not only extend through all levels of society, but
span the entire first half of the twentieth century as well. Earlier, I discussed the analogous parallel structure of *Part II* as working to contrast
Michael's cold-blooded destruction of the family to Vito's formation of
it through affectionate ties and support. However, it also reveals the
son's similarity to the father and their symbiotic relationship: Vito's rise
to power through crime not only parallels Michael's consolidation of
power through crime, but also plants the seeds for Michael's moral
downfall in the later generation. Several of the early transitions between
the Vito and Michael sequences reinforce this association through visual
means provided by superimpositions and fades, which separate or unite
the Michael and Vito figures, depending on their respective status in
relation to each other. In the first transition, the nine-year-old Vito sits
on a chair in the quarantine room on Ellis Island in 1901 in the middle
of the frame; as the image fades, the superimposition of his seven-year-
old grandson Anthony, marching down the aisle to his first communion
in 1958, overlays the figure of the young Vito, pairing the two and, by
implication, contrasting both in their innocence to Michael, the present
godfather. In the second transition, Michael bids farewell to Anthony
after the attempt on his life, his profile in close-up on the left of the
screen; as the scene fades, the figure of the twenty-five-year-old Vito in
1917 appears on the right of the screen, leaning against a door frame
watching his first son, Sonny. Though the fade and superimposition suggest a doubling, the figures are separate, since Vito, a grocer's assistant,
is not yet involved in criminal activities. However, in the fourth transition, the fade and superimposition join the two figures as one blends
into the other. Michael learns of Kay's "miscarriage" from Tom after his

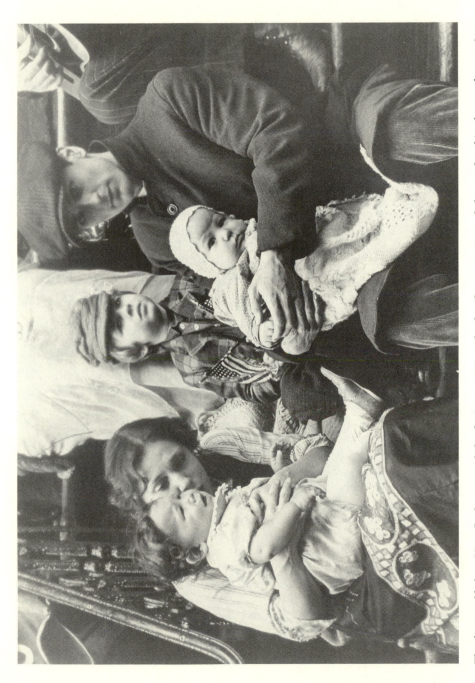

The first godfather, Vito Corleone, and the first generation: the family as utopia and the seeds of its future destruction. Courtesy of Museum of Modern Art Film Stills Archive; Copyright Paramount, 1974.

return from Cuba, his profile in close-up on the left of the screen; the superimposition positions Vito on the same side of the screen over Michael's profile as he leans against the doorway watching his second son, Fredo, a newborn in 1919. The two figures are now one, as Vito has since joined a gang of petty thieves. Also, the sequence which follows chronicles Vito's assassination of Fanucci, catapulting him to the position of godfather. The visual identification of Vito and Michael in the fourth transition not only implicates both, but, more significantly, establishes the father's initiation into crime as the root of the son's condition and ultimate moral disintegration.

Ideology and *Part III* as Summation

In "Reification and Utopia in Mass Culture," *Signatures of the Visible* (New York 1990), Frederic Jameson clarifies the ideological relationship between *Parts I* and *II* of *The Godfather*. For Jameson, *Part II*'s explicit critique of American capitalism unmasks the ideological and utopian function of the earlier film. The ideological function of *Part I* is to disguise the economic cause at the heart of America's problems. The Mafia acts as a displacement for American capitalism, a displacement which encourages us to believe that the cause for the deterioration of life in the United States today is not economic but ethical, not derived from a profit motive, but from the mythic source of "the pure Evil of the Mafiosi" (32). Meanwhile, the utopian function of *Part I* provides the fantasy of an integrated community formed by patriarchal and authoritarian bonds for an audience given over to social fragmentation and atomization. *Part II* deconstructs both the ideological and the utopian content of *Part I*, as the mythic content of *Part I* falls into history itself. The Mafiosi actually turn into businessmen in their attempt to invest in legitimate schemes with the Batista government, and American business and imperialism "meet that supreme ultimate obstacle to their internal dynamism and structurally necessary expansion which is the Cuban Revolution" (34). Meanwhile, *Part II* undercuts the utopian content of the family in *Part I* by tracing its roots back to feudal Sicily and showing that its survival depends on "forms of repression and sexism and violence" (34).

Jameson's insights may well apply to *Part III* of the *Godfather* saga, made sixteen years after *Part I* and *Part II* and released on Christmas Day 1990.[5] The fall from myth into history, from mystification into critique, continues in *Part III*. The movie completes the process of Michael's transformation from Mafioso to legitimate businessman when he sells his gambling investments and buys into a European conglomerate, International Immobiliare. Michael's secularization fulfills the critique of capitalism, since he discovers that the world of legitimate business is just as corrupt as the Mafia's, forcing him to resort to the same ruthlessness and violence in order to survive and be successful in the "real" world. Immobiliare proves to be capitalism in its most dehumanized, multinational, and corporate form, implicating even papal history in its corruption, since the movie incorporates the death of Pope John Paul I in 1979 as part of a plot to gain control of the company.

Part III also recapitulates the utopian myth of the family and its deconstruction in the earlier films. It rejuvenates the myth of the family's solidarity and integration we find in *Part I.* Michael has moved the family back to its roots in New York City; he revives the family's relationship with the church by contributing $200 million to a Sicilian fund for the needy, receiving in return the medal of San Sebastian; at the reception after the religious ceremony, Connie leads the orchestra and guests in the singing of the traditional Italian tarantella played at her own wedding in *Part I*; Michael craves family gatherings and togetherness, asking Anthony and Mary (Sofia Coppola) to include their mother in the Corleone parties; he is flexible and loving in allowing Anthony to pursue a singing career; he agonizes over the murder of Fredo and confesses his sins to Cardinal Lamberto; he even confesses his transgressions to Kay and asks for her forgiveness; he takes in Sonny's bastard son, Vinnie (Andy Garcia), and trains him to take his own place as godfather; and Connie assumes a powerful role as an unofficial godmother. The family, though broken, shows strong signs of coming together at the same time that Michael attempts to become legitimate. Ironically, it is this attempt to legitimatize that destroys any desired family unity. For in selling off the Corleone family business, Michael incurs the wrath of Joey Zasa (Joe Mantegna) and is pulled back into the intrigue and violence of the gangsters. In maneuvering to control International Immobiliare through his purchase of the majority of its stocks, he invites the disfavor of its board, headed by Lucchesi, who plots to regain control by delaying tactics, betrayal, and assassination. In other words, try as he may, Michael cannot extricate the family from the web of destruction woven by Vito and by him in the past. As in *Part II*, the lie at the heart of the family's utopian image undermines it again in *Part III* as the violence which erupts from the ruthlessness inherent in the multinational capitalist system destroys Michael's beloved daughter, Mary. Mary's death reconfirms for Kay the danger that Michael represents and permanently fractures his attempts to reestablish cordial relations with her.

Part III reflects on the earlier films in other ways as well. Kay continues to act as chorus to the corruption which Michael represents. At the beginning, she tells him he is more dangerous than ever, now that he has become "respectable." When she momentarily softens to him in Sicily, word comes of Don Tommasino's death by an assassin. As Michael vows vengeance, Kay looks on from another room. The camera subjectivizes her in a medium long shot as she listens, then walks out of sight behind the side wall, shielding herself from the Michael she recognizes only too well. *Part III* also reprises the two forms of narrative we find in *Part I* and *Part II*, namely the classic narrative of conflict and resolution of *Part I* and the modernist narrative of characterization and theme in *Part II*. The classic plot of action centers on Vincent, who reprises the earlier roles of Vito and Michael in their rise to the top of the gangster world. Vinnie's story includes the maneuverings to secure the family's power and fortune from its enemies in both the Mafia world (Joey Zasa, Altobello) and the world of international capitalism (Lucchesi, Archbishop Gilday). Meanwhile, the modernist plot of character centers on Michael's internal struggle to come to terms with his guilt, his need for forgiveness and redemption, and his desire to bury the past. In the end, he fails for the weakness within and for the world of corruption which overwhelms. And finally, *Part III* is reflexive as *Part I* and *Part II* are. In addition to the overall reflexivity of *Part III* in relation to its genre and to the earlier films, we find analogies at work in its references to Shakespeare's *Lear*, Mascagni's *Cavalleria Rusticana*, and the puppet act of family honor from the Sicilian *teatro dei pupi*.

I do not wish to offer an extended analysis of *Part III*, which falls outside the period of the American film renaissance. I only intend to indicate by these brief remarks the symbiotic relationship which exists among all three films, though sixteen years separate the last from the earlier two. In a sense, *The Godfather, Part III* is a 1970s film made in the late 1980s. It reinscribes many of the features of the earlier films, so much in tune with the darkened attitudes in the era of Vietnam, Nixon, and Watergate. Its cynicism may seem an anachronism in the era of Reagan, Bush, the Gulf War, and flag waving patriotism. Like *Part I* and *Part II* together, *Part III* portrays an America vexed with contradictions, offers no simple solutions, and implicates the whole system and everyone in its deterioration.

THE DETECTIVE GENRE IN THE 1970s: *CHINATOWN* (1974)

If the Academy Awards are a barometer of the temper of the times, then the best picture nominees of 1974 may be a measure of the epidemic pessimism of the midseventies. 1974 was the year of Watergate and Nixon's resignation. The following year saw the fall of Saigon to the Viet Cong after America had withdrawn its military support under heavy pressure from the American public. The mood of the country was at its darkest, and the year's most significant movies mirror the American public's loss of faith in its country and its leaders. The best picture nominees for 1974 were *The Godfather, Part II*, *Chinatown*, *The Conversation*, *Lenny*, and *The Towering Inferno*. The last may seem an anomaly among the other four; the first three depict the alienation and disillusionment consequent upon the discovery of corruption in the very highest places in society and government, while the fourth is iconoclastic in its treatment of the irreverent Lenny Bruce's lifelong struggle with censorship and drugs. However, even the highly commercial fifth nominee is not without its unflattering picture of American capitalism. A disaster picture, *The Towering Inferno* contains a generic conflict between man and circumstances that arises as a result of the vanity of corporate leaders. The decision to save money by cutting corners on the construction of the world's tallest building causes flaws which leave the building vulnerable to the disastrous conflagration. After the fire starts, the company boss complicates the situation by denying any danger with a smug attitude of invincibility. The disaster picture's positive resolution, however, is clearly out of sync with those of its fellow nominees. Steve McQueen's fire chief and Paul Newman's architect are moral heroes who make a difference; they triumph over both the fire and the company magnates. In contrast, Michael's villainy controls the world of *The Godfather, Part II*; Jack Nicholson's detective, Jake Gittes, and Gene Hackman's surveillance expert, Harry Caul, in *Chinatown* and *The Conversation*, respectively, are impotent in the face of an ever widening circle of deception and intrigue; and Dustin Hoffman's Lenny dies tragically, ostensibly a victim of a drug-ridden culture, but really a victim of a hypocritical, puritanical society.

Of *The Godfather, Part II*, *Chinatown*, *The Conversation*, and *Lenny*, the first two had the greatest impact, achieving both financial and critical success.[6] Like *The Godfather, Part II*, *Chinatown* addresses the loss of faith in American society by appealing to, then overturning generic expectations.[7]

Private Eyes Past and Present

Polanski's film includes all the elements of the private eye *noir* genre: the hard-boiled but vulnerable detective, the femme fatale, antagonistic cops, henchmen and heavies, and a complex plot of murder and deceit, which the detective eventually exposes. Polanski's modernist narrative, however, complicates the genre and eventually explodes the moral security of its prosocial myth. Films such as *The Maltese Falcon* (1941), *Murder, My Sweet* (1945), and *The Big Sleep* (1946) promote the prosocial myth by locating it in the figure of the private eye who calls upon both his moral idealism and his street savvy to counteract the infestation of crime. Bogart's Sam Spade and Phillip Marlowe doggedly adhere to a personal code of honor, an element of balance and sanity in a whirlpool of deceit and betrayal. In *The Maltese Falcon*, for example, Spade spurns the inappropriate, tasteless advances of the widow of his just-killed partner, Archer; he returns all but $1,000 of the $9,000 which Gutman (Sidney J.

Greenstreet) paid him to find the black bird because the statue turns out to be a fake; and in the end, he sends Brigid O'Shaughnessy (Mary Astor), the femme fatale whom he loves, to the chair for the murder of Archer. His last confrontation with Brigid is a textbook illustration not only of the code, but of his tough-guy practicality as well. He tells her that he won't play the sap for her (personal honor); that she has to pay for what she's done (justice); that it would be bad for business if his partner's killer got away (moral obligation to his partner); and that if she were free, he could never trust her, as she could never trust him (self-preservation). In the end, he tosses off a typical tough-guy remark to dispel any sentimentality that may compromise his decision, "Maybe you love me, and maybe I love you. I'll have some rotten nights over you, but that will pass."

The Spades and Marlowes of the past are certainly not saints. The shadowy world of *noir* rubs off on them. The widow Archer's hopeful question "Did you kill my husband?" implicates Sam in an illicit past relation. His love affair with Brigid takes full advantage of her vulnerability, since she needs his help in the falcon conspiracy. In other words, Sam succumbs to common human weaknesses. That is, after all, part of his appeal. However, his failings prove to be only temporary aberrations. He affirms his integrity through his single-minded action to solve the crime and attain justice. During the investigation, he preserves his integrity by keeping his isolation intact in several ways: physically, through his bare, almost spartan office; occupationally, through his engagement in the pursuit of truth opposed to financial reward; emotionally, through a life-style which rejects prolonged human interaction and commitment; and morally, through his personal code of honor (Schatz, *Hollywood Genres* 128). At the end, he retreats to his office until an alluring woman or the death of a friend draws him back into the whirlpool of corruption which defines the *noir* universe.

Chinatown shatters the sanctuaries of immunity the detective clings to in order to protect himself from the incursions of the world. Jake Gittes has sold out and bought into the system. Like Bogart's Sam Spade, Gittes quit the police force out of disillusionment over its lack of integrity and its ineffectiveness and became a private eye. However, unlike Spade, Gittes buys into society's materialism by specializing in lucrative divorce cases, a practice which consists in snooping into people's intimate affairs. At the beginning, Gittes shows off a well-furnished agency with several offices, two assistants, and a secretary, a far cry from the bare, spartan rooms of his predecessors. A conversation between Gittes and his former colleagues on the police force, Escobar and Loach, reinforces his deconstruction of the private eye. At the scene of Mulwray's death, Escobar chides Gittes, "Look like you done well for yourself"; Gittes replies, "I get by." Escobar says with a trace of sarcasm, "Well, sometimes it takes

Jack Nicholson's Jake Gittes: the modernist private eye and his lucrative business—well heeled, well stocked, and highly compromised. *Courtesy of Museum of Modern Art Film Stills Archive; Copyright Paramount, 1974.*

a while for a man to find himself; maybe you have"; to which Loach adds more explicitly, "Going through other people's dirty linen." Furthermore, Gittes's confrontation with the banker in the barber shop links him with the capitalistic imperative that propels men like Noah Cross to become greedy entrepreneurs. The banker snidely remarks over the headlines of the Mulwray love nest scandal that Gittes helped expose, "You got a hell of a way to make a living"; to which Gittes replies, "Tell me, did you foreclose on many families this week?"

Narrative and Narration as Moral Commentary

Gittes's narrative function in *Chinatown*'s transformed myth of the private eye differs from that of the traditional detective. As a function of the narrative, the private eye character unfolds the mysteries of the plot and provides the point of view or acts as filter for the events. Traditionally, he exposes the layers of deceit and betrayals and brings the perpetrators to justice, either by killing them (defending himself or having them kill each other) or by turning them over to authorities. The ultimate conflict in the genre pits the hero's value system against the corrupt social environment. Because this remains an ongoing struggle, the genre's overriding theme is an existential one; the private eye rejects a society whose values he cannot accept and exists as a marginal figure, a self-willed individual clinging to a personal code of honor (Cawelti 499–500). As a function of the narration's point of view, the classic *noir* detective is the subject of the narrative, the perceptual center through which the events are filtered and a figure of power, unraveling the complex web of intrigue and deception. As a significant factor in the narrative's closure, he successfully creates an intersection of his uncompromised sensibilities with the *noir* world of corruption, an endorsement of his personal code of honor as an operable force.

Jack Nicholson's Jake Gittes also functions centrally in the plot, theme, and point of view of *Chinatown*, but the effects and ramifications differ from those of the classic *noir* film. As a function of plot, Gittes repeats the mythic actions of his predecessors by uncovering a malicious conspiracy while investigating a seemingly simple affair between an older married man and a young girl. His snooping on Hollis Mulwray (Darrell Swerling) exposes a double plot of incest, murder, land swindle, and profiteering. However, though Gittes solves the crime by identifying Noah Cross (John Huston) as the man who murdered Mulwray and masterminded the dam project, the water shortage, and the land swindle to make a profit, he is powerless to do anything about it. Cross proves invulnerable, a powerful political figure who owns the police. Gittes's reenactment of an earlier disaster he tried to prevent signifies his lack of control over a common situation which continues to haunt him. A force greater than anything he can imagine determines the outcome, whether that force be Noah Cross, the evil he represents, or the fate that awaits those who dare to think they can dent the overwhelming corruption within the modern landscape. At the end, Chinatown becomes the mythic ground of lawlessness where modern man in the person of Jake Gittes ritualizes his futile gestures. The police kill an innocent victim, Evelyn Mulwray (Faye Dunaway), who they suspect murdered her husband over an alleged affair with a young girl. The young girl is really her daughter, Katherine, by her father Noah Cross. Evelyn had been hiding Katherine from Cross, who wants custody. Escobar and his men conveniently pin the murder on the dead Evelyn, while Cross goes free to realize his money-making scheme and to victimize Katherine. Gittes's revelation about the real murderer falls on deaf ears, and his colleagues try to console him by advising him, "Forget it, Jake; it's Chinatown."[8]

As a function of plot, Gittes is empowered only to the extent that he uncovers a series of crimes and exposes its perpetrator; that Cross goes unpunished prevents him from effecting a just resolution. The ramifications of Gittes's futile actions suggest his function in the thematic significance of the film's ultimate vision. The tragic injustice of Evelyn's death and her inscription as Mulwray's murderer by the forces of law and order confirm for Gittes the impotence of individuals and society to achieve justice in the face of widespread corruption. Those who are untainted offer no alternative. Evelyn, Katherine, and Hollis fall easy prey to powerful forces beyond their control. The hard-boiled detective himself lacks the traditional mythic power to resolve at least an isolated instance of injustice, a deficiency inscribed from the very beginning, of course, in the signs of his compromise. Gittes will no doubt incur yet more guilt over this present reenactment of his past, but he will also become more resolved in his cynicism to pursue the lucrative business of divorce work.

Point of view also functions to deconstruct the traditional myth of the private eye in *Chinatown*. In the classic *noir* film, the primary function of point of view was to reveal both the complex plottings and the hard-boiled detective's integrity as he deflected compromises to his code, while seeking a just solution. In *Chinatown*, point of view functions only secondarily to reveal plot. Its main function is to reveal Gittes's compromised character and muddled, limited vision. In other words, the use of point of view is an ironic and reflexive one, undercutting Gittes's perspective as it uses it to present the story.

The filmic apparatus deconstructs the private eye myth from the very beginning with self-conscious references to the genre's code and an objective point of view in the first sequence. The washed out brown tones of the titles framed by shadows on both sides of the screen approximate the black and white photography of classic film *noir* projected in the old ratio of 1:1.33. The sound track isolates the melancholy jaded tone of a trumpet, enumerating the *noir* emotion and atmosphere. The titles and credits are followed by close-ups of black and white photographs of a couple in various positions of lovemaking; the photos are lowered to reveal Gittes, sitting at his desk in the background. His client Curly puts down the photos and starts clawing the venetian blinds on the window, another pointed generic reference. The point of view of the first sequence is objective. Though Curly views the photos, the camera frames him as object as he walks to the window, then cuts to Gittes as object also, as he tells Curly to mind the venetian blinds since they were just put in yesterday. The objective perspective functions not only to present the scene, but to scrutinize Gittes as well; we note his three-piece white suit meticulously set off by a black and yellow tie, his slicked-back hair, his new venetian blinds, his well-stocked liquor cabinet, and his questionable line of work. We note, in other words, signs of his compromise in contrast to the classic *noir* detective.

After the first sequence, the narration switches to a subjective point of view, the filmic apparatus inscribing Gittes's perspective as a filter for the events when he starts to tail Mulwray to gain incriminating evidence. The point of Gittes's subjectivity is not so much to reveal the nefarious plotting as it is to emphasize his limited vision. At the beginning of his inquiry, he is in the dark as to the real nature of what he is hired to do. He thinks he has been hired by Evelyn Mulwray to get proof of her husband's affair with a young girl. He doesn't know that it was really an impostor, Ida Sessions (Diane Ladd), who hired him for the hidden purpose of discrediting Mulwray because of his opposition to the dam project. When Gittes pursues the fiction of Mulwray's affair with Katherine, the real plots, of which he is unaware, are in plain sight before his eyes. He begins following Mulwray by attending the civic hearing on the proposed water dam, which Mulwray testifies against. Later, he tails Mulwray to the dry L.A. riverbed and to the ocean, where Mulwray stays all night to conduct his own investigation of the water runoff from the reservoirs into the ocean. Gittes finally has the opportunity to take pictures of Mulwray and "the young girl" the next day at Griffith Park and at her El Macondo apartment. He thinks both meetings are lovers' rendezvous, not knowing that Mulwray is Katherine's stepfather and the only parent she has known in her deprived upbringing. After Gittes figures out the outlines of the water plot, he hypothesizes correctly that Mulwray was killed because he knew someone was dumping water from the reservoirs, but this clarification is undercut by the still mysterious second plot of incest. He gets sidetracked by this plot when he begins to suspect Evelyn as Mulwray's murderer after following her to what he thinks is a kidnapped Katherine. Instead of acting on his first insight, he instinctively trusts his limited experience in divorce work. He acts on the cliché of the jealous wife in accusing Evelyn of the killing after he discovers salt water and what he thinks are Mulwray's glasses in the garden pond on Mulwray's estate (Mulwray drowned in salt water). He suspects that Evelyn is keeping Katherine under wraps because the girl witnessed the killing. When Evelyn reveals to him that Katherine is her sister *and* her daughter, he tries to explain it with another cliché, ''He raped you.'' With a shake of her head, Evelyn clarifies the second plot. She ran away to Mexico when she learned of her pregnancy. Hollis came and took care of both of them, but after a while, she left Katherine to Hollis's care: ''I couldn't see her; I was fifteen; I wanted to, but I couldn't. And now I want to be with her; I want to take care of her.'' Evelyn has hidden Katherine in fear that her father, Noah Cross, may step forward and claim her for his own. ''Evelyn, how many years have I got? She's mine too,'' Cross pleads with her in Chinatown.

Not only does Evelyn reveal the details of the second plot to Gittes, she also helps him solve the mystery of the first plot. She tells him that the glasses he found in the pond are not her husband's because he never wore bifocals. With this clue, Gittes correctly deduces that the glasses belong to Cross and that Cross murdered Mulwray after Mulwray found out about the water dumping and the real estate scheme. Earlier, Gittes's clarified vision had been clouded by his clichéd response to the jealous wife stereotype. Now, his corrected vision wilts before forces which have greater consequences than its own circumscribed capacity may contain. First, Noah Cross's larger, more powerful vision co-opts the limited one of Mulwray's murder and the demand for its restitution that Gittes entertains. To Gittes's accusation that Cross will take the water from L.A. and pour it into the valley once the dam is built, Cross replies that plans have already been formed to incorporate the valley into the city in order ''to bring L.A. to the water.'' To Gittes's uncomprehending question, ''What can you buy that you can't already afford?'' Cross replies, ''The future, Mr. Gittes, the future.'' Cross also knows that the law won't touch him because of his influence, a fact lost on Gittes when he tries to tell Escobar the truth in Chinatown. Gittes's clarified vision is further undercut by the compromised vision of those in authority. Escobar's decision to pin the murder on Evelyn and let everyone else go scot free in order to prevent any embarrassment and inconvenience nullifies Gittes's desire to bring Cross to justice. Gittes tells Evelyn that he and Escobar did ''as little as possible'' when they worked in Chinatown for the district attorney. He repeats these words over Evelyn's bloody corpse, a motto for the skewed vision of those in authority. Finally, Gittes's own imprisonment in his guilty past dooms him to repeat actions which lead to the destruction of an innocent victim. He explains to Evelyn the disillusionment which forced him to leave the police force, ''I was trying to keep someone from getting hurt. I ended up making sure she was hurt.''

SSCT-9-9A

Faye Dunaway's Evelyn Mulwray: daughter/mistress, mother/sister—the vulnerable, fractured femme fatale. *Courtesy of Museum of Modern Art Film Stills Archive; Copyright Paramount, 1974.*

When Evelyn reveals the address of her servant's house, 1712 Alameda in Chinatown, Gittes feels an onrush of déjà vu. In this sequence, the filmic apparatus underlines Gittes's sense of fatalism by the use of a high-angle shot of him combined with a zoom-in close-up of his stunned face.

The filmic apparatus also utilizes deep focus photography, mise-en-scène, and positioning within the frame to diminish the figure of Gittes even as it empowers him as subject and filter of the narrative. In *Roman Polanski* (1985), Virginia Wright Wexman discusses the use of these techniques to function in this capacity. In an early scene after he has exposed Mulwray's alleged affair, Gittes tears into his office to tell his male associates (he shoos his secretary from the office) a racist Chinaman joke. The deep focus photography undercuts his central position in the frame by revealing the real Evelyn Mulwray behind his back, privy to both his bigotry and his ignorance of her identity, which she is about to spring on him (100). In scenes involving Gittes and officials such as Escobar, Loach, Yelburton, and Mulvihill, Gittes is often boxed in or pushed to the side of the frame. In scenes involving Noah Cross, Cross's superior size dominates the frame, diminishing Gittes's smaller figure. However, deep focus photography and positioning also work to usurp Gittes's central position in his scenes with Cross. Cross is first introduced to Gittes and the film audience in a deep focus shot, centered in the frame and surrounded by his men, from Gittes's point of view through the windshield of Gittes's automobile as he arrives at the Albacore Club to meet Cross for lunch. At one point during the lunch, Cross talks to Gittes at cross purposes as his figure dominates the frame in the foreground screen left, facing the audience, while Gittes sits in the background screen right with his back to both Cross and the audience. Later, when Cross arrives at the Mulwray residence to meet with Gittes, he is centered in a shot from Gittes's point of view as he enters the garden framed by the patio door which is further framed by the front door behind. Wexman observes that the formal symmetry of these scenes "designates Cross as a person of entrenched power, the man at the center of things, and also as a figure toward whom all paths will inevitably lead" (96–97).[9]

Conclusion

Chinatown is one of three hard-boiled private eye movies in the 1970s to transform the traditional myth of the genre and to employ a modernist narration in doing so. The other two are Robert Altman's *The Long Goodbye* (1973) and Arthur Penn's *Night Moves* (1975). All three films subvert the prosocial myth in their representation of a systemic corruption. The three films represent a progression of nihilism within the genre. Altman's Phillip Marlowe (Elliot Gould) uncovers a plot of deception, which he cannot alleviate, except by revenging himself on the perpetrator, a long-time trusted friend who betrays him throughout the movie. Polanski's Jake Gittes cannot even act on his own victimization. He is advised to "forget it" and accepts the inevitability of defeat in the wasteland of modern society. And Penn's Harry Moseby's (Gene Hackman) vision is so vitiated that he cannot even begin to detect, much less solve anything. The title *Night Moves* suggests the darkness at the center of man and his environment to obfuscate vision and corrode moral action. No one wins; everyone loses. "Who's winning?" asks Harry's wife as he watches a football game on television. "Nobody," he answers. "One side's just losing slower than the other." In *A Cinema of Loneliness* (New York 1988), Robert Phillip Kolker observes, "Harry's job becomes not so much detecting as confirming the existence of a moral swamp, an unclear, liquid state of feelings and relation in which the drowning of the spirit is perpetual (69)."[10]

The breakdown of the myth of the self-sufficient, hard-boiled private detective in *The Long Goodbye*, *Chinatown*, and *Night Moves* in the middle of the decade signaled the twilight of the renaissance period begun by *Bonnie and Clyde* and *The Graduate* in 1967. The modernist narratives, mythic restructurings, and moral visions of the films of the period would culminate, fittingly, with the apocalypses of *Nashville* (1975) and *Taxi Driver* (1976).

CHAPTER SIX

Apocalypse: *Nashville* and *Taxi Driver*

The beginning of the renaissance era in American films in 1967 produced a cautious optimism that the oppressive elements in American society could be resisted and changed. Though *Bonnie and Clyde* ended tragically with a testament to the system's power over the individual, it was also an exhilarating paean to personal expression both in its characters and in its art. Bonnie's and Clyde's romantic myth of the self infected the nation at a time when liberal sentiments and demonstrations were knocking down repressive, conservative barriers. Benjamin Braddock's revolt against parents and the plastic culture of suburban America was in sync with the agitation against the war in Vietnam, the youth-hippie movement, and black civil disobedience at the time *The Graduate* hit the screen. And *2001's* free-floating wide-eyed fetus announced the beginning of a new era in human development, and by transference, in society as well. However, the breakdown of genres and their prosocial myths in these films and those which followed hardly signaled a complementary vision of an alternative politics. In the end, the critique of the system was only that, revealing finally its entrenchment and staying power. Whether it was Altman's Harrison-Shaughnessy monopoly, Coppola's Mafia America, Polanski's Chinatown, Nichols's plastic suburbia, or Kubrick's sanitized space station, the films reminded us of the politics of money, greed, convention, and power that textualize our lives and relationships. Increasingly, the significant American films of the period turned either outward to expose the capitalistic disease infecting America (*McCabe and Mrs. Miller, The Godfather* films, *Chinatown*) or inward into the dynamics of the confused, alienated individual at odds with a system callous in its lack of empathy (*Five Easy Pieces, Midnight Cowboy, Lenny, The Conversation*). These two strains climaxed in Altman's *Nashville* (1975) and Scorsese's *Taxi Driver* (1976), respectively. Both films signal the end of the decade-long period in an apocalyptic manner. The desperation caused by the broken promises of a nation that caved in to the attractions of power and commodification and shattered the ideals of the 60s erupts in explosive, unexpected acts of violence. Things fall apart and as they do, anti-heroes take pot shots at the icons of material and political decadence: a presidential candidate, a country and western singer, and a prostitute's pimp.

In several ways, of course, the Vietnam films of the late 1970s are also apocalyptic in nature and may represent for some a summing up of the renaissance period. However, except for *Coming Home* (1977), they remain problematic as culminating expressions of the period's themes. Coppola's *Apocalypse Now*, which appeared in 1978, conveys a profound sense of destruction and damnation through an expressionistic cinema. However, it shifts the critique of the American system to its imperialistic, colonialist side, and it does this by also shifting the scene from the agitation and alienation felt at home to the disillusionment felt in the war itself. In shifting the locus of critique to Vietnam, the movie distances its audience from the reality of issues that had been promulgated by those set in the American scene. Add to this the surreal quality of the images and editing, the literary allusions to the Conradian theme, and the confused, bloated, indulged last sequence (like Brando's performance of Kurtz), which attempts to reach for an ultimate statement only to fail in its pretension, and the distantiation is complete. Michael Cimino's *The Deer Hunter* (1977) probed the devastating psychological and emotional effects of the war on the individual in a narrative significant for its deliberate characterization, its moving camera, and its Grand Guignol effects. However, the critique of America's capitalist venture overseas is undercut by the film's dominant conservative attitude, one that reinscribes the myths of the World War II combat films and the cold war films of the 50s: myths about Asia, Asians, Communism, and aliens, myths that frame oppositions between "Us" and the "Other" different from us. *Coming Home* (1977) is the Vietnam film of the period that captures the spirit of the renaissance films of the 60s and 70s because it depicts the radicalization of its characters through the war experience as lived back home. Luke Martin (Jon Voight), the Vietnam veteran crippled in body and soul, participates in the agitation against the war at home, and Sally Hyde (Jane Fonda) discovers a liberation from the confining patriarchal and military values of her officer husband, whose suicide follows from his unwillingness to accept the profound changes wrought by the war at home.

In the characters of Luke Martin and Sally Hyde, American audiences glimpsed the possibilities for individual development in a time of turmoil and upheaval. However, the end of the renaissance period leaned more heavily on the side of disillusionment, alienation, and a cynical acknowledgment of a corruption entrenched in our politics and culture. After Watergate, the correlation between unbridled laissez-faire capitalism and the political structure of the nation was easy to make. *The Godfather, Part II* depicted corrupt politicians, such as Senator Geary, on the payroll of the Corleone family; *Chinatown* revealed widespread graft in the city politics of 1939 Los Angeles; and *All The President's Men* (1976) detailed the Watergate scandal itself in a breathtaking investigative, documentary style. It was inevitable that *Nashville* and *Taxi Driver* would locate corruption in the highest levels of government by targeting presidential campaigns and candidates as complicit in the crass materialism of the country. The former film would do this through a reflexive narration formed in part by the principles and aesthetics of a satiric realism and by the generic conventions of the American film musical; the latter would do so through an expressionistic narrative whose protagonist represents yet another modern commentary on the myth of the classic Hollywood western hero.

NASHVILLE (1975)

The Credit Sequence

Nashville's kaleidoscopic credit sequence initiates its satire and subversion of America's prosocial myths and demonstrates its reflexive narrative technique. The title and performers' credits take the form of an ad for the film itself; a whirling poster zooms forward and stops, showing us the title *Nashville* at the top and a picture of the performers below. A voice-over begins to hype the movie and announces each star as his/her picture appears in close-up on the poster screen right and the name rolls up on the left. At the same time, a sound montage of the songs of *Nashville* is heard along with the salesman's voice intoning the name of each performer. The original poster showing all the stars appears again and whirls into the background and into oblivion as the ad man promotes the spectacle of entertainment about to begin, "And along with the magnificent stars—the magic of stereo sound and living color picture—right before your very eyes, without commercial interruption."

The title *Nashville* in white is all that remains against the black background. Another voice, a politician's, is heard as the word "Nashville" becomes part of the sign in the next scene advertising the Tennessee state headquarters of Hal Phillip Walker, the presidential candidate for the Replacement Party. Through the sound bridge and the common title of "Nashville," the filmic apparatus connects the world of entertainment with the world of politics. The garage door of the headquarters opens and a van emerges, blaring Walker's speech. The politician's hype to buy voters parallels the ad man's hype of the movie. As the van makes its way through the streets, another sound bridge occurs, the strumming of guitars that signals the start of Haven Hamilton's (Henry Gibson) patriotic song, "200 Years." The apparatus cuts to a recording studio, the camera panning from spectators to musicians to the background singers to Haven Hamilton himself in a recording booth singing, "Oh we must be doin' something right to last 200 years." The rest of the credits begin in red, white, and blue and continue to the end of the recording session. Hamilton's recording session intercuts with that of a black choir, all male except for a white female, Linnea (Lily Tomlin), who leads the choir in singing a gospel song, "Yes, I Do." The credit sequence ends when a short-tempered Hamilton stops the session because Frog, the piano player (Richard Baskin), is playing erratically. Hamilton stomps out of the studio telling Frog, "You get your hair cut; you don't belong in Nashville." The apparatus makes an ironic cut to a close-up of a sign, "Welcome to Nashville," at the airport, where TV cameras, reporters, celebrities, and fans await the arrival of country western star, Barbara Jean (Ronee Blakley).

The parallel structure of the credit sequence intersects show business and politics with commercialism and justifies Altman's claim that *Nashville* is his metaphor for America: "Nashville is a metaphor for my personal view of our society. . . . Nashville is the New Hollywood, where people are tuned in by instant stars, instant music and instant politics" (Gardner 26); and, "I think country music stars and politicians are alike in this country. Basically, they're just involved in popularity contests" (Michener 47). The credit sequence also incorporates the generic conventions of the American film musical, conventions that will later be subverted. First of all, the film promotes itself from the very beginning as a movie about show business. As with most musicals, *Nashville* is self-referential and self-reflexive at the same time. The ad man's hype announcing the film's title, songs, and stars alerts the audience to the conventions of the musical film which perpetuate what Jane Feuer calls the "myth of entertainment," a construct that resolves tensions and results in a utopian vision of spontaneity, integration, and audience participation.[1] Moreover, the credit sequence contrasts two styles of performance that recall the conflict between artificial, self-important, highbrow productions and natural, effortless, popular ones in the genre, the former being ponderous and unsuccessful, the latter irrepressible and triumphant. Haven Hamilton's performance is calculated and preening, while Linnea's is spontaneous and unassuming. Hamilton interrupts his recording session to throw out Opal (Geraldine Chaplin), the BBC reporter who "wandered" into the studio uninvited. His objections indicate his lack of flexibility, his insistence on etiquette, and his commercial instinct: "Bob, Buddy, both of you—you know I don't allow no people visitin' when I'm recording," and "I want no recording equipment in that studio. . . . If she wants a copy of this record, she can buy it when it's released." Hamilton's businesslike approach to his take contrasts with Linnea's absolute joy in hers as she loses herself in the music, becoming one with it. With the introduction of John Triplette (Michael Murphy) at the airport gathering for Barbara Jean, the movie incorporates yet another aspect of the American film musical into its narrative. Triplette's main task is to persuade singers to perform at a rally for Walker at the Parthenon. The gathering of talent for this rally recalls one of the staple plots of the musical, people cooperating to put on a rousing and successful show, a plot undercut by *Nashville*'s shattering climax.

Nashville's credit sequence weaves a satire that targets the American myth of success and the myth of entertainment perpetrated by the traditional Hollywood musical. The rest of this discussion will focus on the film's subversion of these two myths.

Satire and the American Dream

Altman fashions *Nashville*'s satire on a documentarylike realism.[2] His use of the wide-screen process and his experimentation with overlapping sound are contributions to the development of the physical apparatus to achieve a greater illusion of realism that Andre Bazin first traced through the realistic styles of Flaherty, Murnau, the Italian neorealists, Welles, and Hollywood's use of deep focus photography in "The Evolution of the Language of Cinema" (*What Is Cinema?* Vol. I 23–40). Furthermore, backgrounds in *Nashville* function in a neorealist vein; they do not merely serve as backdrops to the story in the foreground, but contain other stories as well. Peripheral characters not essential to the double plot of Barbara Jean's homecoming and Walker's political rally pass in and out of the picture as in real life: L. A. Joan (Shelley Duvall), the motorcyclist (Jeff Goldblum), the Vietnam veteran (Scott Glenn), Opal, Albuquerque (Barbara Harris), and Kenny the assassin (David Hayward). Even the double plot seems plotless. As one commentator puts it, "*Nashville* doesn't really lead up to the 'assassination' nor does it end with it. The murder simply happens and people are already singing again by the final backwards zoom" (Byrne and Lopez 13). However, *Nashville*'s episodic structure does not give the impression of being entirely open and spontaneous. The impression of fortuitousness, of privileged moments that we find in Italian neorealism seems lacking in Altman's film. Instead, we sense a *selectivity* of events and movement that recalls Fellini's *La Dolce Vita* (1959). Fellini works within the neorealist tradition, but he transforms it from cinema verité to dramatic social satire. He "chooses" episodes not so much to reveal the social milieu of modern day Rome as to expose its moral malaise. Altman does the same in *Nashville*; the movie's "open" episodic events are selected—maybe "edited" would be the more correct term—in order to achieve a satiric vision of American culture and society.³ *Nashville* may be "plotless," but its whole is held together by thematic motifs and analogues. Its style of realism works in concert with a coherent satiric vision of America in the midseventies.

The time is the Bicentennial summer of 1976. Haven Hamilton's song "200 Years" is in celebration of this event, a paean to America's growth and power. However, the movie is anything but a celebration of America as it approaches its 200th birthday. For one thing, it inscribes the recent history of turmoil and moral decadence to remind audiences of America's shortcomings. The presence of Pfc Kelly hovering in adoration over Barbara Jean's every move and Opal's brief interview with him during the Opry Belle sequence are grim reminders of the Vietnam conflict; Wade's (Robert Doqui) chiding "Tommy Brown's the whitest nigger in town!" in the Picking Parlor bar recalls the racial tensions of the civil rights protests; Lady Pearl's sentimental memories of the Kennedys, Barbara Jean's assassination, and Haven's shocked cry "This isn't Dallas; this is Nashville" invoke the trauma of the country's political assassinations; and the song that we hear on the soundtrack as Walker's entourage wends its way to the Parthenon in the last sequence refers to the latest scandal of Watergate.

The references to national political events punctuate the movie's satire of the American dream of material success centered in the relationships among the film's characters. Greed, ego, and power motivate the interactions of those who pursue star celebrity. Connie White (Karen Black), who subs for an ailing Barbara Jean at the Grand Old Opry, snubs the grateful gift of Barnett, Barbara Jean's manager and husband (Allan Garfield), who in turn controls and talks down to Barbara Jean; Tom (Keith Carradine) is a Lothario who beds and then discards any woman willing to submit herself; L. A. Joan is too busy pursuing men to care about her uncle's (Keenan Wynn) wife, who is dying of cancer; Opal from the BBC imposes upon everyone for her documentary on Nashville, insulting those she considers unimportant (Norman the chauffeur, Haven Hamilton's son Buddy) while currying favor with the celebrities; Triplette, with the help of Del Reese (Ned Beatty), manipulates Sueleen (Gwen Welles) into doing a striptease at a fundraising smoker for Walker, after which Del Reese propositions her on taking her home; Triplette persuades Bill and Mary to perform at the Walker rally by saying they would be the only rock group on the program and could walk away with the show; he bribes Haven to perform by implying Walker's support for Haven's possible political ambitions for the Tennessee governorship; and Barnett finally agrees to include Barbara Jean on the Walker program only to appease her fans after her breakdown on the Opry Belle stage, with no regard for her health.

Haven Hamilton's recording session: music as big business and the irony of the Bicentennial song "200 Years." *Courtesy of Museum of Modern Art Film Stills Archive; Copyright Paramount, 1975.*

Nashville reinforces the emotional and moral callousness of its characters by its juxtaposition of parallel action both between and within scenes. Three sequences cut back and forth between parallel action in different locations: The Grand Old Opry sequence cuts from the Opry to Sueleen in her bedroom and then later to Barnett and Barbara Jean in the hospital room; the Sunday morning sequence cuts from the different church services and the automobile junkyard; and finally, Tom's "I'm Easy" in the Exit Club alternates with Sueleen's singing and striptease at the Walker campaign smoker at the Red Barn Dinner Theater. In each case, the juxtapositions comment significantly on the characters and their relationships. The action at the Grand Old Opry reveals the commercialism of the Goo-Goo Candy–sponsored show, Haven's hypocrisy as he sings of the need to be faithful "For the Sake of the Children" (Lady Pearl [Barbara Baxley] has been his longtime mistress), and the preening self-involvement of Connie White. This action alternates with Sueleen's own preening before a mirror as she practices "I Never Get Enough" for the smoker, off key and pathetic in her false hopes and dreams for success, and then with the scene between Barnett and Barbara Jean in the hospital room revealing Barbara Jean's childish dependency on Barnett and his surly dominance. The Sunday morning sequence contrasts America's spiritual worship in its churches to its worship of material goods, as it cuts from the church services to the junkyard of cars piled high on one another, a kind of index to the wasteland of our disposable culture. And finally, Tom's song, "I'm Easy" dedicated to "someone kind of special," signifies his betrayal of Mary, Opal, and L. A. Joan, as he passes over his former conquests in favor of his new one, Linnea, which compares to Triplette's and Del's betrayal and manipulation of Sueleen, who is forced to strip before an ogling male audience.

A good illustration of parallel action within a scene occurs after the Grand Ole Opry sequence when the performers gather at the King of the Road nightclub. On two occasions, the filmic apparatus frames Connie White's table in a full deep-focus shot with Haven and Triplette in the foreground; Del, Connie, her manager and friends in the center; and Lady Pearl and Opal in the background, using the sixteen-track sound system to record simultaneous dialogue. The first occurs when Haven's public relations manager introduces Julie Christie to the table, and the second is when Barnett arrives to give Connie a corsage to thank her for substituting for Barbara Jean at the Grand Old Opry. In each case, the camera reveals Connie's overweening pride. She ignores Julie Christie and underplays her accomplishments, reacting incredulously to Haven's informing her of Christie's Academy Award, "Come on, Haven, she can't even comb her hair"; then she snubs Barnett's offer.

Interspersed with these group shots of the table are cuts to medium shots of couples at Connie's table, Bill and Norman at another table, and the action on stage. The parallel action made by these cuts displays further the comedy of human foibles and vulnerability as the characters give in to ego or pride or reveal feelings of betrayal and loss. At one point, a medium closeup shot of Haven and Triplette pans to one of Barnett and Connie's manager. In the first, we hear Haven explaining to Triplette the sensitive "etiquette" governing the professional relationship between Connie and Barbara Jean and his own preference for an advantageous appearance: "Connie White and Barbara Jean never appear on the same stage together. . . . And as for Haven Hamilton, well, I'll appear wherever Barbara Jean appears." In the second, the tension underlying the competition between Connie and Barbara Jean surfaces in a heated exchange between their respective managers. Haven and Connie are in another medium shot when the MC announces that someone special is in attendance; Haven prepares to rise as Connie's name is called. Lady Pearl and Opal are in several two shots, Lady Pearl unburdening her sentimental disappointment over the loss of the Kennedys to a visibly uncomfortable Opal. Meanwhile, in another series of two shots, Bill complains to Norman about his suspicions about Mary's extramarital affair. The whole sequence ends on Norman's expression of disbelief in Bill's suggestion of Mary's infidelity, the apparatus making a parallel cut to Mary in bed with Tom in Tom's apartment.

Subversion of Genre

Nashville's subversion of the American musical film is its crowning testament to the grim reality underlying the glitter of the American dream of material success. In shattering the utopian myth of entertainment promulgated by the Hollywood dream factory, *Nashville* offers a dystopian vision of fragmentation and dissolution. It undercuts the ideological function of the musical, which is to champion the show business values of Hollywood itself. Hollywood's genre productions raise audience expectations and then fulfill them. In other words, they *entertain*. The Hollywood musical doesn't pretend to be anything other than it is, a construct which sacrifices plausibility in order to heighten its essential quality of fantasy. Its myth of entertainment promotes a world in which joy and spontaneity overcome convention and studied professionalism, integration of individuals resolves conflicts and tensions, and participation of the audience ensures its satisfaction and signals the success of the movie's goal to please (Feuer, "The Self Reflexive Musical" 331–338). In *The American Film Musical* (1987), Rick Altman divides the genre into three categories: the fairy tale musical, the show musical, and the folk musical. All three categories include values promulgated by the genre as a whole. For example, each usually ends with the integration of the male and female couple after a series of conflicts, an integration replicated on other levels as well. Each category, however, stresses a certain kind of replication. In the fairy tale musical, the unity of the couple accompanies the restoration of order to an imaginary kingdom; in the show musical, the creation of the couple parallels the creation of a work of art, usually the successful production of a show; while in the folk musical, the marriage of the couple signals the integration of the community with each other and with the land which sustains them. In addition to stressing a different replication of the primary integration, each category also valorizes one particular aspect of the genre. The fairy tale musical plays up the fantastic element; the show musical maximizes the general expression of joy through music and dance; and the folk musical emphasizes the togetherness and communitarianism characteristic of the genre's choral tendencies (126).

Altman analyzes *Nashville* as a folk musical which undermines the folk musical in two ways: the lack of community in the film and the commercial, manufactured nature of its music, which undercuts the music's function to promote and preserve folk values within the modern industrial complex. The disintegration of the community is evident in the dissolution of family ties, infidelities among its characters, and the separation of its internal audiences from the performers through physical barriers, dissatisfaction (with Barbara Jean at the Opry Belle), or lack of talent to join in and become one with the performers (Sueleen). The commercial, manufactured nature of the music is evident in *Nashville*'s self-reflexive credits, in Haven Hamilton's recording session, and especially in its finale, where show business is not glorious entertainment, but a pawn in a political gambit. Music no longer expresses a love of the land and community; instead, performers prostitute it for pay, political influence, and the seduction of married women (324–327).

As a complement to Rick Altman's commentary, I offer the following as further evidence of *Nashville*'s jarring of the Hollywood musical by focusing on ways in which it undermines the musical's myth of joy and spontaneity in performance and its myth of audience integration. Part of *Nashville*'s appeal lies in its music and in its renditions of songs. This being the case, however, do the performances conform to the myth of spontaneity that we find in the traditional musical film? In other words, do they transcend the social and political environment, so that they stand on their own as expressions of true joy and exuberance, where both singer and audience lose themselves in the magic world of music making? As Tom Schatz says, utopia in the Hollywood musical exists not only at the end when all the conflicts are resolved in the production of a successful show, but also at various points when the performers transcend their interpersonal differences and express themselves in song and dance (*Hollywood Genres* 188). Though appealing, each of the performances in *Nashville* remains in some way tied to conflicts, tensions, and/

or social, political, or commercial realities. Haven Hamilton's recording session of "200 Years" plays up the business end of the industry; the song is also ironic in the context of the film's depiction of the social and political realities of the time. Hamilton's Grand Old Opry stint turns into a self-congratulatory retrospective on his career, and his duet with Barbara Jean at the Parthenon counts as a political favor for the Walker campaign. Meanwhile, whenever Connie White performs, she does so in conscious competition with Barbara Jean. Tom, Bill, and Mary's "Since You've Gone" turns into Mary's angry lament to Tom for his betrayal. Tom's "I'm Easy" connects with Linnea, to whom he sings, but creates tension within Mary, Opal, and L. A. Joan.

One singer, however, seems able to rise above the grasping world of Nashville in her performances—Barbara Jean. Barbara Jean commands attention whenever she is on stage/screen. Her performances radiate sincerity, love, and joy, and they create, for brief moments, a transport into a magic world. The filmic apparatus enhances her charisma by consistently shooting her from a low angle in a medium long shot and then slowly zooming forward to a close-up of her face as she performs. The low angle accentuates her magnetism, while the slow zoom to a close-up insulates her within her world of magic at the same time that it draws us into that world. Cuts to the audience within the movie indicate that it too is affected by her aura as she sings in the hospital chapel, at the Opry Belle, and at the Parthenon. However, these cuts also operate to compromise the transcendent quality of her performance by contrasting it to reality and situating it, finally, not in the wonderful, but in the *petty* world of show business.

In the hospital chapel, Barbara Jean's soulful rendition of "In the Garden" mesmerizes the chapel audience, Pfc Kelly its touchstone, as the apparatus cuts from Barbara Jean to his rapt presence. Instead of cutting back to Barbara Jean to complete the magic of her performance, however, the apparatus ends the sequence by enumerating the reality of Vietnam and the casualties of war. Mr. Green, sitting next to Pfc Kelly, intrudes upon the moment by leaning over to tell Kelly about his son, who died in World War II while serving in the navy.

In the Opry Belle sequence, cuts to the audience again feature a starstruck Pfc Kelly; this time Opal interrupts his identification with Barbara Jean's magic by questioning him about Vietnam. The apparatus then focuses on Kenny. Barbara Jean's magnetism affects him as he listens with deep emotion to her singing. At the same time, however, the apparatus indicates that this is the moment he may have decided to target Barbara Jean for an assassination. A slow zoom to a close-up of Kenny's face punctuates the moment of both his identification and his decision to shatter the object of his identification. His face shows anguished emotion as he seems to be moved by Barbara Jean's expression of heartfelt suffering and victimization as she sings the words to "Dues": "You've got your own private world / I wouldn't have it no other way. / But lately, you've been hidin' your blues, / Pretendin' what you say. / It hurts so bad, it gets me down, down, down. / I want to walk away from the battle ground." It's as if Kenny has found a soulmate, one who needs to be put out of her misery, a target to express his own suffering and to "save" someone at the same time. Kenny's identification with Barbara Jean is analogous to that produced by the cinematic apparatus; for both, identification is the initial stage in the process of destruction. The apparatus enhances Barbara Jean's captivating presence as she sways into song, only to disrupt her magic by cutting to Opal's callousness during the performance and by enumerating Kenny's growing threat; Kenny relates to Barbara Jean's deeply felt emotions, but that only motivates him to blow her away at the Parthenon.

The transcendence of Barbara Jean's performance at the Opry Belle is further undercut by her breakdown on the stage after her two songs. Her nostalgic reminiscence as she wanders in her "talk" interrupts the show and alienates her audience. Barnett can placate the audience only by promising them a free show the next day at the Parthenon. Moreover, Barbara Jean's wandering back into the past is an attempt to capture a lost innocent rural existence before the pressure filled world of commercial entertainment overwhelmed her. She longs for the time when, as a little girl, she sang merely for the pleasure it gave her: "Well I can sing like a munchkin myself. I don't know about you, and I'm real fond of the Wizard of Oz an' plus I live out y'know just a ways out here on— offa Highway Interstate 24 on the road to Chattanooga." Then she relates the first time she sang for money, when her mother made her memorize two songs to sing to the "advertisin' man" at the Frigidaire store. He paid her fifty cents for her singing, and "Ever since then I been workin', I don't—I think ever since then I been workin' and doin' my . . . supportin' myself, anyway. . . ." From what she says, it is clear that Barbara Jean's breakdown is symptomatic of her deep sense of rootlessness, the loss of folk values to the commercialization of her art.[4]

At the Parthenon, Sueleen and Albuquerque join Pfc Kelly as barometers of audience adulation of Barbara Jean as she sings "One, I Love You" with Haven and "My Idaho Home" in solo. Albuquerque lies on the stage looking up at Barbara Jean, while Sueleen stands off to the side against a pillar swaying to the music and mouthing the words. However, three things detract from Barbara Jean's performance at the Parthenon. For one thing, the movie frames the Parthenon sequence in the context of its political nature, never allowing Barbara Jean a moment in which her performance can soar. Instead, the encroaching political reality makes her vulnerable to assassination. Howard K. Smith's commentary on Hal Philip Walker introduces the sequence; Barnett argues with Triplette over the Walker banner above the stage; and the American flag fills the screen at the beginning of Barbara Jean's performance with Haven and then later just before her assassination. Second, the apparatus is more intent on enumerating the ensemble nature of the event than on isolating one particular drama. Barbara Jean's performance is merely one part of this ensemble. As Barbara Jean sings, the apparatus reintroduces all the characters in cuts to the audience, each entrance a reminder of that individual story: Albuquerque's husband looking for her through the crowd; Wade searching for Sueleen; Opal with her tape recorder; L. A. Joan with a new wig and man as she leads Bill through the crowd; Mr. Green and Kenny just arrived from Mrs. Green's funeral; Pfc Kelly walking to a central front position below the stage; Albuquerque and Sueleen living their dreams on stage; Tom and Mary together without Bill; Triplette and Del in the rear wearing self-congratulatory smiles; and Barnett lurking in back of the musicians, keeping close watch on his singer/wife. After the assassination, the apparatus follows the exit of each of the characters as they disperse, leaving Albuquerque on stage to wrap up the show in the wake of the disaster. In other words, the Parthenon sequence is a capsule version of the episodic quality of the film as a whole, Barbara Jean's performance engulfed in its pattern.

Third, within this ensemble, the particular drama of the assassination produces tension during Barbara Jean's performance, thereby undercutting its entertainment value. The tension builds through a series of shot-reverse-shots between Kenny, Barbara Jean, and the American flag. The subject of these shots is Kenny, who looks intensely at Barbara Jean as she sings "My Idaho Home," another icon of her lost rural innocence. The shots of Barbara Jean are tight close-ups, hemming her in within Kenny's narrowing focus and heightening the tension of the moment. The world is too much for Barbara Jean. The intention of the apparatus undercuts the fantasy that she would weave for her audience. Unlike the artist-protagonists of the conventional musical, she fails to transform her environment into the stuff of her imagination. Instead, she falls prey to an assassin's bullet.[5]

The Assassination and the End of the American Dream

The violence of the assassination is carefully choreographed to contrast starkly with other cinematic depictions of violence in the 70s. Its staging deconstructs the elaborate mechanism devoted to screen violence since *Bonnie and Clyde* (1967) and *The Wild Bunch* (1969). In *McCabe and Mrs. Miller* (1971), Altman had aped the examples of Penn and Peckinpah, prolonging and sharpening the moment of violence through slow motion and close-ups in the killing of the young cowboy and in the showdown between McCabe and the hired guns at the end. In *Nashville*, however, he

Barbara Jean singing ''My Idaho Home'' before her assassination: nostalgia for a lost rural innocence. *Courtesy of Museum of Modern Art Film Stills Archive; Copyright Paramount, 1967.*

distances the violence and covers it up as quickly as Barnett, Del, and Triplette can clear Barbara Jean off the stage. He shoots the moment of assassination in an extreme long shot of the stage from the rear of the audience. Barbara Jean and Haven stand in the right center of the stage dwarfed on the screen. A shot rings out; Barbara Jean falls backward; Haven collapses over her; cut to a medium shot of Kenny with gun in hand shooting at the stage, while Pfc Kelly and others grab and subdue him; cut to a medium shot of a wounded Haven rising, while Barnett and others lift Barbara Jean and hustle her off the stage; Haven calms the crowd and hands the mike to Johnny-on-the-spot Albuquerque, who starts singing "It Don't Worry Me." The violence is sudden; it comes as a shock, but it is not dwelt on. Unembellished, it blends in with the other events of the rally, in sync with the episodic rhythm of the film. Like Haven's politically motivated presence, Sueleen's chance for stardom, Mr. Green's anger over L. A. Joan's insensitivity, and Barbara Jean's singing, Kenny's violent action occurs as but one event in the tapestry which is *Nashville*. It is not even given a chance to stand out because of inexplicableness. Kenny's action may be sudden, but the film has prepared for it, so that it all makes sense. The greed, opportunism, self-involvement, bitchy competitiveness, material grasping, and overwhelming bearishness of those in politics and show business mirror the commodification of people and relationships, which has alienated Kenny, who is a sensitive soul. Bullied by an overbearing mother, angered over the capitalistic venture of a Vietnam and its senseless destruction of lives, and touched by the hurt and despair of Barbara Jean, Kenny performs an act of anger, frustration, desperation, and compassion. We don't need a detailed rendering of his personal life to clarify his actions; the causes are everywhere apparent in Altman's savage view of the American scene.

Nashville's ending is consistent with its deconstruction of national and generic myths and its undercutting of audience identification with the characters. It caps the bleak satiric vision offered by the movie as a whole. There are some who think that *Nashville*'s end is positive and moving in portraying the American common folk as resourceful and resilient after the assassination. One argument goes this way: though the words to "It Don't Worry Me" indicate a passive acceptance of economic exploitation ("You may say that I ain't free, but it don't worry me"), the people sing passionately in a tone of hope and strength, which help them overcome the violence in their midst. A corollary to this is that the film is an attack not on the American people but on the system which victimizes them, and that it signals the possibility of change in the portrayal of certain of its characters, Barbara Jean, Sueleen, and Linnea.[6] However, this interpretation presents several problems. The only use to which resourcefulness has been put in the film is in the service of "getting ahead." The film provides no clear assurance that this quality presages a change in attitude or politics. Moreover, the characters who provide glimpses of decency and integrity sadly buy into the system and become perpetrators as well as victims. Barbara Jean's integrity lies only in the recognition of a lost innocence, not in any strength that allows her to break out of the rut of commercialization; Sueleen's "innocence" is a naïveté which fools her into a dream that is as false as her talent is nil; Linnea's loving and supportive relationship with her deaf children is framed in a loveless marriage to Del, which leaves her vulnerable to shallow one-night stands with uncaring studs like Tom.

No, the satire and deconstruction of myths which are *Nashville* plays itself out to the bitter end, keeping us at a moral distance from the events and the characters.[7] Our relationship with the characters remains short-circuited not only because we never know what finally happens to them, but also because it doesn't really matter. So what if Barbara Jean survived the shooting; if Sueleen decided to go to Detroit with Wade; if Albuquerque went on to become a star; if Tom, Bill, and Mary split up as a group; if Mr. Green finally confronted L. A. Joan; if Haven ran for governor; or if Walker ever got elected? Nothing would change anyway. We don't have to look beyond the last sequence at the Parthenon to infer this dismal prediction. The assassination attempt and its effects, symptoms of a sick society, are quickly glossed over and covered up. Barnett and Bud whisk Barbara Jean's body off the stage; Triplette and Del orchestrate a swift cleanup; Haven appeases the crowd, "This isn't Dallas; this is Nashville," and urges them to sing as he thrusts the mike into Albuquerque's hand. The amazing thing about this, of course, is that Albuquerque, the choir, and the crowd *do* sing. In the midst of the tragedy, they conduct a singalong as if nothing had happened; like sheep, they do what they're told. The words to the song are not a denial that they're not free, but an acceptance of the way things are: "You may say that I ain't free, / But it don't worry me." Furthermore, Albuquerque's singing is not an attempt to rally the people's spirit; it is another example of opportunism. When Haven hands her the mike, her expression is one of disbelief, but her eyes are star-filled. Moreover, Albuquerque's singing exacerbates rather than dissipates the tensions of the moment. She shrieks the words and strains the rhythm; the notes tug against one another. The dissonant quality of her singing distances the movie audience and reminds it of the troubled nature of the rally and its aftermath. Similarly, the filmic apparatus distances the movie audience by shooting the stage in a penultimate extreme long shot from behind the crowd as it did during the assassination. And as if it can no longer bear the ironies and tensions it itself has exposed and can no longer gaze at the mythless landscape of its own agenda, it pans up above the Parthenon and the American flag to the serene, indifferent sky, an escape from the harsh glare of the human scene below.

TAXI DRIVER (1976)

Subterranean Vision

The apocalyptic descent of Martin Scorsese's *Taxi Driver* is more sub-terranean than that of Altman's *Nashville*. If *Nashville*'s vision represents an outer circle of crass commercialism figured in a landscape of mani-cured lawns, slick ads, and show business glitter, then *Taxi Driver*'s plummets further to an inner circle of prostitution where the landscape becomes the tawdry glare, steamy smell, and sticky grime of New York's Manhattan streets. *Taxi Driver*'s vision is explored through a narration that is expressionistic and subjective in contrast to *Nashville*'s realistic and objective one. It's credit sequence begins with a slow-motion wide-angle shot of a taxi cab driving through steam from a manhole and looming ominously before disappearing offscreen, followed by the title *Taxi Driver* against the background of the white steam; then it cuts to an extreme close-up of Travis Bickle's (Robert de Niro) observing, pene-trating eyes as he drives through the streets, lights flashing on his face. The two images suggest a two-pronged narration, the self-conscious styl-ized slant of the omniscient camera and the subjective filter of Travis Bickle. In other words, the narration is largely filtered through the con-sciousness of Travis, but not always; at times, the omniscient apparatus separates itself from Travis's subjectivity to present other scenes and characters, comment on its central character, create atmosphere, or reflect on its own cinematic activity. For example, Travis is not present during the conversations between Betsy (Cybill Shepherd) and Tom (Albert Brooks) in the Palantine campaign headquarters or when Iris (Jodie Fos-ter) and Sport (Harvey Keitel) dance together in her apartment. The strik-ing shot when the camera pans from Travis on the phone pleading with Betsy to see him again to the empty hallway is a commentary on Travis's alienation and loneliness; the bird's-eye-view shot of the carnage at the end heightens the fatalism of Travis's act, while the slow track and dis-solves out of the room and down the hallway and stairs trace in reverse the process of the carnage, expanding the moment while dissipating its tension. And finally, the apparatus summarizes the aftermath of the kill-ings through a pan of newspaper headlines pasted on the wall of Travis's apartment and through the simultaneous voice-over of Iris's father read-ing the letter he wrote expressing gratitude to Travis for the rescue of his daughter. One of the clippings shows a picture of the carnage that is the exact bird's-eye-view shot in the preceding sequence, just one in-stance of the narration's reflexivity.

Taxi Driver's two-pronged narration provides a moral commentary on contemporary American society of the mid-1970s. We see what Travis experiences and we hear his commentary on the social scene. In voice-over, Travis says, "All the animals come out at night: whores, skunk pussies, buggers, queens, fairies, dopers, junkies, sick, venal. Someday a *real* rain will come and wash all this scum off the streets," and "Each night when I return the cab to the garage I have to clean the cum off the back seat. Some nights I clean off the blood." His one desire, voiced to Palantine in his cab, is that the president should "clean up this city here. It's full of filth and scum; scum and filth. It's like an open sewer." Travis's perception of a corrupt city of night follows upon his encounters as a taxi driver: the hooker and the businessman john who do it in the back seat; Wizard's (Peter Boyle) crude joke about the woman changing her pantyhose in his cab; Iris's attempt to escape her pimp by running into Travis's cab and Sport's $20 payoff for keeping his mouth shut about the incident; Scorsese's mad husband who tells Travis, in graphic details, how he plans to kill his unfaithful wife.

The prostitution that defines relationships in the sewers and streets operates in the upper echelons of society as well. Betsy pimps for Palantine, "First push the man, then the issue. Senator Palantine is a dynamic man, an intelligent, interesting, fascinating man." Tom tells her, "Sounds like you're selling mouthwash," to which she replies, "We are selling mouthwash." Palantine's campaign promises are slick clichés to appeal to uninformed voters, much like Sport's unctuous two-liners to reassure a doubtful Iris. Sport says to Iris, "I depend on you; I'd be lost without you. . . . I only wish every man could know what it's like to be loved by you. That every woman everywhere had a man who loves her like I love you." Palantine curries the voters' favor with such empty rhetoric as "No longer will we the people suffer for the few. . . . We the people know the right roads and the good. Today I say to you, we are the people, you and I; and it is time to let the people rule."

The crux of the film lies in the relationship between its corrupt environment and its protagonist. Is Travis God's lonely man and "avenging angel," cleansing society with his violent action, if only temporarily? Or is he a reflection of the city itself, a disordered self-destructive personality symptomatic of its own seedy, repressed, and violent environment?[8] Each interpretation raises more questions than it can answer. Does Travis's role as God's "avenging angel" justify the utter savagery of his violence? How does it jibe with his intentions to assassinate Palantine because of Betsy's rejection and his thirst for notoriety as a means toward self-identity? Conversely, if Travis is merely a reflection of the city's madness, bent on self-destruction, how does one account for his sincere attempts to help Iris, for his outrage against the corruption on the streets? The only way out of these difficulties, of course, is to accept both accounts of Travis. He is both good and bad. However, he is not schizophrenic. The dual parts of his personality are not separate, the one dominating at one time, the other at another. Nor is there a tension or

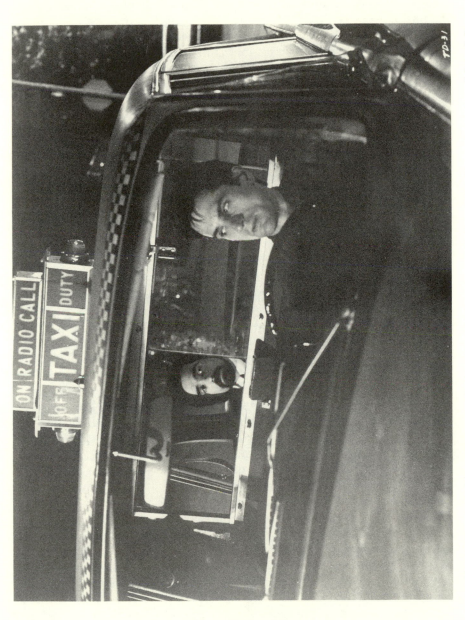

De Niro's Travis Bickle and Scorsese's disturbed husband: encounters with the corrupt city of the night. *Courtesy of Museum of Modern Art Film Stills Archive; Copyright Columbia, 1976.*

balance between the two. Instead we find a mixture, or better, a *confusion* between the two, a confusion of values that reflects the moral turmoil within Travis and within the society of the midseventies. A blurring of the line between civilized values and street values had already been embodied in earlier films of the renaissance decade, in the anti-westerns of Peckinpah and Altman. I think that a meaningful way to understand *Taxi Driver*, its protagonist, and his relation to his environment is to see Scorsese's film as yet another modern commentary on the classic Hollywood western and its mythic hero.

Travis Bickle and the Western Hero

By the time of Peckinpah's *The Wild Bunch* (1969), the dividing line between the frontier and civilization had broken down to the point where the whole environment mirrored the savage qualities of the former. In the myth of the West, the dark side of the western hero had become the dominant factor in defining its protagonist as an anti-hero and society as morally fractured. The only honor left to Peckinpah's antiheroes was an existential integrity, a banding together in a show of loyalty and courage for the maintenance of the group. That was all. Earlier, Clint Eastwood's Man with No Name in the Sergio Leone spaghetti westerns of the 60s had eschewed even that in a high stakes survival game where the only rules were those of the wilderness, "Draw first, draw faster, or shoot 'em in the back." The society of law and order in the classic westerns had all but disappeared in a landscape rife with deception and greed. By the time of Altman's *McCabe and Mrs. Miller* (1971), huge commercial monopolies had taken the place of unscrupulous individuals. McCabe's conscious adoption of the role of the classic westerner turns out to be a foolish gesture in an unaccommodating world of ruthless corporate expansion. Altman's film put the gravestone on the myth in contemporary times, a death prefigured earlier in *The Searchers* (1956) and *The Man Who Shot Liberty Valance* (1962).

Taxi Driver, for all its modern urban setting, fits squarely into this subversive tradition. To some extent, Travis Bickle represents a balance between the classic westerner and the anti-heroes of the modern western. He is neither a reluctant hero in the classic mode nor an unscrupulous one in the modern mode. Rather, he is a skewed hero, caught between two worlds that he cannot understand. Travis is the alienated, morally confused individual of the seventies who wants desperately to fit in, but cannot. David Boyd, in the 1976 article "Prisoner of the Night," likens him to John Wayne's Ethan Edwards in *The Searchers*. Both Travis and Ethan are alienated from society but commit acts of violence in its name; both are sexually frustrated by the women of their dreams, Betsy and Martha, respectively; both rescue child-women, Iris and Debbie, who are surrogates for Betsy and Martha; both obscure the dichotomy between civilization and the wilderness in their preference for violent behavior, aping the savage characteristics of their enemy, the Indian Scar and the Indian dressed Sport; and both represent the general social malaise within their environment. In the end, their acts of purgation are only temporary; they achieve no self-recognition, nor do they change society by their actions on its behalf; Travis returns to the streets and Ethan to the desert (29–30).

The following discussion expands, in more detail, Boyd's suggestion of the pattern of civilized and savage behavior in *Taxi Driver*. Travis's dark side and his alienation from society are evident from his solitary existence, the untold horrors of his Vietnam experience, his war veteran's inability to fit back smoothly into society, his insomnia, his obsessive voyeurism on the streets and in porno theaters, and his lack of everyday knowledge ("What's moonlighting?" and "Who's Kris Kristofferson?"). At the same time, however, he abhors the scum and filth he sees on the streets, wants to save Iris from the degradation of prostitution, and attempts to overcome his isolation by forming relationships ("All my life needed was a sense of someplace to go. I don't believe one should devote his life to morbid self-attention, but should become a person like other people"). Each of his attempts to communicate with others fails. His boss doesn't take his jokes kindly; the concessions girl at the porno theater ignores his advances, then threatens him; his fellow cab driver Wizard (Peter Boyle) misunderstands his needs and offers him shallow advice; and finally, though Betsy entertains a relationship at first, she rebuffs him in the end. Two events before the end highlight the confusion of the civilized and the anti-social within Travis. The first occurs when Travis takes Betsy to a porno flick on their first date. Travis is so caught up in his own alienated world that he can't see the impropriety of this decision. The second occurs when Travis kills the robber during a deli holdup. On the one hand, this is a social act; on the other, Travis has to escape before the police arrive because his gun is illegal and an investigation may turn up the arsenal in his apartment. The storekeeper himself obscures the line between civilized and savage behavior as he beats the dead body with a crowbar.

Betsy's refusal to get together after their first date destroys Travis's link to the outside world, and the outlaw side of his personality takes over. He decides to assassinate Betsy's boss, Palantine. Contrary to the opinion that Travis's motives for targeting Palantine are mysterious, my opinion is that they are clear.[9] Travis acts out of revenge. Earlier, he had supported Palantine wholeheartedly after his first success with Betsy ("I'm one of your biggest supporters; I tell everybody that comes in this cab that they should vote for you"). Later, he reverses his support after Betsy's rejection. Hurt, angry, frustrated, and bent on self-destruction,

Disastrous first date to a porno flick: insulated man and the failure to communicate. *Courtesy of Museum of Modern Art Film Stills Archive; Copyright Columbia, 1976.*

Travis plans his attack on Palantine to get back at Betsy and to gain self-esteem and a sense of identity in the process. He will make his mark by the only means left open to him, a highly visible act of notoriety ("My whole life has pointed in one direction. I see that now. There never has been any choice for me"). After the assassination attempt fails, events happen very quickly. Travis goes straight to Sport and Iris from the Palantine rally. The immediate response indicates that Travis is still acting out of the same frustration and anger, held in check for so long and now reaching a boiling point. It is no wonder that what follows is an explosive unleashing of energy, an all-consuming fury of violence. It does not matter who the target is; Travis chooses Sport and those who victimize Iris because of his prior disgust with the street scum and desire to help Iris. But that does not mean his intentions are noble at this moment. If we view Travis as a man driven by sexual frustration, we can say that his bottled up sexual energy needs a theater for expression after the attempt on Palantine's life falls through. Sport and his corps of pimps just happen to be around. The orgasmic explosion that follows is a life-in-death act, meant to be both a consummation and a suicide. After Travis shoots Sport abruptly and without warning at point blank range, blasts the corrupt cop who is with Iris, and splatters the brain of Sport's associate, he turns the gun on his throat and presses the trigger of the empty gun three times. When the police arrive, he points an imaginary gun with his fingers to his temple and fires, imitating the sounds of the explosion. Wasted and spent, he falls into a deep sleep, a substitution for the death that has eluded him.

The confusion of the civilized and the savage in *Taxi Driver* is nowhere more apparent than in its epilogue. Travis's violent action is uncompromising in its intention and execution. However, he awakens to the gratitude of Iris's parents and to the applause of the public. Though his intent was criminal and self-destructive, Travis discovers the acceptable social identity he had hoped to achieve earlier in his normal relationship with Betsy. However, he doesn't take advantage of this ironic turn of events. Instead, he reverts to his true form, not to the untrammeled rugged individualism of the classic westerner, but to the disturbed alienation of contemporary man. When Betsy attempts to reestablish their relationship, he refuses her offer, leaves her at the curb, and rides off into the darkness of the night. The disorder within Travis remains. His violent nature hovers beneath the surface of his seemingly civilized self. The expressionistic editing at the end conveys the tension within. The last sequence of shots wrenches and disturbs. From a close-up of Travis's eyes in the rear view mirror, the apparatus cuts quickly to his face as he does a sudden double take into the mirror. The apparatus then cuts to his eyes in the mirror and finally to the inside of the windshield as the end credits come on. What did Travis glimpse? Was it a fleeting insight into what he was rejecting as Betsy's figure receded from him? Was it the darkness at the back of the cab? Did Travis recognize for a moment the horror within, which he has failed to comprehend during his odyssey and even now as he cruises the city's forbidden streets?

The Ethics of Violence

While Altman underplays the mechanism of screen violence in *Nashville*, Scorcese pays homage to it in *Taxi Driver*. Slow motion and close-ups expand Travis's relentless fury and his victims' shock and consequent rage. The action is swift, but drawn out through speed changes and editing of parallel action. Travis shoots Sport in the stomach at point blank range, goes into the building, confronts the timekeeper, and shoots the fingers off his left hand; Sport stumbles into the entrance and shoots Travis in the neck before Travis finishes him off; the off-duty cop who is in session with Iris shoots Travis in the arm at point blank range; Travis fills his face with bullets; the timekeeper wrestles Travis to the floor; Travis stabs his hand, shoots him point blank in the temple, then attempts to shoot himself in the throat; the police arrive. At this point, the speed slows considerably as if the heretofore slower than normal speed and close-ups hadn't been enough to convey the wrathful, self-destructive nature of Travis's act. The audience, which had gotten it full in the face, is forced now to relive the event as the camera pans the room and retraces the sequence in reverse down the hall, down the stairs, and out into the street.

The atmosphere painted is lurid, the pain and brutality excruciating. But this is the desired effect. The self-indulgence of the filmmaker reinforces the self-indulgent nature of the act of violence of the protagonist, an act useful only to the self in its moment of frustration and revenge. The violence possesses a paranoid quality, slightly off edge, discordant. It does not raise Travis to any level beyond his disorder and disturbance. The contrast to the function of violence in *Bonnie and Clyde* (1967) and *The Wild Bunch* (1969) signifies the changing fate of the individual from the beginning of the renaissance period to its end. In *Bonnie and Clyde*, the violence was integral to the romance of the individual at odds with an authoritarian society, raising the couple in the end to the level of myth in the consciousness of a public hungry for new heroes. In *The Wild Bunch*, the violent conflagration at the end was an honorable act to maintain the integrity of the self as westerners in the face of a dying frontier.

By the time of the *Godfather* films (1972 and 1974) and *Chinatown* (1974), however, violence acted as a moral commentary on the ruthlessness of capitalistic self-interest, figured in a Mafia don and an entrepreneur, respectively. Coppola's and Polanski's visions were conscious indictments of a pervasive complicity in a compromised materialism. In *Taxi Driver*,

the violence caps the tragedy of the individual mired in the moral turmoil within the wasteland of the self and of society. The period that had
begun with promise ends then in defeat. *Nashville* exposes America's
capitulation to the glitter and gold of its dream on the eve of its Bicentennial, while *Taxi Driver* mirrors its paranoia and confusion over a par-
adise lost.

Epilogue

The renaissance text of 1967–1976 that combined, in various ways, modernist narration, mixed modes, genre transformation, unsettling of traditional cultural myths, and a liberal moral perspective was on the wane by 1977. Such films would continue to be made, but sporadically as isolated instances of what had once been a whole school. The turn to a more traditional, conservative dynamics within Hollywood took its lead from such precursors within the renaissance period as *Love Story* (1970), *The Poseidon Adventure* (1972), *The Towering Inferno* (1974), *The Texas Chainsaw Massacre* (1974), and *Jaws* (1975). The films that significantly define the period since 1977 are those that solidify genre as a success formula and the classical paradigm as a suturing narrative inducing spectator involvement with story and identification with character, a process that functions to naturalize and reinforce traditionally constructed cultural and gender attitudes.[1]

The new films would incorporate the stylistic pyrotechnics and mixture of genres and styles of the American renaissance new wave and would develop new techniques in the area of special effects, but would utilize these in the service of story, spectacle, and formula. Prime examples of this slick handling of mixed modes, scintillating technique, and special effects are the Spielberg-Lucas films—*Close Encounters of the Third Kind* (1977), the Indiana Jones series beginning with *Raiders of the Lost Ark* (1981), *E. T.* (1982), the *Star Wars* trilogy starting with *Star Wars* in 1977—and the *Back to the Future* movies initiated in 1985.

Given a reliance on the inherent commercial qualities of the classical paradigm and their tendency to naturalize conservative attitudes, the postrenaissance films reflect a backlash against the radical sentiments of the late 60s and early 70s. In welcoming "the return of the myths," they project a need to resuscitate the values that unified American society in the past and recuperate those that had eroded its foundations (Mast, *Short History* 496). Films such as *Kramer vs. Kramer* (1979) and *Ordinary People* (1980) critique the feminism of the 70s in their empowerment of the male as both a paternal and a maternal figure within the family after its abandonment by the mother. *Kramer vs. Kramer* is especially significant since it signals the dangers of female independence to the nuclear American family. Meryl Streep's frustrated housewife who leaves her husband and son to pursue her own career would by 1987 mutate into Glenn Close's career woman monster who threatens the secure middle-class home life of Michael Douglas in *Fatal Attraction* and is destroyed, appropriately, by Anne Archer's faithful, committed wife. *Looking for Mr. Goodbar* (1977), *The Postman Always Rings Twice* (1981), and *The Good Mother* (1988) are three films in which the woman is punished (the first two by death) for pursuing her own desires independent of society's mores. But the primary example of this kind of reaction in the late 70s and 80s is the horror/slasher film in which sexually aggressive females are punished by a monster male figure because they fan male castration anxieties and threaten male dominance: *Halloween* (1978) and its sequels, *Friday the 13th* (1980) and its sequels, *Dressed to Kill* (1980), *Cat People* (1981), *Student Bodies* (1981), *Slumber Party Massacre* (1982), and *Sorority House Massacre* (1987). In the 1990s, we see a transmutation of the genre where the woman *is the monster*, a fact that is always implicit in the horror/slasher film in which both woman and monster are identified as threats to society and therefore victims of its wrath.[2] *The Hand That Rocks the Cradle* (1992), *Candyman* (1993), *Single White Female* (1993), and *The Crush* (1993) are all examples of this particular subgenre.

While the slasher films figuratively put women in their proper place, other films of the late 70s, the 80s, and the 90s complete the agenda by reinforcing traditional patriarchal values. *Star Wars, The Deer Hunter* (1978), *Superman* (1978), *Raiders of the Lost Ark*, and *Rambo* (1985) glorify the white American male as patriotic leader in his destruction of "others" different in kind from his own. Other films of the period uphold the sanctity of the American family or the bonds between husband and wife: *Poltergeist* (1982), *Tender Mercies* (1982), *On Golden Pond* (1982), *Terms of Endearment* (1983), *Someone to Watch over Me* (1987), *Fatal Attraction* (1987), *Running on Empty* (1988), *Baby Boom* (1988), *The Abyss* (1989), *Parenthood* (1989), *Dad* (1989), *Steel Magnolias* (1989), and *Men Don't Leave* (1990), a far cry from the subversion of the American family found in such late 60s and early 70s films as Romero's horror allegory *The Night of the Living Dead* (1968) and Cassavetes's *A Woman under the Influence* (1974).[3] Also, breezy feel-good romantic comedies surface during this period, in contrast to the satirization of romance a decade before in *The Graduate, Five*

Easy Pieces, and *Carnal Knowledge.* Films such as *Heaven Can Wait* (1979), *An Officer and a Gentleman* (1982), *Romancing the Stone* (1984), *Moonstruck* (1987), *Dirty Dancing* (1987), *Big* (1988), *Working Girl* (1988), *Crossing Delancey* (1988), *When Harry Met Sally* (1989), *Cousins* (1989), *Chances Are* (1989), and *Pretty Woman* (1990) happily celebrate the mating rituals of the American male and female within traditional gendered constructions.

In contrast, the renaissance films of 1967–1976 had challenged the narrative style and structure of the classical paradigm and the myths it perpetuates. They did this by working within the paradigm, rupturing its form and content. In this way, they compare with the most extreme examples of what Comolli and Narboni refer to as "e" films, those Hollywood films whose radical elements disrupt the text and conflict with its inherent conservatism. The extreme "e" film resists a successful recuperation of its radical elements so that the disturbance to the dominant form and ideology remains at the end (687).[4] In "Ideology, Genre, Auteur," Robin Wood illustrates this kind of failed attempt at recuperation in Hitchcock's Hollywood small town genre film *Shadow of a Doubt* (1943) (482–485). In this film, the heart and foundation of society, the traditionally gendered American family, is threatened by suggestions of a prefeminist attitude in the daughter, Charlie (Teresa Wright), and the mother, Emmy (Patricia Collinge); of incestuous desires between Uncle Charlie (Joseph Cotten) and Young Charlie and between Uncle Charlie and his sister Emmy; of a fallen corrupt world that not only surrounds the town of Santa Rosa, but also infects it with the arrival of Uncle Charlie, the merry widow murderer, who unleashes Young Charlie's and Emmy's repressed desires. The film attempts to recuperate these subversive elements by Young Charlie's investigation into the murders and her suspicion of Uncle Charlie as the culprit and by the coupling of Young Charlie with the wholesome male detective (MacDonald Carey). However, though Uncle Charlie gets his just desserts and dies attempting to kill Young Charlie, the police believe another person to be the merry widow murderer, and the townspeople extoll Uncle Charlie as an exemplary citizen at his funeral. The irony of this is not lost on Young Charlie, whose family remains fractured at the end (Emmy's last words are "You grow up, you get married, and you become known as your husband's wife") and whose symbolic marriage to the scion of law and order belies the turmoil beneath the neat facade of small town Americana.[5]

Hitchcock's *Shadow of a Doubt* disrupts the dominant system to such an extent that it resists its own attempt to recoup the losses to a cardboard ideological agenda. The renaissance texts of 1967–1976 align themselves with the radical agenda of Hitchcock's film, but move beyond it as well. They develop radically from and along the lines of Hitchcock's own suggested radicalism and become, in my estimation, progressive texts. I use the term "progressive" in light of Barbara Klinger's discussion of the "progressive genre," that takes its cue from Comolli's and Narboni's seminal suggestions about the "e" film. In " 'Cinema/Ideology/Criticism' Revisited: The Progressive Genre," Klinger identifies certain Hollywood genres that fit into the "e" category particularly well as evidenced by their production of disruptive elements:

> Difference from the environment of conventions within which these films exist, then, is a paramount feature of their progressive status, and the rationale by which they are accorded a radical valence. The diverse critical positions that address film noir, the woman's film, the sophisticated family melodrama of the forties and fifties, the horror film of the seventies, and the exploitation and B film are united in particular by an emphasis on the identity of these film groups as alternative or "countercinemas" within the province of dominant cinematic practice. (79)

Klinger's criterion for the progressive text is that it produces an "alternative or 'countercinemas' within the province of dominant cinematic practice." A further criterion she focuses on is the anti-realist effect of disruptions within the system, shattering the transparency and illusionism of the classical text, and therefore its hold on an audience susceptible to its naturalization of constructed myths (78). The renaissance films of 1967–1976 exhibit Klinger's definition of the progressive genre in a most generous way since their conscious attempt to explore new narrative strategies and alternative generic patterns yields transformations of the classical paradigm and its genres that suggest new myths as well.

And so *The Graduate* and *Taxi Driver* both mock their own suggestions of recuperation. The end of *The Graduate* is so highly ambiguous as to complicate any hint that Ben and Elaine, beaters of the system, will end up like their parents; society's treatment of Travis as a hero at the end of *Taxi Driver* is as laden with irony as is Uncle Charlie's status as an upright citizen at the end of *Shadow of a Doubt*. In most renaissance films, the process of recuperation exists not even in token form; it is eschewed altogether. A film such as *2001: A Space Odyssey* offers radical narrative strategies and a dazzling display of ambiguities that leave its audience unsettled rather than satisfied. Altman's films subvert genres and their traditional mythic baggages as a common enterprise. *McCabe and Mrs. Miller* and *Nashville* overturn the western and the musical, respectively, and lay bare the self-interested laissez faire that undergirds the myths of the pioneer spirit on the one hand and folk and rural values on the other. The *Godfather* films construct parallel and self-referential narrations in their scathing critique of American capitalism, while the counterculture films assume the bankruptcy of bourgeois myths from the start in exposing their hypocrisy, oppression, and repression in narrative styles that range from the expressive to the neorealistic. Films such as *Bonnie and Clyde* and *The Wild Bunch* radically transform their genres and raise their protagonists to heroic proportions to satisfy the thirst for new heroes, alternative gods such as Penn's romantic rebel-artist couple, or Peckinpah's strangely compelling outlaws who refuse at the end to surrender their integrity in a landscape rife with compromise.

I can only suggest here the sporadic legacy of the renaissance films since 1977, but it seems to me that the following films (and there may be others) carry on the progressive tradition, in Klinger's words, " 'countercinemas' within the province of dominant cinematic practice": *Annie Hall* (1977) and the string of Woody Allen films since then, *Interiors* (1978), *Manhattan* (1979), *Stardust Memories* (1980), *The Purple Rose of Cairo* (1985), *Hannah and Her Sisters* (1986), *Crimes and Misdemeanors* (1989), and *Husbands and Wives* (1992); Fosse's *All That Jazz* (1979); Scorsese's *Raging Bull* (1980) and *The King of Comedy* (1983); Kubrick's *The Shining* (1980) and *Full Metal Jacket* (1987); Michael Cimino's *Heaven's Gate* (1980); Lawrence Kasdan's *Body Heat* (1981); Ridley Scott's *Blade Runner* (1982) and *Thelma and Louise* (1991); David Lynch's *Blue Velvet* (1986); Oliver Stone's *Platoon* (1986); Spike Lee's *Do the Right Thing* (1989), *Jungle Fever* (1990), and *Malcolm X* (1992); Coppola's *The Godfather, Part III* (1990); Altman's *The Player* (1992); and Clint Eastwood's *Unforgiven* (1992).

The five most recent of these films, all made since 1990, signify the tenacity of the progressive spirit in dominant Hollywood cinema. Allen's *Husbands and Wives* is yet another one of his experimental modernist narratives about the urban condition, a black comedy that probes the fractured relationships that define the personal lives of the professionally successful American middle class. Altman's *The Player* employs a highly reflexive and allusive narrative in a satire on the rapacity of the Hollywood industry that extends the critique of such other films about Hollywood as *Sunset Boulevard* (1950), *The Bad and the Beautiful* (1952), *The Big Knife* (1955), and *The Last Tycoon* (1977). Spike Lee's *Malcolm X* is both an auteurist transformation of the standard Hollywood biopic and a searing revelation of the Afro-American experience seen through the eyes of the radical black leader. Ridley Scott's *Thelma and Louise*'s rich play on the western genre, male buddy movies, road pictures, and the woman's film allows it to undermine settled notions of gendered constructions and to resist its own attempt to recuperate its women protagonists as they soar into a trajectory that catapults them out of the bounds of male narratives. Finally, Eastwood's *Unforgiven* proves the enduring plasticity of the western genre in this darkly brooding, ambiguous tale of a modernist western hero whose capitalistic impulse and vengefulness override the civilizing influence of woman and family, but whose desire for revenge encompasses a compassion for the marginalized, the women prostitutes cheated out of justice and his black sidekick murdered by the forces of law and order.

Looking back ten years from now, will we view this handful of recent films as announcing a new period in the Hollywood cinema akin to that of the American film renaissance of 1967–1976? Not likely, but their existence ensures the vitality of that legacy.

Notes

INTRODUCTION

1. Some critics/historians like David Cook, *A History of Narrative Film* (1990), underplay the period as an artistic renaissance. Cook argues that the most-often-mentioned directors of the period (he cites Peckinpah, Penn, Wexler, Hopper, and Kubrick), with the exception of Kubrick, never fulfilled the promise expected of them, never made a film that equaled in stature their films of the late 60s (886). But this is beside the point. The new freedom of the period gave filmmakers the opportunity to become auteurs overnight and to influence other films that followed in the decade ahead. In addition to Cook's listing, one can add Nichols, Bogdanovich, Altman, and Coppola as new wave directors who began to make their mark in the late 60s and who sustained their level of achievement into the mid-70s. That they may not have sustained that same level beyond the period does not undercut the period's renaissance quality and its most representative characteristics of imagination, originality, and the questioning and transformation of traditional Hollywood genres and styles.

2. In his *A Cinema of Loneliness: Penn, Kubrick, Coppola, Scorsese, Altman* (1980), (5–6), Robert Kolker emphasizes the inevitable compromise in the production and making of a commercial film even within this time of artistic freedom. His thesis is that the promise of artistic freedom was illusory. For even if filmmakers used their talents in a critical way, examining the assumptions and forms of the commercial narrative, their experimentation was carried out in the context of an economic structure that permitted experimentation only if it created a profit. (Kolker toned down this idea in his Second Edition [1988], putting less stress on the economic determinants of commercial filmmaking in order to achieve a more balanced viewpoint.)

3. The idea of genre's potential for greater expressiveness as a condition for

its continued development, expansion, and deepening is articulated by Stanley Cavell in his study of the comedy of remarriage, *Pursuits of Happiness*:

a new member (of a genre) gets his distinction by investigating a particular set of features in a way that makes them, or their relation, more explicit than in its companions. Then as these exercises in explicitness reflect upon one another, looping back and forth among the members, we may say that the genre is striving toward a state of absolute explicitness, of expressive saturation. (30)

4. The trend of big-budgeted musicals and spectacles continued into the period 1967–1976, but musicals like *Dr. Doolittle* (1967), *Finian's Rainbow* (1968), *Star!* (1968), *Paint Your Wagon* (1969), and *Darling Lili* (1970) flopped at the box office; and even such commercial successes as the Bond movies, the *Planet of the Apes* series, *Love Story* (1970), *The Poseidon Adventure* (1972), *The Sting* (1973), and *Jaws* (1975) were overshadowed by the new American cinema and the new American auteurs. The latter films are, in retrospect, pre-postrenaissance films; they prepared the way for the return of spectacle and mass-marketed genre pictures of the late 70s and the 80s.

5. The targeting of the period as a renaissance ranges from tentative contemporary reactions to brief summaries in film history texts. See, for example, Stefan Kanfer, "Hollywood, the Shock of Freedom in Films," *Time* (December 8, 1967): 66–76; Thomas W. Bohn, Richard L. Stromgren, and Daniel H. Johnson, *Light and Shadows: A History of Motion Pictures* (Sherman Oaks 1975); Gerald Mast, *A Short History of the Movies*, Fourth Edition (New York 1986); and David Cook, *A History of Narrative Film*, Second Edition (New York 1990).

6. Three earlier works on the period differ from mine in several ways. Both Diane Jacob's *Hollywood Renaissance* (1977) and Robert Phillip Kolker's *A Cinema of Loneliness*, Second Edition (1988), organize their discussions by auteurs. Jacobs outlines the period rather loosely; she has it beginning in 1970, but includes a discussion of Cassavetes and his work of the 1960s. Kolker focuses more definitively on auteurist canons and the existential theme of alienation. Meanwhile Thomas Schatz's *Old Hollywood/New Hollywood* (1983) looks at the films of the period primarily from a cultural and socioeconomic perspective.

CHAPTER ONE: 1967–1968, THE WONDER YEAR, PART I: *BONNIE AND CLYDE*

1. Gerald Mast in *A Short History of the Movies*, Fourth Edition (1986), notes that several films in the early 1960s led up to *Bonnie and Clyde*: *Psycho* (1960), *The Hustler* (1961), *Lonely Are the Brave* (1962), *Dr. Strangelove* (1963), *The Pawnbroker* (1965), and *Who's Afraid of Virginia Woolf?* (1966). Though Mast singles out no particular film to mark the awakening of the Hollywood cinema, he says that *Bonnie and Clyde* was "perhaps the first full statement of the new cinema's values" (422–423).

2. See, for example, Bosley Crowther, "Review of *Bonnie and Clyde*," *New York Times* (August 14, 1967): 36 and Page Cook, "Review of *Bonnie and Clyde*," *Films in Review* 18:8 (1967): 504–505 for *Bonnie and Clyde*; Stanley Kauffmann, "Lost in the Stars," *The New Republic* (May 4, 1968): 24–41, and Renata Adler, "*2001* Is Up, Up and Away," *New York Times* (April 4, 1968) for *2001*; and Richard

Schickel, "Fine Debut for a Square Anti-Hero," *Life* (January 19, 1968): 16 for *The Graduate*.

3. Other examples of retractions during the period include Andrew Sarris's on *2001* in *The Village Voice* issue of August 7, 1970 and Arthur Knight's on *McCabe and Mrs. Miller* in *The Saturday Review* issue of August 7, 1971. Sarris's earlier negative reviews had appeared in *The Village Voice* of April 11, 1968, and February 20, 1969; Knight's had appeared in *The Saturday Review* of July 24, 1971.

4. See Stefan Kanfer, "The Shock of Freedom in Films," *Time* (December 8, 1967): 66–76, and John Cawelti, "Introduction: *Bonnie and Clyde*: Tradition and Transformation," *Focus on Bonnie and Clyde* (Englewood Cliffs 1973): 1–6.

5. In their account of the writing of the screenplay, David Newman and Robert Benton acknowledge the direct influence of Truffaut, Godard, and the French New Wave, along with Hitchcock, De Broca, Bergman, Kurosawa, Antonioni, and Fellini. They had even approached Truffaut to direct the film, but he had already committed to *Fahrenheit 451*; and for a time, Godard was interested in filming *Bonnie and Clyde* before running into major disagreements with the producers. Eventually, Warren Beatty bought the screenplay and signed Arthur Penn to direct (13–26).

6. For the controversy over the film's violence, see the reviews by Bosley Crowther and Page Cook; see also Joseph Gelmis, "Homicidal Fun Irks While It Spellbinds," *Newsday* (August 14, 1967): 3A.

7. Pauline Kael identifies the image of the bank clerk's startled shot face as a reference to the startled face of the woman shot by the soldiers in the Odessa Steps sequence in Eisenstein's *Potemkin* (1925). She also observes that the audience, which had been laughing up to this point, becomes "the butt of the joke" during this unexpected flare-up of violence (55).

8. For more on the techniques and characteristics of art cinema narration, see David Bordwell, "The Art Cinema as a Mode of Film Practice," *Film Criticism* 4 (1979): 56–64, and *Narration in the Fiction Film* (1985), Chapter 10, "Art-Cinema Narration," 205–213.

9. "Privileged moments" in a film are moments which are especially felicitous. They reveal, in a sympathetic way, the humanity of its characters. The privileged moments of *Bonnie and Clyde* (the episode with Eugene and Velma is another) are yet another indication of its debt to the art cinema of neorealism and the French New Wave. Neorealism sought to present life whole and uninterrupted on the screen, and, in this way, to reveal the little, undramatic, but no less revealing moments of human existence. Kracauer calls this "the flow of life," which may contain here and there the "found story." See *Theory of Film* 60–73, 245–251, and 300–309, and Andre Bazin, "The Evolution of the Language of Cinema," *What Is Cinema?* Vol. I.

The French New Wave appropriated the "found story" by including moments that had nothing to do with the main action but were revelatory of the human condition. Truffaut's *The 400 Blows* and *Shoot the Piano Player* contain such moments, spontaneous happenings that are brief tender glimpses of humanity: the faces of children as they watch a puppet show and the bird's-eye view of the children breaking off from the human chain formed by their teacher and running away in the streets in *The 400 Blows*; Chico's conversation with a passerby about the passerby's love for his wife and the waiter's endless song with silly lyrics in the restaurant in *Shoot the Piano Player*. But perhaps *Bonnie and Clyde* has more in common with Truffaut's *Jules and Jim* than with the earlier films. For, after all, the privileged moments of *Bonnie and Clyde* are not irrelevant, spontaneous happenings, but integrated into the film's plot of character and theme of illusion/disillusionment. The privileged moments of *Jules and Jim* are also integrated into its plot of character and theme of commitment and freedom in love. Two examples are Catherine's joyous, uninhibited singing of Albert's song and Therese's candid conversation with Jim about her lovers and husbands, and about her present husband, who is an undertaker.

10. The best studies of the prototypical gangster films of the 30s, *Little Caesar* (1930), *Public Enemy* (1931), and *Scarface* (1932), are Robert Warshow's seminal essay "The Gangster as Tragic Hero," from *The Immediate Experience* (1971): 127–133; Jack Shadoian's *Dreams and Dead Ends: The American Gangster/Crime Film* (1977): 15–58; and Thomas Schatz's *Hollywood Genres: Formulas, Filmmaking, and the Studio System* (1981): 81–95.

11. In *Howard Hawks* (1968), Robin Wood links Camonte's incapacity for self-awareness to his basic innocence and naïveté: "He is funny and touching because he is an overgrown child, emotionally arrested at an early stage, with no sympathetic awareness of others and no self-awareness" (60–61).

12. Shadoian views the gangster film as a vehicle to expose the basic contradiction in the American culture between the two opposing ideologies of the individual and the community, America as a land of opportunity and as a classless, democratic society (5).

13. Some may assert that Fritz Lang's *You Only Live Once* (1937) compares with *Bonnie and Clyde* since it depicts a biased, unjust society, but important differences between the two films mitigate any claim that Lang's film predates the later film as a generic transformer. In the first place, Eddie and Joan Taylor (Henry Fonda and Sylvia Sidney) are victims rather than heroes, and pitiful ones at that. They are victimized not only by the obviously biased society (no one wants to give Eddie a chance in life because of his criminal background, and the court convicts him of a crime he didn't commit), but also by the manipulative melodramatic plot which pushes home the Langian theme of the innocent individual done in by an uncaring, self-serving society. Moreover, the protagonists lack the individual appeal we find in Bonnie and Clyde—joie de vivre, spontaneity, wit, and imagination. *You Only Live Once* seems more an expression of a depressed European sensibility during the Hitler years (Lang was forced to leave Germany in 1933) than an expression of the genre itself.

CHAPTER TWO: 1967–1968, THE WONDER YEAR, PART II: *THE GRADUATE* AND *2001: A SPACE ODYSSEY*

1. In his book *See No Evil* (1970), Jack Vizzard, a member of the Production Code Administration, recounts the significant role played by *Who's Afraid of Virginia Woolf?* in the transition to the new Production Code of 1968. Along with *Alfie* (1966), Nichols's film garnered a special S.M.A. (Suggested for Mature Audiences) rating, paving the way for the new categories two years later. See the

excerpt from *See No Evil* in *The Movies in Our Midst*, ed. Gerald Mast (Chicago 1982) 693–704.

2. As early as 1969, Nichols seems to have been in search of an unself-conscious style. While filming *Catch 22*, he said, "It seems to me that the highest achievement in a film is for no technique to be visible at all" ("Filmmaker as Ascendant Star" 51). In an interview in *Film Comment* (May–June 1991), Nichols pinpointed *Silkwood* as the movie in which he began to utilize a transparent style in contrast to the self-conscious techniques of his earlier films. Presently, he feels that technique should be as unself-conscious as possible to preserve the audience's relationship with the story and its characters: "That's the fun of making movies: you use these technical things to make people completely unaware of technical things" (Smith 32), and "My basic assumption is that the things that are happening to the characters, and thus to the audience, must be strong enough to burn away the technique, so there is no technique" (Smith 36).

3. Other traditional forms of overt narration in fiction include irony (implicit commentary), interpretation, judgment, generalization, and reflexivity (commentary on the discourse). For more on overt and covert narration, or the degree of perceptibility of the narrator in the story, see Seymour Chatman, *Story and Discourse, Narrative Structure in Fiction and Film* (1978): 196–253, and Shlomith Rimmon-Kenan, *Narrative Fiction, Contemporary Poetics* (1983): 86–116.

4. H. Wayne Schuth offers a perceptive analysis of color in *The Graduate* in *Mike Nichols* (1978): 45–63.

5. See also Hollis Alpert, "*The Graduate* Makes Out," *Saturday Review* (July 6, 1968): 15, and Andrew Sarris, "*The Graduate*," *The Village Voice* (December 28, 1967): 33.

6. Andrew Sarris calls the action of Ben's late arrival at the church followed by Elaine's running off with him anyway an "anti-cliché improvisation," shattering the "monogamous mythology . . . in the name of a truer love." See his review, "*The Graduate*": 33.

7. See, for example, Stanley Kauffman, "Lost in the Stars," *The New Republic* (May 4, 1968): 24, 41; Renata Adler, "*2001* Is Up, Up and Away," *New York Times* (April 4, 1968): 58; Kathleen Carroll, "Space Film Is Way Out Experience," *Daily News* (April 4, 1968): 67; Judith Crist, "Stanley Kubrick, Please Come Down," *New Yorker* (April 27, 1968): 52–53; Judith Shatnoff, "A Gorilla to Remember," *Film Quarterly* (Fall 1968): 56–62; and Archer Winsten, "*2001: A Space Odyssey* at Capitol," *New York Post* (April 4, 1968): 68.

8. Examples of critics who rely on Clarke's novel to one extent or the other to "explain" the film include Norman Kagan, *The Cinema of Stanley Kubrick* (New York 1972); Thomas Allen Nelson, *Kubrick: Inside a Film Artist's Maze* (Bloomington 1982); Gene D. Phillips, *Stanley Kubrick: A Film Odyssey* (New York 1975); and Kenneth Von Gunden and Stuart H. Stock, *Twenty All Time Great Science Fiction Films* (New York 1982).

9. In *Screening Space*, Sobchack contrasts the science fiction film monster, whose evil is in wreaking physical destruction, to the horror film monster, whose evil is internal. She says that the horror monster's external appearance is really a clue to the moral chaos within and that sin, guilt, and moral struggle are the horror monster film's main concerns (52).

10. For a useful discussion of sci-fi films after *2001* and before *Star Wars*, see

Joan F. Dean, "Between *2001* and *Star Wars*," *Journal of Popular Film and Television* 7: 1 (1978): 32–41. Dean says that with *Star Wars* and *Close Encounters of the Third Kind* in 1977 yet another era in science fiction film began, in which aliens are friendly and technology an accepted way of life.

CHAPTER THREE: WESTERNS IN MODERN DRESS: *THE WILD BUNCH* AND *MCCABE AND MRS. MILLER*

1. Thomas Elsaesser in "Pathos of Failure: American Films in the 70s," *Monogram* no. 6 (1975): 13–19, says that unlike their European counterparts who experimented with the nature of narrative outside the conventional supports of genre, American film directors of the 70s worked within an "audience-oriented cinema" and that the "innovatory line in the American cinema can be seen to progress not via conceptual abstraction but by shifting and modifying traditional genres and themes, while never quite shedding their support, be it to facilitate recognition or for structuring the narrative" (18).

2. See, for example, Andre Bazin, who writes of the western's centrality in the development of the cinema in "The Western: or the American Film Par Excellence," *What Is Cinema?* Vol. II (Berkeley 1972): 140–148: "The Western is the only genre whose origins are almost identical with those of the cinema itself and which is as alive as ever after almost half a century of uninterrupted success" (140). Bazin wrote this in 1953. Meanwhile, Thomas Schatz points out the western's function as a mirror for the myths underlying American society: "The meaning of the western or of any other genre does not reside 'in' the films but rather in the consciousness—both individual and collective—of those who consume and interpret them. We may dismiss this or that western as mere 'entertainment' but for it to hold the viewers' interest it must somehow appeal to what is meaningful in his or her own experience" ("The Western" 42).

3. See Jack Nachbar, "Riding Shotgun: The Scattered Formula in Contemporary Western Movies," *Focus on the Western* (Englewood Cliffs 1974): 101–112, in which he defines the personal western as first and foremost its director's vision with a different set of themes and motivations, but that they also "continue to be constructed around the epic moment and violent-but-honorable hero of the traditional Western" (105). Thomas Schatz, in "The Western," *Handbook of American Film Genres* (New York 1988): 25–46, emphasizes the modernist element in these westerns, their self-conscious concern with style and genre (34–35).

4. Like many classic American genre films, *My Darling Clementine* promotes prosocial values over any internal subversive and radical elements by offering simple solutions to complex problems. In "Genre Films and the Status Quo," Judith Hess Wright argues that classic Hollywood genres such as science fiction, the horror film, the gangster film, and the western launder the contradictions and ambiguities involved in a combination of prosocial and radical forces by favoring the former over the latter, thereby upholding the status quo. For example, one of the ways in which the western reduces the tension between the values of the community and the individual, between civilization and the wilderness is to co-opt the latter as a function of the former. In other words, the western sanctions violence as long as it is used to preserve law and order. There-

fore, violence is not a criminal, but a necessary part of the westerner's code, used to protect prosocial forces (41–44).

5. Schatz sees the initiate hero operating in such diverse westerns as *Red River* (1948), *Shane* (1952), *The Searchers* (1956), *Rio Bravo* (1957), *The Magnificent Seven* (1960), *Ride the High Country* (1962), *El Dorado* (1967), *Little Big Man* (1970), *The Cowboys* (1972), and *The Shootist* (1976) ("The Western" 31).

6. The flashbacks in *The Wild Bunch* have been the subject of great controversy because they were cut from the original 148–minute release print which premiered on June 25, 1969. In July, Warner Brothers recalled the original release print and distributed a widely released print of 135 minutes. The most significant flashbacks cut were those involving Pike and his past relationships with Deke Thornton and his mistress Aurora; they are crucial to an understanding of character and motivation. Other cuts included the flashback of Crazy Lee in the railroad office, part of the festivities in Angel's village, and Villa's attack on Mapache at a railroad station. See Vincent Canby, "Which Version Did You See?" *New York Times* (July 20, 1969): 1, 7; Doug McKinney, *Sam Peckinpah* (Boston 1979): 89–90; and Paul Seydor, *Peckinpah, The Western Films* (Urbana 1980): 84–94.

7. Examples of criticism against the violence in *The Wild Bunch* are Hollis Alpert, "Variations on a Western Theme," *Saturday Review* (September 27, 1969): 39; Tracy Hotchner, "Is the *Bunch* Too Wild?" *New York Times* (July 20, 1969): 29; and Archer Winsten, "*The Wild Bunch* Arrives at Trans-Lux East and West," *New York Post* (June 26, 1969): 59. Examples of criticism in defense of the film's violence are Lewis Beale, "The American Way West," *Films and Filming* (April 1972): 24–30; and Stephen Farber, "Peckinpah's Return," *Film Quarterly* (Fall 1969): 2–11.

In interviews, Peckinpah defended the graphic depiction of violence as honest and educationally revelatory to an audience attracted to it. See John Cutts, "Shoot!" *Films and Filming* (October 1969): 4–6, 8; Joe Medjuck, "Sam Peckinpah Lets It All Hang Out," *Take One* (January–February 1969): 18–20; and William Murray, "*Playboy* Interview: Sam Peckinpah," *Playboy* (August 1972): 65–74, 192.

8. Stephen Farber in "Peckinpah's Return" explains the twofold vision of *The Wild Bunch* in this way: "(*The Wild Bunch*) wavers between a harsh, very contemporary cynicism and an older, mellower belief in grand human possibilities that has always been the most sentimental affirmation of the Western" (6).

9. In his seminal essay on the anti-western elements in Altman's film, "*McCabe and Mrs. Miller*: Robert Altman's Anti-Western," *Journal of Popular Film* (Fall 1972): 268–287, Gary Engle notes McCabe's diminishment as the film undercuts his humor, his business acumen, and his role as leader of the community; he also notes McCabe's racism and exploitative actions; he contends that Mrs. Miller's greater love for McCabe than his for her undercuts his stature as her lover; and concludes by observing that McCabe's death is not existentially noble because it is totally unnecessary and should have been avoided.

10. See Robert Self, "The Art Cinema and Robert Altman," *Velvet Light Trap*, no. 19 (1982): 30–34, for a discussion of art cinema narration in Altman's works.

11. The history of Godard's and Antonioni's films has been the history of the subversion of classical cinema by the European masters. Godard's first feature film, *Breathless* (1959), was both a tribute to and an explosion of American genre films and their classical narrative style. The films which followed, especially *Vivre*

sa Vie (1962), *Les Carabiniers* (1963), *Masculin-Feminin* (1966), *La Chinoise* (1967), and *Weekend* (1968), exploited this subversion even further and are textbook examples of anti-classical narration. Antonioni's first masterpiece, *L'Avventura* (1960), was wildly booed and hissed at its Cannes Festival showing for its meandering plot, lingering shots, and cryptic open-endedness. It upset audience expectations and introduced a unique personally developed narrative to reveal the plight of alienated modern man and woman in an industrial, bourgeois society. Antonioni would extend this theme and narrative style uncompromisingly in *La Notte* (1961), *L'Eclisse* (1962), and *The Passenger* (1975).

12. In his book on genres and American popular culture, *Adventure, Mystery, and Romance* (Chicago 1976), John Cawelti notes that one of the themes in westerns of the late 60s and early 70s, which reflect their pessimism with society, is white America's monolithic destructive attitude toward "other ways of life" both in the past and, by implication, in the present: "The search for a new western myth expresses the view that violence has been the underlying force in the development of American society and that all modern white Americans are implicated in guilt for their aggressive destruction of other ways of life" (259).

CHAPTER FOUR: COUNTERCULTURE: *MIDNIGHT COWBOY, FIVE EASY PIECES, CARNAL KNOWLEDGE, AMERICAN GRAFFITI, LENNY*

1. See Michael Ryan and Douglas Kellner, *Camera Politica, The Politics and Ideology of Contemporary Hollywood Film* (Bloomington 1988), for a discussion of the conservative backlash against the counterculture in 1970s Hollywood films such as *Straw Dogs, Dirty Harry, The French Connection, Star Wars, Rocky,* and *Grease.* See especially chapter one, "From Counterculture to Counterrevolution, 1967–1971," and chapter three, "Genre Transformations and the Failure of Liberalism."

See also Andrew Sarris, "After *The Graduate*," *American Film* 3:9 (July–August 1978): 32–37. Sarris observes that the promise of *The Graduate* fizzled in the 1970s when audiences stayed away in droves from the downbeat counterculture films of the period and began flocking to less realistic, less critical films that incorporated fantasy, sentimentality, and violence.

2. See Joan Mellen, *Big Bad Wolves, Masculinity in the American Film* (New York 1977), pp. 287–292, for more on the homosexual subtext in relation to the depiction of the women characters in *Midnight Cowboy*. Her thesis is that the erotic preference of Joe and Ratso for each other is dependent on Joe's humiliation by women and that the two men are not allowed fulfillment because "the homosexual relationship they seem in all respects but the physical to have chosen were still taboo" (287).

3. See note 9 in chapter one for a discussion of the "privileged moments" in Italian neorealism and the French New Wave.

4. Frank Kofsky's *Lenny Bruce, The Comedian as Social Critic and Secular Moralist* (New York 1974) summarizes the canonization process of Bruce as a liberal saint in the late 1960s and early 1970s; see especially 52–62. It itself contributes significantly to this process, as does the Julian Barry play *Lenny* (1971), upon which the Bob Fosse film is based. For a bracing retort to this attempt to raise Bruce to

counterculture hero, see Pauline Kael's review of the film *Lenny*, "When the Saints Come Marching In," *Reeling* (New York 1976): 494–502.

CHAPTER FIVE: GANGSTERS AND PRIVATE EYES: *THE GODFATHER* FILMS AND *CHINATOWN*

1. Apropos to this, Coppola said, "I wanted him to be destroyed by forces inside of himself; the very forces that had created him. I leave *Godfather, Part Two*, with Michael very possibly the most powerful man in America. But he is a corpse." Quoted in John Hess, "*Godfather II*: A Deal Coppola Couldn't Refuse," *Jump Cut* no. 7 (May–July 1975): 10.

2. See Robert Warshow, "The Gangster as Tragic Hero," *The Immediate Experience* (New York 1971): (the gangster) "is what we want to be and what we are afraid we may become" (131); and Pauline Kael, "Alchemy," *Deeper into Movies* (Boston 1973): "When 'Americanism' was a form of cheerful, bland official optimism, the gangster used to be destroyed at the end of the movie and our feelings resolved" (425).

3. In "Coppola and *The Godfather*," Stephen Farber observes that this accepted division in American life represents a confusion of values, an assumption that there is "no correlation between what a man is personally and what he may be forced to do in his work ... trading the Judeo-Christian ethic for jungle ethics when the dollar is at stake" (218).

4. Marxist critics agree that Coppola doesn't go far enough in his progressive attitude. He shows the negative effects of capitalism, but fails to analyze the root of capitalism and to provide an alternative. In the Cuba sequence, Coppola gives us only a glimpse of a counterforce, the revolutionaries who are fighting the corrupt money-backed Batista government. See Leonard Quart, "*The Godfather, Part II*," *Cineaste* 6:4 (1975): 39; and John Hess, "A Deal Coppola Couldn't Refuse," *Jump Cut* no. 7 (May–July 1975): 1.

5. Between *Part II* in 1974 and *Part III* in 1990, a reedited version of *I* and *II* appeared on network television in November 1977. Coppola himself restructured his own work, piecing together parts of his two films and adding footage which had been originally cut to come up with *The Godfather Saga*, a chronological rendering beginning with the young Vito in Sicily and ending with Michael alone on his Nevada estate. This version played on TV for three nights, November 12–15, totaling 9 hours, with 7 hours 10 minutes of actual movie time. Restored footage not seen in the originals totaled 55 minutes.

The chronological restructuring emphasizes story and waters down commentary. It dissipates the tension between the two films and between the two generations in *Part II*, and it seriously compromises the critique of Michael and the family. For a good overall view of the TV version along with critical commentary, see David Thomson, "The Discreet Charm of the Godfather," *Sight and Sound* 47: 2 (Spring 1978): 76–80.

6. Both *The Godfather, Part II* and *Chinatown* received the highest number of nominations for the Academy Awards of 1974, eleven each. *The Godfather, Part II* won seven awards for best picture, director, supporting actor (De Niro), adapted screenplay, score, art direction, and set decoration. *Chinatown* won one award for best original screenplay (Robert Towne).

7. See John Cawelti's 1979 seminal essay, "*Chinatown* and Generic Transformation in Recent American Film," in *Film Theory and Criticism*, Fourth Edition, edited by Gerald Mast, Marshall Cohen, and Leo Braudy (New York 1992): 498–511, which was one of the first studies to outline the demythologizing process of invoking traditional genres in order to show up the inadequacy of their myths not only in *Chinatown*, but in other films of the period as well.

8. Robert Towne's original ending to *Chinatown* was not as bleak as Polanski's final version. In the original ending, Evelyn kills her father, Noah Cross, and goes to jail for it, unable to tell the truth of Katherine's identity. Gittes manages to ferret Katherine out of the country and save her from further exploitation. Of his original ending, Towne says that he was looking for some balance: the larger crime may go unpunished, but Evelyn kills Cross and frees her daughter from his influence. He is quoted as saying: "My own feeling is if a scene is relentlessly bleak—as the revised ending is—it isn't as powerful as it can be if there's a little light there to underscore the bleakness. If you show something decent happening, it makes what's bad almost worse." Quoted in "Dialog on Film," *American Film* 1:3 (December 1975): 35.

On the other hand, Polanski, who insisted on the revised ending, reveals a sensibility more modernist and Brechtian in his statement" What I want is to finish a film without giving the audience the feeling of being satisfied." Quoted in James Leach, "Notes on Polanski's Cinema of Cruelty," *Wide Angle* 7:1 (1978): 39.

9. Wexman also sees another way in which *Chinatown* undercuts the myth of the private eye—by revealing his chauvinistic, racist attitudes, another sign of his compromised nature (97). She also views him as acting out the myth of the hard-boiled detective in order to validate his white male value system, a validation possible in the 1940s, but not in the 1970s (97).

10. See Robert Phillip Kolker, *A Cinema of Loneliness*, Second Edition (New York 1988), for a discussion of *The Long Goodbye* and *Night Moves* in the context of the *film noir* detective, modernist narrative, and the auteurist concerns of Altman and Penn, respectively. See 340–352 for *The Long Goodbye* and 65–71 for *Night Moves*.

CHAPTER SIX: APOCALYPSE: *NASHVILLE* AND *TAXI DRIVER*

1. See Jane Feuer, "The Self-Reflexive Musical and the Myth of Entertainment," *Film Genre Reader*, ed. Barry Keith Grant (Austin 1986): 329–343. I am indebted to four sources in my discussion of the Hollywood musical: Feuer's essay, her book *The Hollywood Musical* (Bloomington 1982), Thomas Schatz's *Hollywood Genres* (New York 1981), and Rick Altman's *The American Film Musical* (Bloomington 1987).

2. The documentary look of *Nashville* was a deliberate choice by Altman from the start: "The interesting thing is that we're setting up the fabric of a documentary film; we're setting up the events and filming them, instead of having a whole built-up motivation" (Gross 28). One of the film's editors, Sid Levin, concurs: "Because of the improvisational nature of *Nashville* and the variations inherent

in that kind of shooting, editing the film was like cutting an extremely well-covered documentary" (Levin 33).

3. In "Altman's Open Surface," *Jump Cut* 10/11 (June 1976): 31–32, Jane Feuer compares the openness of *Nashville* and its foregrounding of details with Italian neorealism. However, she also says that Altman selects the details to make important points.

Nashville's selectivity of details may prompt some to see its parallel structure not as an elaboration of neorealism but as an extension of the parallel editing of classical Hollywood narrative stretching back to D. W. Griffith's innovative cross-cuttings (see Kolker 355). Such a view needs qualification. The classical technique of parallel editing is used to achieve effects of suspense, to further plot in a teleological manner, or to emphasize emotional and psychological states related to motivation and action. In contrast, Altman's parallel editing is "selective" in another way, primarily in the service of a satiric observation of character and society and only secondarily in the service of plot.

4. For a sympathetic view of Barbara Jean and her breakdown as an example of social tragedy, see Michael Klein, *"Nashville* and the American Dream," *Jump Cut* 9 (October/December 1975): 7, and Ruth McCormick, "In Defense of *Nashville*," *Cineaste* 7:1 (Fall 1975): 24–25.

5. See Thomas Elsaesser, "Vincente Minnelli," *Genre: The Musical*, ed. Rick Altman (London 1981): 8–27, for a discussion of the artist-protagonist's unique ability to transform the plastic environment of the Hollywood musical into the fantasy of his desires, and conversely, the protagonist's inability to do so in the Hollywood family melodrama, in which the external frustrates the internal.

6. See, for example, Klein (6–7) and McCormick (25, 51).

7. Feuer briefly outlines some elements in *Nashville* that distance the viewer from the characters: the use of distant camera, tracks and zooms, the lack of classical cutting for psychological effects, a minimum of close-ups, the lack of a central consciousness, distasteful characters, and intrusive sound. See "Altman's Open Surface" (31–32).

8. Scorsese in separate interviews calls Travis Bickle "this avenging angel floating through the streets of the city" (Thompson and Christie 54) and "a commando for God" (Taylor 15). Frank Rich and Lenny Rubenstein equate Travis with his corrupt environment: "[The environment] is a reflection of his own disordered personality" (Rich 58) and "There is little to distinguish the mad Bickle from his mad environment" (Rubenstein 35).

9. See Kolker (182) and Rubenstein (35).

EPILOGUE

1. For discussions on the system of suture and its ideological effects, see Jean-Louis Baudry, "Ideological Effects of the Basic Cinematographic Apparatus," *Film Quarterly* 28:2 (Winter 1974–75): 39–47; Daniel Dayan, "The Tutor Code of Classical Cinema," *Film Quarterly* 28:1 (Fall 1974): 22–31; and Kaja Silverman, *The Subject of Semiotics* (New York 1983): 194–236.

2. For a compelling argument on the woman-monster identification and the cancellation of the woman's desire and look in the horror film, see Linda Wil-

liams, "When the Woman Looks," *Film Theory and Criticism*, Fourth Edition, ed. Gerald Mast, Marshall Cohen, Leo Braudy (New York 1992): 561–577.

3. Robin Wood's essays on the horror film trace the surfacing of sexual and other repressions in the psyches of parents and their children, claiming that the horror film represents a modern-day critique of the puritan and capitalist American family. See "The American Family Comedy: From *Meet Me in St. Louis* to *The Texas Chain Saw Massacre*," *Wide Angle* 3:2 (1979): 5–11, and *Hollywood from Vietnam to Reagan* (New York 1986): 70–94.

4. In their highly politicized *Cahiers du Cinema* article, "Cinema/Ideology/Criticism," Comolli and Narboni also identify six other categories of film, all in the context of ideology and its depiction. The "a" film conveys the dominant ideology in "pure and unadulterated form"; the "b" film consciously undermines the ideology on both the level of subject matter and the level of discourse; the "c" film critiques the ideology through a discourse that works against the subject matter; the "d" film deals explicitly with a radical political subject matter but adopts the dominant discourse; the "f" film is the documentary that depicts "live" or "real" political events and reflections but adopts the dominant discourse; and the "g" film is the documentary that upsets the ideology in both subject matter and discourse (685–688).

5. In the same article, Wood contrasts Hitchcock's *Shadow of a Doubt* and its failed attempt at recuperation to Capra's *It's a Wonderful Life* (1946) and its successful recuperation of disruptive elements (479–481).

Works Cited

Adler, Renata. "*2001* is Up, Up and Away." *New York Times* 4 April 1968: 58.

Agel, Jerome, ed. *The Making of Kubrick's 2001*. New York: New American Library, 1970.

Aldridge, Leslie. "Who's Afraid of the Undergraduate?" *New York Times* 18 February 1968: 15D.

Alpert, Hollis. "*The Graduate* Makes Out." *Saturday Review* 6 July 1968: 14–15, 32.

———. "Mike Nichols Strikes Again." *Saturday Review* 23 December 1967: 24.

———. "Variations on a Western Theme." *Saturday Review* 27 September 1969: 39.

Altman, Rick. *The American Film Musical*. Bloomington: Indiana University Press, 1987.

Atlas, Jacob and Ann Guerin. "Robert Altman, Julie Christie and Warren Beatty Make the Western Real." *Show* (August 1971): 18–21.

Barry, Julian. *Lenny, a Play by Julian Barry, Based on the Life and Words of Lenny Bruce*. New York: Grove Press, 1971.

Baudry, Jean-Louis. "Ideological Effects of the Basic Cinematographic Apparatus." *Film Quarterly* 28:2 (Winter 1974–1975): 39–47.

Bazin, Andre. *What Is Cinema?* Vol. I. Berkeley: University of California Press, 1967.

———. *What Is Cinema?* Vol. II. Berkeley: University of California Press, 1972.

Beale, Lewis. "The American Way West." *Films and Filming* 18:7 (April 1972): 24–30.

Belton, John. "The Bionic Eye: Zoom Esthetics." *Cineaste* 11:1 (Winter 1980–81): 20–27.

Bohn, Thomas W., Richard L. Stromgren, and Daniel H. Johnson. *Light and Shadows: A History of Motion Pictures*. Sherman Oaks, California: Alfred Publishing Co., 1975.

Bordwell, David. "The Art Cinema as a Mode of Film Practice." *Film Criticism* 4 (1979): 56–64.

———. *Narration in the Fiction Film*. Madison: University of Wisconsin Press, 1985.

Bordwell, David, Janet Staiger, and Kristin Thompson. *The Classical Hollywood Cinema, Film Style and Mode of Production to 1960*. New York: Columbia University Press, 1985.

Boyd, David. "Mode and Meaning in *2001*." *Journal of Popular Film* 6:3 (1978): 202–215.

———. "Prisoner of the Night." *Film Heritage* 12:2 (Winter 1976–77): 24–30.

Brackman, Jacob. "*The Graduate*." *The New Yorker* 44 (27 July 1968): 34–66.

Byrne, Connie and William O. Lopez. "*Nashville*." *Film Quarterly* 29:2 (Winter 1975–76): 13–25.

Canby, Vincent. "Which Version Did You See?" *New York Times* 20 July 1969: 1, 7.

Carens, Carlos. *An Illustrated History of the Horror Film*. New York: Capricorn Books, 1967.

Carroll, Kathleen. "Space Film Is Way Out Experience." *New York Daily News* 4 April 1968: 67.

Cavell, Stanley. *Pursuits of Happiness, The Hollywood Comedy of Remarriage*. Cambridge: Harvard University Press, 1981.

Cawelti, John G. *Adventure, Mystery, and Romance: Formula Stories as Art and Popular Culture*. Chicago: University of Chicago Press, 1976.

———. "*Chinatown* and Generic Transformation in Recent American Films." *Film Theory and Criticism*, Fourth Edition. Ed. Gerald Mast, Marshall Cohen, and Leo Braudy. New York: Oxford University Press, 1992. 498–511.

———. "Introduction: *Bonnie and Clyde*: Tradition and Transformation." *Focus on Bonnie and Clyde*. Ed. John Cawelti. Englewood Cliffs, New Jersey: Prentice-Hall, 1973. 1–6.

———. "Reflections on the New Western Films." *Focus on the Western*. Ed. Jack Nachbar. Englewood Cliffs, New Jersey: Prentice-Hall, 1974. 113–117.

Chatman, Seymour. *Story and Discourse, Narrative Structure in Fiction and Film*. Ithaca, New York: Cornell University Press, 1983.

Clarke, Arthur C. *2001: A Space Odyssey*. New York: New American Library, 1982.

Comolli, Jean-Luc and Jean Narboni. "Cinema/Ideology/Criticism." *Film Theory and Criticism*, Fourth Edition. Ed. Mast, Cohen, Braudy. New York: Oxford University Press, 1992. 682–689.

Cook, David. *A History of Narrative Film*, Second Edition. New York: W. W. Norton & Co., 1990.

Cook, Jim. "*Bonnie and Clyde*." *Screen* 10:4–5 (1969): 101–114.

Cook, Page. Review of *Bonnie and Clyde*. *Films in Review* 18:8 (1967): 504–505.

Crist, Judith. "Stanley Kubrick, Please Come Down." *New York* 27 April 1968: 52–53.

Crowther, Bosley. Review of *Bonnie and Clyde*. *New York Times* 14 August 1967: 36.

Cutts, John. "Shoot!" *Films and Filming* 16:1 (October 1969): 4–6, 8.

Daniels, Don. "*2001*: A New Myth." *Film Heritage* 3:4 (Summer 1968): 1–11.

Dayan, Daniel. "The Tudor-Code of Classical Cinema." *Film Quarterly* 28:1 (Fall 1974): 22–31.

Dean, Joan F. "Between *2001* and *Star Wars.*" *Journal of Popular Film and Television* 7:1 (1978): 32–41.

Elsaesser, Thomas. "The Pathos of Failure: American Films in the 70's." *Monogram* 6 (1975): 13–19.

———. "Vincente Minnelli." *Genre: The Musical.* Ed. Rick Altman. London: Routledge & Kegan Paul, 1981. 8–27.

Engle, Gary. "*McCabe and Mrs. Miller*: Robert Altman's Anti-Western." *Journal of Popular Film* (Fall 1972): 268–287.

Eyman, Scott. "Against Altman." *Focus on Film* 36 (October 1980): 26–28.

Farber, Stephen. "Coppola and *The Godfather.*" *Sight and Sound* 41:4 (Autumn 1972): 217–223.

———. "Peckinpah's Return." *Film Quarterly* 23:1 (Fall 1969): 2–11.

———. "They Made Him Two Offers He Couldn't Refuse." *New York Times* 22 December 1974: Section 2, 1, 19.

Feuer, Jane. "Altman's Open Surface." *Jump Cut* 10/11 (June 1976): 31–32.

———. *The Hollywood Musical.* Bloomington: Indiana University Press, 1982.

———. "The Self-Reflexive Musical and the Myth of Entertainment." *Film Genre Reader.* Ed. Barry Keith Grant. Austin: University of Texas Press, 1986. 329–343.

"The Filmmaker as Ascendant Star." *Time* 4 July 1969: 46–51.

Fisher, Jack. "The End of Sex in *2001.*" *The Film Journal* 2:1 (1972): 65.

Gardner, Paul. "Altman Surveys 'Nashville' and Sees 'Instant' America." *New York Times* 13 June 1975: 26.

Gelmis, Joseph. "Another Look at *Space Odyssey.*" *Newsday* 20 April 1968: 41W.

———. *The Film Director as Superstar.* New York: Doubleday, 1970.

———. "Homicidal Fun Irks While It Spellbinds." *Newsday* 14 August 1967: 3A.

———. "*Space Odyssey* Fails Most Gloriously." *Newsday* 8 April 1968: 3A.

Glushanok, Paul. "*Bonnie and Clyde.*" *Cineaste* 1:2 (1967): 14–17.

Gross, Larry. "An Interview with Robert Altman, on the Set of *Nashville.*" *Millimeter* 3:2 (February 1975): 24–29.

Hanson, Curtis Lee. "An Interview with Arthur Penn." *Cinema* 3:5 (1967): 11–16.

Harmetz, Aljean. "The 15th Man Who Was Asked to Direct *M*A*S*H* (and Did) Makes a Peculiar Western." *New York Times* 20 June 1971: Section C, 10–11, 46–54.

Hess, John. "A Deal Coppola Couldn't Refuse." *Jump Cut* 7 (May–July 1975): 1, 10–11.

Hotchner, Tracy. "Is the *Bunch* Too Wild?" *New York Times* 20 July 1969: 16, 29.

Jacobs, Diane. *Hollywood Renaissance.* South Brunswick, New Jersey: A. S. Barnes & Co., 1977.

Jameson, Frederic. "Reification and Utopia in Mass Culture." *Signatures of the Visible.* New York: Routledge, 1990. 9–34.

Kael, Pauline. "Alchemy." *Deeper into Movies.* Boston: Little, Brown, and Co., 1973. 420–426.

———. "*Bonnie and Clyde.*" *Kiss Kiss Bang Bang.* Boston: Little, Brown, 1968. 47–63.

————. "When the Saints Come Marching in." *Reeling*. New York: Warner Books, 1976. 494–502.

Kagan, Norman. *The Cinema of Stanley Kubrick*. New York: Holt Rinehart & Winston, 1972.

Kanfer, Stefan. "Hollywood, the Shock of Freedom in Films." *Time* 8 December 1967: 66–76.

Kauffmann, Stanley. "Cum Laude." *The New Republic* 23 December 1967: 22, 38.

————. "Lost in the Stars." *The New Republic* 4 May 1968: 24, 41.

————. "Postscript." *The New Republic* 10 February 1968: 20, 37.

Klein, Michael. "*Nashville* and the American Dream." *Jump Cut* 9 (October/December 1975): 6–7.

Klinger, Barbara. " 'Cinema/Ideology/Criticism' Revisited: The Progressive Genre." *Film Genre Reader*. Ed. Barry Keith Grant. Austin: University of Texas Press, 1988. 74–90.

Kloman, William. "*2001* and *Hair*—Are They the Groove of the Future?" *New York Times* 12 May 1968: D15.

Knight, Arthur. "*McCabe and Mrs. Miller*." *Saturday Review* 24 July 1971: 51.

————. "The Technics and Techniques of Film." Review of *McCabe and Mrs. Miller*. *Saturday Review* 7 August 1971: 31.

Kofsky, Frank. *Lenny Bruce, The Comedian as Social Critic and Secular Moralist*. New York: Monad Press, 1974.

Kolker, Robert Phillip. *A Cinema of Loneliness: Penn, Kubrick, Coppola, Scorsese, Altman*. New York: Oxford University Press, 1980.

————. *A Cinema of Loneliness: Penn, Kubrick, Scorsese, Spielberg, Altman*, Second Edition. New York: Oxford University Press, 1988.

Kracauer, Siegfried. *Theory of Film: The Redemption of Physical Reality*. New York: Oxford University Press, 1973.

Lawrence, D. H. *Studies in Classic American Literature*. New York: Viking Press, 1972.

Leach, James. "Notes on Polanski's Cinema of Cruelty." *Wide Angle* 7:1 (1978): 32–39.

Levin, Sid. "The Art of the Editor: *Nashville*." *Filmmakers Newsletter* 8:10 (August 1975): 29–33.

Mast, Gerald. *The Movies in Our Midst*. Chicago: University of Chicago Press, 1982.

————. *A Short History of the Movies*, Fourth Edition. New York: MacMillan, 1986.

Mast, Gerald, Marshall Cohen, and Leo Braudy, Eds. *Film Theory and Criticism*, Fourth Edition. New York: Oxford University Press, 1992.

McCormick, Ruth. "In Defense of *Nashville*." *Cineaste* 7:1 (Fall 1975): 22–25, 51.

McKinney, Doug. *Sam Peckinpah*. Boston: Twayne Publishers, 1979.

Medjuck, Joe. "Sam Peckinpah Lets It All Hang Out." *Take One* 2:3 (January–February 1969): 18–20.

Mellen, Joan. *Big Bad Wolves, Masculinity in the American Film*. New York: Pantheon Books, 1977.

Michener, Charles and Martin Kasindorf. "Altman's Opry Land Epic." *Newsweek* 30 June 1975: 46–50.

Morgenstern, Joseph. Review of *Bonnie and Clyde*. *Newsweek* 21 August 1967: 65.

————. "A Second Look at *Bonnie and Clyde*." *Newsweek* 28 August 1967: 82.

Murray, William. "*Playboy* Interview: Sam Peckinpah." *Playboy* 19:8 (August 1972): 65–75, 192.

Nachbar, Jack. "Riding Shotgun: The Scattered Formula in Contemporary Western Movies." *Focus on the Western*. Ed. Jack Nachbar. Englewood Cliffs, New Jersey: Prentice-Hall, 1974. 101–112.

Nelson, Thomas Allen. *Kubrick: Inside a Film Artist's Maze*. Bloomington: Indiana University Press, 1982.

Newman, David and Robert Benton. "Lightning in a Bottle." *Bonnie and Clyde*. Ed. Sandra Wake and Nicola Haydon. New York: Lorrimer, 1983. 13–30.

Pechter, William S. "Keeping Up with the Corleones." *Movies Plus One*. New York: Horizon Press, 1982. 86–95.

Penn, Arthur. "*Bonnie and Clyde*: Private Morality and Public Violence." *Take One* 1.6 (1967): 20–22.

Phillips, Gene D. *Stanley Kubrick: A Film Odyssey*. New York: Popular Library, 1975.

Plecki, Gerard. *Robert Altman*. Boston: Twayne Publishers, 1985.

Quart, Leonard and Albert Austen. "*The Godfather, Part II*." *Cineaste* 6:4 (1975): 38–39.

Ragni, Gerome and James Rado. *Hair, The American Tribal Love-Rock Musical*. New York: Pocket Books, 1970.

Ray, Robert. *A Certain Tendency of the Hollywood Cinema, 1930–1980*. Princeton, New Jersey: Princeton University Press, 1985.

Rich, Frank. "Scorsese's Ride Through Hell." *New York Post* 14 February 1976: 16, 58.

Rimmon-Kenan, Shlomith. *Narrative Fiction, Contemporary Poetics*. London: Methuen, 1986.

Rubenstein, Lenny. "*Taxi Driver*." *Cineaste* 7:3 (Fall 1976): 34–35.

Ryan, Michael and Douglas Kellner. *Camera Politica: The Politics and Ideology of Contemporary Hollywood Film*. Bloomington: Indiana University Press, 1988.

Sarris, Andrew. "After *The Graduate*." *American Film* 3:9 (July–August 1978): 32–37.

———. "*The Graduate*." *The Village Voice* 28 December 1967: 33, 35.

———. "*2001: A Space Odyssey*." *The Village Voice* 11 April 1968: 45.

———. "*2001: A Space Odyssey*." *The Village Voice* 20 February 1969: 47.

———. "*2001: A Space Odyssey*." *The Village Voice* 7 May 1970: 57, 62.

Schatz, Thomas. *Hollywood Genres: Formulas, Filmmaking, and the Studio System*. New York: Random House, 1981.

———. *Old Hollywood/New Hollywood: Ritual, Art, and Industry*. Ann Arbor, Michigan: UMI Research Press, 1983.

———. "The Western." *Handbook of American Film Genres*. Ed. Wes D. Gehring. New York: Greenwood Press, 1988. 25–46.

Schickel, Richard. "Fine Debut for a Square Anti-Hero." *Life* 19 January 1968: 16.

Schuth, H. Wayne. *Mike Nichols*. Boston: Twayne Publishers, 1978.

Self, Robert. "The Art Cinema and Robert Altman." *Velvet Light Trap* 19 (1982): 30–34.

Seydor, Paul. *Peckinpah: The Western Films*. Urbana: University of Illinois Press, 1980.

Shadoian, Jack. *Dreams and Dead Ends: The American Gangster/Crime Film*. Cambridge, Massachusetts: MIT Press, 1977.

Shatnoff, Judith. "A Gorilla to Remember." *Film Quarterly* 22:1 (Fall 1968): 56–62.

Silverman, Kaja. *The Subject of Semiotics*. New York: Oxford University Press, 1983.

Smith, Gavin. "Mike Nichols: Without Cutaways." *Film Comment* 27:3 (May–June 1991): 27–42.

Sobchack, Vivian. "Science Fiction." *Handbook of American Film Genres*. Ed. Wes D. Gehring. New York: Greenwood Press, 1988. 229–247.

———. *Screening Space: The American Science Fiction Film*. New York: Ungar Publishing Co., 1987.

Taylor, Clarke. "The Saint and the Taxi Driver." *Soho Arts Weekly* 26 February 1976: 15, 31.

Thompson, David and Ian Christie, ed. *Scorsese on Scorsese*. London: Faber & Faber, 1989.

Thomson, David. "The Discreet Charm of the Godfather." *Sight and Sound* 47:2 (Spring 1978): 76–80.

Towne, Robert. "Dialogue on Film." *American Film* 1:3 (December 1975): 33–48.

Truffaut, François. *The Films of My Life*. New York: Simon and Schuster, 1985.

Vizzard, Jack. "*See No Evil*." *The Movies in Our Midst*. Ed. Gerald Mast. Chicago: University of Chicago Press, 1982. 693–704.

Von Gunden, Kenneth and Stuart H. Stock. *Twenty All Time Great Science Fiction Films*. New York: Arlington House, 1982.

Warshow, Robert. "The Gangster as Tragic Hero." *The Immediate Experience*. New York: Atheneum, 1971. 127–133.

———. "Movie Chronicle: The Westerner." *The Immediate Experience*. New York: Atheneum, 1971. 135–154.

Webb, Charles. *The Graduate*. New York: New American Library, 1963.

Weiss, Miriam. "She Identifies with *The Graduate*." *New York Times* 9 June 1968: D19.

Wexman, Virginia Wright. *Roman Polanski*. Boston: Twayne Publishers, 1985.

Williams, Linda. "When the Woman Looks." *Film Theory and Criticism*, Fourth Edition. Ed. Mast, Cohen, and Braudy. New York: Oxford University Press, 1992. 561–577.

Winsten, Archer. "*2001: A Space Odyssey* at Capitol." *New York Post* 4 April 1968: 68.

———. "*The Wild Bunch* Arrives at Trans-Lux East and West." *New York Post* 26 June 1969: 59.

Wood, Robin. "The American Family Comedy: From *Meet Me in St. Louis* to *The Texas Chain Saw Massacre*." *Wide Angle* 3:2 (1979): 5–11.

———. *Arthur Penn*. New York: Frederick A. Praeger, 1970.

———. *Hollywood from Vietnam to Reagan*. New York: Columbia University Press, 1986.

———. *Howard Hawks*. New York: Doubleday, 1968.

———. "Ideology, Genre, Auteur." *Film Theory and Criticism*, Fourth Edition. Ed. Mast, Cohen, and Braudy. New York: Oxford University Press, 1992. 475–485.

————. "Smart-Ass and Cutie Pie: Notes Toward an Evaluation of Altman."
    Movie 21 (Autumn 1975): 1–17.
Wright, Judith Hess. "Genre Films and the Status Quo." *Film Genre Reader*. Ed.
    Barry Keith Grant. Austin: University of Texas Press, 1986. 41–49.

Filmography (Arranged by Chronology)

BONNIE AND CLYDE (WARNER BROTHERS, 1967)

Producer: Warren Beatty
Director: Arthur Penn
Screenplay: David Newman and Robert Benton
Cinematographer: Burnett Guffey
Art Director: Dean Tavoularis
Editor: Dede Allen
Music: Charles Strouse, Flatt and Scruggs
Costumes: Theadora van Runkle
Special Consultant: Robert Towne
Cast: Warren Beatty (Clyde Barrow), Faye Dunaway (Bonnie Parker), Michael J.
  Pollard (C. W. Moss), Gene Hackman (Buck Barrow), Estelle Parsons (Blanche
  Barrow), Denver Pyle (Frank Hamer), Dub Taylor (Ivan Moss), Evans Evans
  (Velma Davis), Gene Wilder (Eugene Grizzard)
Running time: 111 minutes; released July 1967

THE GRADUATE (AVCO EMBASSY, 1967)

Producer: Lawrence Turman
Director: Mike Nichols
Screenplay: Calder Willingham and Buck Henry, based on the novel by Charles
  Webb
Cinematographer: Robert Surtees
Production Designer: Richard Sylbert
Editor: Sam O'Steen
Songs: Paul Simon (sung by Simon and Garfunkel)
Additional Music: Dave Grusin
Sound: Jack Solomon

Costumes: Patricia Zipprodt
Cast: Anne Bancroft (Mrs. Robinson), Dustin Hoffman (Benjamin Braddock), Katharine Ross (Elaine Robinson), William Daniels (Mr. Braddock), Elizabeth Wilson (Mrs. Braddock), Buck Henry (Room Clerk), Brian Avery (Carl Smith)
Running Time: 105 minutes; released December 1967

2001: A SPACE ODYSSEY (MGM, 1968)

Producer: Stanley Kubrick
Director: Stanley Kubrick
Screenplay: Stanley Kubrick and Arthur C. Clarke, based on Clarke's story "The Sentinel"
Cinematographer: Geoffrey Unsworth
Additional Cinematography: John Alcott
Production Design: Tony Masters, Harry Lange, Ernie Archer
Special Effects: Stanley Kubrick, Wally Veevers, Douglas Trumbull, Con Pederson, Tom Howard
Editor: Ray Lovejoy
Music: Richard Strauss, Johann Strauss, Aram Khachaturian, Gyorgy Ligeti
Costumes: Hardy Amies
Cast: Keir Dullea (David Bowman), Gary Lockwood (Frank Poole), William Sylvester (Dr. Heywood Floyd), Daniel Richter (Moonwatcher), Douglas Rain (Voice of HAL 9000), Leonard Rossiter (Smyslov), Margaret Tyzack (Elena), Robert Beatty (Halvorsen), Sean Sullivan (Michaels), Frank Miller (Mission Control), Penny Brahms (Stewardess), Alan Gifford (Poole's Father)
Running Time: 141 minutes; released April 1968

MIDNIGHT COWBOY (UNITED ARTISTS, 1969)

Producer: Jerome Hellman
Director: John Schlesinger
Screenplay: Waldo Salt, from the novel by James Leo Herlihy
Cinematographer: Adam Holender
Production Design: John Robert Lloyd
Editor: Hugh A. Robertson, Jr.
Music: John Barry
Sound Editors: Jack Fitzstephens, Vincent Connelly
Costumes: Ann Roth
Cast: Dustin Hoffman (Ratso Rizzo), Jon Voight (Joe Buck), John McGiver (Mr. O'Daniel), Brenda Vaccaro (Shirley), Barnard Hughes (Towny), Sylvia Miles (Cass), Ruth White (Sally Buck), Jennifer Salt (Crazy Annie)
Running Time: 113 minutes; released May 1969

THE WILD BUNCH (WARNER BROTHERS-SEVEN ARTS, 1969)

Producer: Phil Feldman
Director: Sam Peckinpah

Screenplay: Walon Green and Sam Peckinpah, based on a story by Walon Green and Roy N. Sickner
Cinematographer: Lucien Ballard
Art Director: Edward Carrere
Editor: Louis Lombardo
Music: Jerry Fielding
Sound: Robert J. Miller
Special Effects: Bud Hulburd
Cast: William Holden (Pike Bishop), Ernest Borgnine (Dutch Engstrom), Robert Ryan (Deke Thornton), Edmond O'Brien (Freddy Sykes), Warren Oates (Lyle Gorch), Jaime Sanchez (Angel), Ben Johnson (Tector Gorch), Emilio Fernandez (Mapache), Strother Martin (Coffer), L. Q. Jones (T. C.), Albert Dekker (Harrigan), Bo Hopkins (Crazy Lee)
Original Running Time: 148 minutes, later cut to 135 minutes; released June 1969

FIVE EASY PIECES (COLUMBIA, 1970)

Producer: Bob Rafelson and Richard Wechsler
Director: Bob Rafelson
Screenplay: Adrien Joyce, from a story by Adrien Joyce and Bob Rafelson
Cinematographer: Laszlo Kovacs
Editor: Gerald Shepard
Cast: Jack Nicholson (Bobby Dupea), Karen Black (Rayette Dipesto), Susan Anspach (Catherine Van Ost), Ralph Waite (Carl Dupea), Billy "Green" Bush (Elton), Fannie Flagg (Stoney), Sally Ann Struthers (Betty), Marlena MacGuire (Twinky), Lois Smith (Partita Dupea), Helena Kallianiotes (Palm Apodaca)
Running Time: 96 minutes; released September 1970

CARNAL KNOWLEDGE (AVCO EMBASSY, 1971)

Producer: Mike Nichols
Executive Producer: Joseph E. Levine
Director: Mike Nichols
Screenplay: Jules Feiffer
Cinematographer: Giuseppe Rotunno
Production Designer: Richard Sylbert
Art Director: Robert Luthardt
Editor: Sam O'Steen
Sound: Lawrence O. Jost
Costumes: Anthea Sylbert
Cast: Jack Nicholson (Jonathan), Arthur Garfunkel (Sandy), Candice Bergen (Susan), Ann-Margret (Bobbie), Rita Moreno (Louise), Cynthia O'Neal (Cindy), Carol Kane (Jennifer)
Running Time: 100 minutes; released June 1971

McCABE AND MRS. MILLER (WARNER BROTHERS, 1971)

Producers: David Foster and Mitchell Brower
Director: Robert Altman
Screenplay: Robert Altman, Brian McKay, from Edmund Naughton's novel
  McCabe
Cinematographer: Vilmos Zsigmond
Art Directors: Philip Thomas and Al Locatelli
Production Designer: Leon Erickson
Editor: Louis Lombardo
Music: Leonard Cohen
Sound: John V. Gusselle and William A. Thompson
Cast: Warren Beatty (John McCabe), Julie Christie (Constance Miller), Rene Au-
  berjonois (Sheehan), Hugh Millais (Dog Butler), Shelley Duvall (Ida Coyle),
  Michael Murphy (Sears), John Schuck (Smalley), Corey Fischer (Mr. Elliott)
Running Time: 121 minutes; released July 1971

THE GODFATHER (PARAMOUNT, 1972)

Producer: Albert S. Ruddy
Director: Francis Ford Coppola
Screenplay: Francis Ford Coppola and Mario Puzo, based on the novel by Mario
  Puzo
Cinematographer: Gordon Willis
Art Direction: Waren Clymer
Editors: William Reynolds, Peter Zinner, Marc Laub, Murray Solomon
Music: Nino Rota
Sound: Bud Grenzbach, Richard Portman, Christopher Newman, Les Lazarowitz
Costumes: Anna Hill Johnstone
Cast: Marlon Brando (Don Vito Corleone), Al Pacino (Michael Corleone), James
  Caan (Sonny Corleone), Richard Castellano (Clemenza), Robert Duvall (Tom
  Hagen), Diane Keaton (Kay Adams), Sterling Hayden (McCluskey), Talia Shire
  (Connie Rizzi), John Cazale (Fredo Corleone)
Running Time: 175 minutes; released March 1972

AMERICAN GRAFFITI (UNIVERSAL, 1973)

Producer: Francis Ford Coppola
Director: George Lucas
Screenplay: George Lucas, Gloria Katz, Willard Huyck
Cinematographers: Ron Everslage and Jan D'Alquen
Art Direction: Dennis Clark
Editors: Verna Fields, Marcia Lucas
Sound Editor: James Nelson
Costumes: Aggie Guerard Rodgers
Cast: Richard Dreyfuss (Curt), Ron Howard (Steve), Paul Le Mat (John), Charlie

Martin Smith (Terry), Cindy Williams (Laurie), Candy Clark (Debbie), Mac-
Kenzie Phillips (Carol), Wolfman Jack (Disc Jockey), Harrison Ford (Bob Falfa)
Running Time: 110 minutes; released July 1973

CHINATOWN (PARAMOUNT, 1974)

Producer: Robert Evans
Director: Roman Polanski
Screenplay: Robert Towne
Cinematographer: John A. Alonzo
Art Direction: W. Stewart Campbell
Production Designer: Richard Sylbert
Editor: Sam O'Steen
Music: Jerry Goldsmith
Sound Editor: Robert Cornett
Costumes: Anthea Sylbert
Cast: Jack Nicholson (J. J. Gittes), Faye Dunaway (Evelyn Mulwray), John Huston
    (Noah Cross), Perry Lopez (Escobar), John Hillerman (Yelburton), Darrell
    Swerling (Hollis Mulwray), Diane Ladd (Ida Sessions), Roy Jenson (Mulvihill),
    Roman Polanski (Man with Knife)
Running Time: 130 minutes; released June 1974

LENNY (UNITED ARTISTS, 1974)

Producer: Marvin Worth
Director: Bob Fosse
Screenplay: Julian Barry, based on his play
Cinematographer: Bruce Surtees
Production Designer: Joel Schiller
Editor: Alan Heim
Costumes: Albert Wolsky
Cast: Dustin Hoffman (Lenny Bruce), Valerie Perrine (Honey Bruce), Jan Miner
    (Sally Marr), Stanley Beck (Artie Silver), Gary Morton (Sherman Hart)
Running Time: 111 minutes; released November 1974

THE GODFATHER, PART II (PARAMOUNT, 1974)

Producers: Francis Ford Coppola, Gray Frederickson, Fred Roos
Director: Francis Ford Coppola
Screenplay: Francis Ford Coppola, Mario Puzo, based on the novel by Mario
    Puzo
Cinematographer: Gordon Willis
Art Direction: Angelo Graham
Production Design: Dean Tavoularis
Editors: Peter Zinner, Barry Malkin, Richard Marks
Music: Nino Rota

Additional Music: Carmine Coppola
Costumes: Theodora Van Runkle
Cast: Al Pacino (Michael Corleone), Robert Duvall (Tom Hagen), Diane Keaton (Kay), Robert De Niro (Vito Corleone), John Cazale (Fredo Corleone), Talia Shire (Connie Corleone), Lee Strasberg (Hyman Roth), Michael V. Gazzo (Frankie Pentangeli)
Running Time: 200 minutes; released December 1974

NASHVILLE (PARAMOUNT, 1975)

Producer: Robert Altman
Executive Producers: Martin Starger and Jerry Weintraub
Director: Robert Altman
Screenplay: Joan Tewkesbury
Cinematographer: Paul Lohmann
Editor: Sidney Levin and Dennis Hill
Music: Richard Baskin
Sound: Jim Webb and Chris McLaughlin
Cast: David Arkin (Norman), Barbara Baxley (Lady Pearl), Ned Beatty (Delbert Reese), Karen Black (Connie White), Ronee Blakley (Barbara Jean), Timothy Brown (Timothy Brown), Keith Carradine (Tom), Geraldine Chaplin (Opal), Robert Doqui (Wade), Shelley Duvall (L. A. Joan), Allen Garfield (Barnett), Henry Gibson (Haven Hamilton), Scott Glenn (Pfc Glenn Kelly), Jeff Goldblum (Tricycle Man), Barbara Harris (Albuquerque), David Hayward (Kenny Fraiser), Michael Murphy (John Triplette), Allan Nicholls (Bill), Dave Peel (Bud Hamilton), Cristina Raines (Mary), Bert Remsen (Star), Lily Tomlin (Linnea Reese), Gwen Welles (Sueleen Gay), Keenan Wynn (Mr. Green), Richard Baskin (Frog), Elliot Gould and Julie Christie (themselves)
Running Time: 159 minutes; released June 1975

TAXI DRIVER (COLUMBIA, 1976)

Producers: Michael and Julia Phillips
Director: Martin Scorsese
Screenplay: Paul Schrader
Cinematographer: Michael Chapman
Art Direction: Charles Rosen
Editors: Marcia Lucas, Tom Rolf, and Melvin Shapiro
Music: Bernard Herrmann
Creative Consultant: Sandra Weintraub
Cast: Robert De Niro (Travis Bickle), Cybill Shepherd (Betsy), Jodie Foster (Iris), Harvey Keitel (Sport), Peter Boyle (Wizard), Albert Brooks (Tom), Leonard Harris (Charles Palantine), Diahnne Abbott (Concession Girl), Martin Scorsese (Passenger)
Running Time: 112 minutes; released February 1976

THE GODFATHER, PART III (PARAMOUNT, 1990)

Producers: Fred Roos, Gray Frederickson, Chuck Mulvehill
Executive Producer: Fred Fuchs
Director: Francis Ford Coppola
Screenplay: Francis Ford Coppola and Mario Puzo
Cinematographer: Gordon Willis
Production Design: Dean Tavoularis
Art Direction: Alex Tavoularis
Editors: Barry Malkin, Diane Asnes
Music: Carmine Coppola
Sound: Richard Beggs
Costumes: Milena Canonero
Cast: Al Pacino (Michael Corleone), Talia Shire (Connie), Diane Keaton (Kay),
   Andy Garcia (Vincent), Franc D'Ambrosio (Anthony Corleone), Sofia Coppola
   (Mary Corleone), John Savage (Andrew Hagen), Eli Wallach (Don Altobello),
   Donal Donnelly (Archbishop), Richard Bright (Al Neri), Al Martino (Johnny
   Fontane), Joe Mantegna (Joey Zasa), George Hamilton (B. J. Harrison), Bridget
   Fonda (Grace), Raf Vallone (Lamberto), Helmut Berger (Keinszig), Enzo Ro-
   butti (Lucchesi)
Running Time: 170 minutes; released December 1990

Index

ABOUT THE AUTHOR

GLENN MAN is Associate Professor and Chair, English Department, University of Hawaii at Manoa, where he teaches courses in film and literature. His articles on film and on film and literature have appeared in *New Orleans Review*, *Literature/Film Quarterly*, *East-West Film Journal*, and *Film Criticism*.

ISBN 0-313-29306-6

90000>

EAN

9 780313 293061

HARDCOVER BAR CODE